JUSTICE ACROSS BOUNDARIES

Who ought to do what, and for whom, if global justice is to progress? In this collection of essays on justice beyond borders, Onora O'Neill criticises theoretical approaches that concentrate on rights yet ignore both the obligations that must be met to realise those rights, and the capacities needed by those who shoulder these obligations. She notes that states are profoundly anti-cosmopolitan institutions, and even those committed to justice and universal rights often lack the competence and the will to secure them, let alone to secure them beyond their borders. She argues for a wider conception of global justice, in which obligations may be held either by states or by competent non-state actors, and in which borders themselves must meet standards of justice. This rich and wide-ranging collection will appeal to a broad array of academic researchers and advanced students of political philosophy, political theory, international relations and philosophy of law.

ONORA O'NEILL, BARONESS O'NEILL of Bengarve, is a former Principal of Newnham College Cambridge, sits as a cross-bench peer in the House of Lords and is Emeritus Honorary Professor of Philosophy at the University of Cambridge. She has published widely on Kant's philosophy and her most recent publications include *Acting on Principle*, second edition (Cambridge, 2013).

JUSTICE ACROSS BOUNDARIES: WHOSE OBLIGATIONS?

ONORA O'NEILL

CAMBRIDGE
UNIVERSITY PRESS

CAMBRIDGE
UNIVERSITY PRESS

University Printing House, Cambridge CB2 8BS, United Kingdom

Cambridge University Press is part of the University of Cambridge.

It furthers the University's mission by disseminating knowledge in the pursuit of education, learning and research at the highest international levels of excellence.

www.cambridge.org
Information on this title: www.cambridge.org/9781107538177

© Onora O'Neill 2016

First published 2016

Printed in the United Kingdom by Clays, St Ives plc

A catalogue record for this publication is available from the British Library

Library of Congress Cataloguing in Publication data
O'Neill, Onora.
Justice across boundaries : whose obligations? / Onora O'Neill.
pages cm
Includes bibliographical references and index.
ISBN 978-1-107-11630-6 (Hardback) – ISBN 978-1-107-53817-7 (Paperback)
1. International relations–Moral and ethical aspects.   2. Justice (Philosophy)   3. Distributive justice.
4. Transitional justice.   5. Human rights.   6. Globalization–Moral and ethical aspects.
7. Globalization–Political aspects.   I. Title.
JZ1306.O64 2016
341–dc23   2015031125

ISBN 978-1-107-11630-6 Hardback
ISBN 978-1-107-53817-7 Paperback

Contents

Acknowledgements

I am deeply grateful to many friends, colleagues and students, and to wider audiences, who have commented on and improved my thinking on justice and boundaries across several decades.

Introduction

Do good fences make good neighbours?

In his simple and deep poem *Mending Wall* Robert Frost imagines a
dialogue with his New England neighbour about mending the crumbling
drystone wall that separates their farms, where cattle no longer run.
He points out that the wall is now not needed:

> There where it is we do not need the wall:
> He is all pine and I am apple orchard.
> My apple trees will never get across
> And eat the cones under his pines, I tell him.

His taciturn neighbour remains unconvinced:

> He only says, 'Good fences make good neighbours.'

Frost then poses questions that now animate many discussions of justice in
a globalising world:

> Spring is the mischief in me, and I wonder
> If I could put a notion in his head:
> 'Why do they make good neighbours? Isn't it
> Where there are cows? But here there are no cows.
> Before I built a wall I'd ask to know
> What I was walling in or walling out,
> And to whom I was like to give offence.
> Something there is that doesn't love a wall,
> That wants it down.'

Are walls and fences, borders and boundaries, needed for good relations
and for justice? Or do they impose and perpetuate injustice? What
violations are likely if they are no longer maintained? Can the 'walling
in or walling out' that borders create and maintain be justified? Is
the 'mischief' that tempts Frost to be rejected or embraced? Walls
have been built and mended to exclude and include since time

I

immemorial: walled cities and forts, garden walls and farm fences, the Great Wall of China, Hadrian's Wall, the Berlin Wall, the walls of apartheid townships and the West Bank Barrier (its very name disputed) all aim to 'wall in and wall out'. But when and how do the exclusions they maintain make for a more and when for a less just world?

Boundaries and borders

We live in a world of innumerable structures that 'wall in and wall out', and in particular of countless boundaries and countless boundary crossings. The boundaries that we often think of as borders usually separate states or lesser jurisdictions, and for the most part form clear demarcations. Other boundaries are fuzzier. They include boundaries between societies and nations, between languages and religions, between ideologies and cultures, between ecologies and economies.

Those who control well-defined borders may seek to regulate the passage of people (especially of foreigners), of goods, of aid and trade, of money and weapons, and even of ideas and information. Typically they aim to control who and what will be allowed to cross, and who or what will be detained, obstructed or prevented from crossing (at times with patchy success). So a fundamental task for political philosophy is to consider whether and how varying sorts of borders, and the inclusions and exclusions they create, can be justified; and whether and how appeals to less sharply defined boundaries – national and cultural, religious and ideological – may be relevant to justifications of state borders. Although many accounts of justice insist that its principles are universal, this does not determine the reach of justice: principles can combine universal form with restricted scope.

So it is not surprising that both state borders and other boundaries pose deep and interesting problems for discussions of justice. Borders can be used to secure, alter, undermine or destroy justice, variously understood. This is not generally because their location is disputed: although that happens often enough, it is usually not philosophically interesting. The deeper problems have less to do with the locations of borders, than with their configuration, that is with the types of action they permit or prevent, and with the justification of the inclusions and exclusions that they impose. All justification is demanding, but the justification of inclusions and exclusions often raises particularly difficult demands: do arguments that seek to establish the scope of justice have to address both those included and those excluded? Does it matter if demarcations are not justified to 'outsiders'?[1]

Aspirational versions of moral cosmopolitanism often claim that the borders of states should be made more porous in more ways to more sorts of people and to a greater range of activities. Some point towards a better institutionalised cosmopolitan future, in which various sorts of differences are not seen as justifying exclusions or inclusions, and so to a more extensive institutional cosmopolitanism. Yet it is evident ·that many would-be enthusiasts for cosmopolitan justice are reluctant to endorse a monolithic world state, and are uncertain whether a world of fewer or more porous boundaries could provide greater stability, or security or justice.

Less ambitious, and seemingly more modest and realistic accounts of global justice insist, on the contrary, that at least some of the demarcations that are defined by state borders, and the inclusions and exclusions they maintain, may be needed for justice. The old saying that *good fences make good neighbours* expresses a wary anti-cosmopolitanism, that sees some inclusions and exclusions as helpful, perhaps even as necessary, if justice is to be realised or maintained. These themes animate claims both about moral cosmopolitanism and about institutional anti-cosmopolitanism, and have become central to philosophical and practical discussions of justice in a globalising world. Here I aim to explore and hope to contribute to the underlying arguments that matter for these debates.[2]

Part I Hunger across boundaries

With high hopes I decided in the mid 1970s that a focus on the rights of the hungry would offer a useful approach to establishing at least some of the basic claims of justice in a world where some suffer extreme yet remediable deprivation. In the postwar world, appeals to rights – often, but not always, specifically to the human rights proclaimed in the Universal Declaration of 1948 – were on the way to becoming the most salient ethical vocabulary. While there were then few detailed philosophical investigations of rights, I thought there was headway to be made.

---

[1] Cf. Simon Caney, *Justice beyond Borders: A Global Political Theory* (Oxford University Press, 2005), on borders as shaping justifications.
[2] Several earlier essays on justice and borders are included in my *Bounds of Justice* (Cambridge University Press, 2000).

There were certainly problems to be addressed: the news at that time was full of reports of famine and extreme poverty in many parts of the world, including Biafra, Cambodia and Ethiopia (few knew about the great Chinese famine of 1958–62); of hurtling population growth; and of the effects of the 1973 oil crisis on the poorest. Despite the ongoing green revolution, there was scant evidence of any demographic transition, of any end to the Cold War, of the surging economic growth later achieved in some (but not other) poor states, or of the mushrooming of cross-border activities that fuelled not only greater prosperity for many, but rampant global corruption and the emergence of a peripatetic class of the super-rich. All these profound changes lay far ahead: indeed many of them emerged only because of changes in the effectiveness and effects of border controls that came about with the end of the Cold War and the spread of various forms of economic liberalisation.

Unsurprisingly, much of the ethical literature on poverty and development before these changes focused on the extreme case of hunger and famine. The most widely accepted ethical approach was utilitarian, and the most discussed contribution was Peter Singer's 'Famine, affluence and morality'.[3] I admired his work, but thought that utilitarian approaches depended on extravagant assumptions that could not do the required heavy ethical lifting. I aspired to do more with less, and hoped that an appeal to rights would provide a more economical and plausible starting point to address ethical questions about hunger and famine. The first three chapters in the collection start from considerations about rights. But they also reveal difficulties in that starting point, and put forward reasons for locating rights in a wider framework in which obligations and agency are seen as more basic. In these papers, as in most of the later chapters here, I relied on traditional conceptions of rights – of natural rights, moral rights, fundamental rights – rather than appealing only and specifically to human rights. However, in some of the later chapters I consider both the justification and some of the practical implications of human rights as set out in the Universal Declaration of 1948.[4]

In Chapter 1 'Lifeboat Earth' I tried to show that we can do without either utilitarian or broader consequentialist assumptions, and argued that robust conclusions could be established by starting with rights. However,

---

[3] Peter Singer, 'Famine, affluence, and morality', *Philosophy and Public Affairs* 1 (1972), 229–43.
[4] Chapter 7 'Positivists, pluralists and the justification of human rights', below, 120–33, focuses on the justification of human rights; Chapter 12 'The dark side of human rights', below, 193–207, considers what has to be added to human rights if they are to guide action.

I deliberately did not invoke the temptingly capacious yet amorphous 'right to life'[5] that has been central to so many ethical debates, particularly in bioethics. I hoped that starting from a more modest, widely accepted assumption that everyone has (at least!) a right not to be killed unjustifiably would beg fewer questions, and would be enough to show that action violates rights if its distributive effects unjustifiably lead to additional deaths. 'Lifeboat Earth' has probably had more readers than any other paper I have published, and I have been persuaded to include it unamended in this collection, despite the fact that I soon reached the disappointing conclusion that a minimal right not to be killed unjustifiably does not provide a sufficient ethical basis for an approach to the ethical questions raised by hunger and famine, let alone for a wider view of global justice. The reasons that led me to this conclusion are developed in other papers in this collection.

Although I remain convinced that utilitarian arguments are inadequate for guiding action, I came to think that appeals to rights could have bite only if combined with arguments to show *who* should act, and *what* they should do. Rights could be realised only if the counterpart obligations were held by competent agents. The second paper, Chapter 2 'Hunger, rights and obligations', was written as something of a 'manifesto piece' for this line of thought, which it sets out in plain and direct terms. During the 1980s I developed this approach in more detail in a number of other articles, and in a book.[6]

The third chapter in Part I, 'Rights to compensation', examines a different, perennially popular, rights-based approach. Rights to compensation seek to assign obligations to address poverty and famine to those whose action caused them. An apparent advantage of the approach is that it provides clarity about who is to carry the counterpart obligations. With some regret, I concluded that this approach too does not offer a convincing way of responding to distant hunger or destitution, and may indeed be a distraction. Rights to compensation are relevant where hunger and poverty and hunger have demonstrably arisen from the wrongdoing of identifiable

---

[5] Disagreements about the right to life became and remain central in philosophical and more popular discussions of the legalisation of abortion, and of other novel reproductive technologies.

[6] They include 'The moral perplexities of famine relief' in Tom Regan (ed.), *Matters of Life and Death* (New York: Random House, 1980), 260–98; extensively revised editions, 1986, 1993 (with the title changed to 'Ending world hunger' and pagination to 235–79 in the latter); 'Rights, obligations and needs', *Logos* 6 (1985), 29–47, most recently reprinted in Thomas Pogge and Keith Horton (eds.), *Global Ethics: Seminal Essays* (St. Paul, MN: Paragon, 2008); and *Faces of Hunger: An Essay on Poverty, Development and Justice* (London: George Allen & Unwin, 1986).

others. While it is all too true that there have been great historic injustices, it is also all too often uncertain whose unjust action contributed to whose present poverty, and all too clear that much present poverty and hunger has multiple causes, and is often in large part unattributable to any competent agents who could be required to compensate. Appeals to rights to compensation gesture towards competent agents who are to shoulder obligations to compensate, but they do so with a wavering finger. I concluded that only a clearer focus on action and obligation could support a convincing and broader account of obligations of justice.

Part II Justifications across boundaries

From the early 1980s my understanding of global poverty was transformed by reading Amartya Sen's wonderful *Poverty and Famines.*[7] Once I had fully grasped how deeply hunger and deprivation are shaped both by institutional structures and by everyday economic transactions, the idea that rights to compensation can make a major contribution to global justice seemed unconvincing, although it remains perennially popular. From then on I tried to take a strictly forward-looking and practical view of just responses to hunger and destitution. A practical approach cannot assume that culprits can generally be identified and made to compensate for all injury or harm suffered. Yet if justice is to be secured it is necessary to specify the obligations of competent agents of change.

The chapters in Part II address questions that arise if justifications are to reach across boundaries. Western political philosophy has been deeply shaped by the thought that justice is internal to communities, cities or states, so may and perhaps must be bounded. Although versions and elements of *ius gentium*, and of international justice and law, have been with of us since antiquity, they have generally been seen as applying only in limited ways to justice between *bounded* communities, cities or states, or to ways in which bounded communities, cities or states deal with *outsiders*. Until recently, few have thought through the institutional and practical implications of abandoning these limited claims in favour of institutional-ised forms of cosmopolitanism.

Arguments for instituting a more cosmopolitan system of justice across boundaries are not merely arguments that the *scope* of justice should be enlarged, in the ways in which it may be when a state adds to its territory

[7] Amartya Sen, *Poverty and Famines: An Essay on Entitlement and Deprivation* (Oxford: Clarendon Press, 1981).

or extends the franchise. They are more often arguments for making borders more porous in specific ways – and thereby perhaps less effective in other specific ways. Interestingly, many of the political arguments invoked for making borders more porous, even during the present era of globalisation, appeal to *state* interests: free trade may increase national (i.e. state) prosperity; free movement of ideas could improve understanding between states and national security; free movement of (some) people would improve national prosperity. Such arguments, it seemed to me, would not be adequate to justify a more complete opening of borders, which would dissolve or undermine the very conceptions of national and state interest to which they appealed. So I proceeded more circumspectly.

Chapter 4 'Justice and boundaries' considers whether the claim that principles of justice are universal provides enough to show that they should stretch across boundaries. I concluded that this move is unconvincing because universal form and universal scope are different matters. The mere fact that principles of justice are universal in form does not entail any specific view about their proper scope, or about the merits or failings of any form of institutional cosmopolitanism. In Chapter 5 'Ethical reasoning and ideological pluralism', I considered some difficulties that can arise where the beliefs and conceptual capacities of those who are separated by various sorts of boundaries differ, with the consequence that they may not follow or be persuaded by reasoning that seems adequate to others on the far side of various boundaries, who do not share their outlook. Chapter 6 'Bounded and cosmopolitan justice' continues these themes and compares communitarian justifications that ostensibly work within certain boundaries (or 'spheres'), that are seen as limits of justice, and the 'semi-cosmopolitan' positions supported by the conceptions of public reason defended by John Rawls and many others.

The last chapter in Part II, 'Positivists, pluralists and the justification of human rights', turns to the prospect of justifying the human rights declared and widely accepted in the post-World War II world. Human rights are but one version of the idea that human beings have rights: a uniquely successful and assertive version, but not immune from philosophical investigation, criticism or (if possible) justification. A number of distinguished political philosophers have done penetrating work on the justification of human rights, especially since the millennium, but all too much discussion and advocacy of human rights is still conducted (and accepted) on the basis of arguments from authority. The agreement of states, of the international community, of the *bien pensants*, is all too often taken as sufficient warrant, even by those who would reject arguments from authority in many other contexts. Here I consider a possible way of justifying the rights set out in the Universal Declaration without either arguing from authority, or building on contentious metaphysical or theological claims.

Part III Action across boundaries

The chapters in Part III turn from justifications to some of the preconditions for respecting and realising rights. They argue that appeals to abstract rights are never enough, yet are indispensable. The indeterminacy of rights – like the indeterminacy of other ethical principles – is essential if agents and agencies are to enact obligations of justice in varying circumstances. Many of the problems said to arise because rights are 'too abstract' reflect no more than unsustainable views both of abstraction and of what it would be to respect rights. These chapters also discuss a range of considerations that matter if rights are to be respected and realised, including the task of assigning the necessary counterpart obligations, the capacities of the agents and agencies to whom they are assigned, and the circumstances in which they act. And once again the final chapter addresses questions about enacting human rights.

Chapter 8 'From Edmund Burke to twenty-first-century human rights' discusses Edmund Burke's classical criticisms of abstraction, and suggests that his line of thought neither targets nor undermines the prospect of institutionalising abstract rights, but rather allows for their varied enactment in differing circumstances. Burke saw abstraction neither as avoidable nor as fatal, but rather as indispensable yet insufficient.

Chapter 9 'From statist to global conceptions of justice' argues that the practical tasks of enacting and securing justice should not question specific borders, but should focus on the capacities for action of the agents and agencies that are to respect or realise justice. In particular, a practical approach to rights needs to take account both of the specific powers and of the diversity of non-state actors, many of them not intrinsically territorial, whose activities often cross state and other boundaries. Chapter 10 'Global justice: whose obligations?' argues that rights are not taken seriously unless they are anchored in obligations, and that obligations are not taken seriously unless they are anchored in realistic accounts of the capabilities and vulnerabilities of the agents and agencies that are to carry them, and that doing so requires attention to the highly variable nature of boundaries and borders, and the specific inclusions and exclusions they maintain.

Chapter 11 'Agents of justice' returns to the lurking statism of many accounts of the practical implications of rights and explores ways in which a wider range of non-state agencies may contribute to justice. It argues that states are not invariably the primary agents of justice, and that, even where they are primary, other non-state agents and agencies may have obligations that go beyond complying with the just requirements of states.

The final chapter in this part, like the last chapter in Part II, turns specifically to human rights. Chapter 12 'The dark side of human rights' looks at some ways in which assigning obligations to respect and realise human rights to states have shaped discussions of their realisation, and discusses some of the costs of linking human rights too closely to state actors. It is unclear how far the scope of justice can be extended if obligations to respect and realise rights are assigned primarily to intrinsically anti-cosmopolitan intuitions.

Part IV Health across boundaries

The essays in the final part address some questions that arise in thinking about health and justice in a globalising world. Health is one of several areas (climate and technological change are others) in which the role of state borders in defining the scope of justice can be particularly problematic. I argue that a great deal of work in bioethics has taken too little account of this reality, usually not because it explicitly relies on statist assumptions (they are often implicit), but because it takes an individualistic approach that is often appropriate for clinical ethics, but not for the ethics of public health, which is always affected by disparities in global health.

Chapter 13 'Public health or clinical ethics: thinking beyond borders' examines some of the costs of the intense focus of much contemporary bioethics on doctor–patient relationships, on informed consent, and on the just distribution of health care to individuals. This focus has often marginalised public health issues, and the importance of sustaining and improving the health of poorer populations, and other global health issues. An adequate public health ethics needs to be anchored in political philosophy rather than in ethics, and to take a realistic view of ways in which both state and non-state actors can affect population health. In consequence neither individual autonomy nor informed consent can be seen as fundamental to the ethics of health.

Chapter 14 'Broadening bioethics: clinical ethics, public health and global health' asks whether public health measures are genuine 'global public goods', in which everybody has an interest. It argues that while many public health measures, including many targeted health interventions, may have beneficial externalities, they are not genuine global public goods.

The papers in this collection criticise certain views of human rights, but maintain that those rights matter for justice. I am critical, in the main, of discussions of human rights that are silent or vague about the agents of justice, or about their specific duties, and assume without argument that the relevant duties all fall on states. In my view we do not take rights seriously unless we seek to show *who* ought to do *what* for *whom*, and the duties that do fall on states are typically second-order duties to enable and require other agents and agencies to act. I am all too aware that the many colleagues, students and audiences on whom I have pressed these thoughts may have become weary of my refrain, but I remain unrepentant.

PART I

Hunger across boundaries

CHAPTER I

Lifeboat Earth[1]

If in the fairly near future millions of people die of starvation, will those who survive be in any way to blame for those deaths? Is there anything which people ought to do now, and from now on, if they are to be able to avoid responsibility for unjustifiable deaths in famine years? I shall argue from the assumption that persons have a right not to be killed unjustifiably to the claim that we have a duty to try to prevent and postpone famine deaths. A corollary of this claim is that if we do nothing we shall bear some blame for some deaths.

Justifiable killing

I shall assume that persons have a right not to be killed and a corresponding duty not to kill. I shall make no assumptions about the other rights persons may have. In particular, I shall not assume that persons have a right not to be allowed to die by those who could prevent it or a duty to prevent others' deaths whenever they could do so. Nor will I assume that persons lack this right.

Even if persons have no rights other than a right not to be killed, this right can justifiably be overridden in certain circumstances. Not all killings are unjustifiable. I shall be particularly concerned with two sorts of circumstances in which the right not to be killed is justifiably overridden. The first of these is the case of unavoidable killings; the second is the case of self-defence.

Unavoidable killings occur in situations where a person doing some act causes some death or deaths which he could not avoid. Often such deaths will be unavoidable because of the killer's ignorance of some relevant circumstance at the time of his decision to act. If *B* is driving a train, and *A* blunders onto the track and is either unnoticed by *B* or noticed too late for *B* to stop the train, and *B* kills *A*, then *B* could not have avoided killing *A*, given his decision

[1] 'Lifeboat Earth', *Philosophy and Public Affairs* 4 (1975), 271–92.

to drive the train. Another sort of case of unavoidable killing occurs when B could avoid killing A or could avoid killing C, but cannot avoid killing one of the two. For example, if B is the carrier of a highly contagious and invariably fatal illness, he might find himself so placed that he cannot avoid meeting and so killing either A or C, though he can choose which of them to meet. In this case the unavoidability of B's killing someone is not relative to some prior decision B made. The cases of unavoidable killings with which I want to deal here are of the latter sort, and I shall argue that in such cases B kills justifiably if certain further conditions are met.

A killing may also be justifiable if it is undertaken in self-defence. I shall not argue here that persons have a right of self-defence which is independent of their right not to be killed, but rather that a minimal right of self-defence is a corollary of a right not to be killed. Hence the notion of self-defence on which I shall rely is in some ways different from, and narrower than, other interpretations of the right of self-defence. I shall also assume that if A has a right to defend himself against B, then third parties ought to defend A's right. If we take seriously the right not to be killed and its corollaries, then we ought to enforce others' rights not to be killed.

The right of self-defence which is a corollary of the right not to be killed is a right to take action to prevent killings. If I have a right not to be killed then I have a right to prevent others from endangering my life, though I may endanger their lives in so doing only if that is the only available way to prevent the danger to my own life. Similarly if another has the right not to be killed then I should, if possible, do something to prevent others from endangering his life, but I may endanger their lives in so doing only if that is the only available way to prevent the danger to his life. This duty to defend others is *not* a general duty of beneficence but a very restricted duty to enforce others' rights not to be killed.

The right to self-defence so construed is quite narrow. It includes no right of action against those who, though they cause or are likely to cause us harm, clearly do not endanger our lives. (However, specific cases are often unclear. The shopkeeper who shoots a person who holds him up with a toy gun was not endangered, but it may have been very reasonable of him to suppose that he was endangered.) And it includes no right to greater than minimal preventive action against a person who endangers one's life. If B is chasing A with a gun, and A could save his life either by closing a bullet-proof door or by shooting B, then if people have only a right not to be killed and a minimal corollary right of self-defence, A would have no right to shoot B. (Again, such cases are often unclear – A may not know that the door is bullet-proof or not think of it or may simply reason that shooting *B* is a better guarantee of prevention.) A right of proportionate self-defence which might justify *A* in shooting *B*, even were it clear that closing the door would have been enough to prevent *B*, is not a corollary of the right not to be killed. Perhaps a right of proportionate retaliation might be justified by some claim such as that aggressors lose certain rights, but I shall take no position on this issue.

In one respect the narrow right of self-defence, which is the corollary of a right not to be killed, is more extensive than some other interpretations of the right of self-defence. For it is a right to take action against others who endanger our lives whether or not they do so intentionally. *A*'s right not to be killed entitles him to take action not only against aggressors but also against those 'innocent threats'[2] who endanger lives without being aggressors. If *B* is likely to cause *A*'s death inadvertently or involuntarily, then *A* has, if he has a right not to be killed, a right to take whatever steps are necessary to prevent *B* from doing so, provided that these do not infringe *B*'s right not to be killed unnecessarily. If *B* approaches *A* with a highly contagious and invariably lethal illness, then *A* *may* try to prevent B from getting near him even if *B* knows nothing about the danger he brings. If other means fail, *A* may kill *B* in self-defence, even though *B* was no aggressor.

We can call situation (1) *the well-equipped lifeboat situation*; situation (2) *the under-equipped lifeboat situation*. There may, of course, be cases where the six survivors are unsure which situation they are in, but for simplicity I shall disregard those here. On a well-equipped lifeboat it is possible for all to survive until rescue. No killing could be justified as unavoidable, and if someone is killed, then the justification could only be self-defence in special situations. Consider the following examples:

(1A) On a well-equipped lifeboat with six persons, *A* threatens to jettison the fresh water, without which some or all would not survive till rescue. *A* may be either hostile or deranged. *B* reasons with *A*, but when this fails, shoots him. *B* can appeal to his own and the others' right of self-defence to justify the killing. 'It was him or us', he may reasonably say, 'for he would have placed us in an under-equipped lifeboat situation.' He may say this both when *A* acts to harm the others and when *A* acts as an innocent threat.

(1B) On a well-equipped lifeboat with six persons *A*, *B*, *C*, *D*, *E* and *F* decide to withhold food from *A*, who consequently dies. In this case they cannot appeal to self-defence – for all could

[2] Cf. Robert Nozick, *Anarchy, State, and Utopia* (Oxford: Basil Blackwell, 1977), 34. Nozick defines an innocent threat as 'someone who is innocently a causal agent in a process such that he would be an aggressor had he chosen to become such an agent'.

have survived. Nor can they claim that they merely let *A* die ('We didn't *do* anything') – for *A* would not otherwise have died. This was not a case of violating the problematic right not to be allowed to die, but of violating the right not to be killed, and the violation is without justification of self-defence or of unavoidability.

On an under-equipped lifeboat it is not possible for all to survive until rescue. Some deaths are unavoidable, but sometimes there is no particular person whose death is unavoidable.

Consider the following examples:

(2A) On an under-equipped lifeboat with six persons, *A* is very ill and needs extra water, which is already scarce. The others decide not to let him have any water, and *A* dies of thirst. If *A* drinks, then not all will survive. On the other hand it is clear that *A* was killed rather than allowed to die. If he had received water he might have survived. Though some death was unavoidable, *A*'s was not and selecting him as the victim requires justification.

(2B) On an under-equipped lifeboat with six persons, water is so scarce that only four can survive (perhaps the distillation unit is designed for supplying four people). But who should go without? Suppose two are chosen to go without, either by lot or by some other method, and consequently die. The others cannot claim that all they did was to allow the two who were deprived of water to die – for these two might otherwise have been among the survivors. Nobody had a greater right to be a survivor, but given that not all could survive, those who did not survive were killed justifiably if the method by which they were chosen was fair. (Of course, a lot needs to be said about what would make a selection procedure fair.)

(2C) The same situation as in (2B) holds, but the two who are not to drink ask to be shot to ease their deaths. Again the survivors cannot claim that they did not kill but at most that they killed justifiably. Whether they did so is not affected by their shooting rather than dehydrating the victims, but only by the unavoidability of some deaths and the fairness of procedures for selecting victims.

(2D) Again the basic situation is as in (2B). But the two who are not to drink rebel. The others shoot them and so keep control of the water. Here it is all too clear that those who died were killed, but they too may have been justifiably killed. Whether the survivors kill justifiably depends neither on the method of killing nor on the victims' cooperation, except insofar as cooperation is relevant to the fairness of selection procedures.

Lifeboat situations do not occur very frequently. We are not often confronted starkly with the choice between killing and being killed by the application of a decision to distribute scarce rations in a certain way. Yet this is becoming the situation of the human species on this globe. The current metaphor 'spaceship Earth' suggests more drama and less danger; if we are feeling sober about the situation, 'lifeboat Earth' may be more suggestive.

Some may object to the metaphor 'lifeboat Earth'. A lifeboat is small; all aboard have equal claims to be there and to share equally in the provisions. Whereas the earth is vast and while all may have equal rights to be there, some also have property rights which give them special rights to consume, while others do not. The starving millions are far away and have no right to what is owned by affluent individuals or nations, even if it could prevent their deaths. If they die, it will be said, this is a violation at most of their right not to be allowed to die. And this I have not established or assumed.

I think that this could reasonably have been said in times past. The poverty and consequent deaths of far-off persons were something which the affluent might perhaps have done something to prevent, but which they had (often) done nothing to bring about. Hence they had not violated the right not to be killed of those living far off. But the economic and technological interdependence of today alters this situation.[3] Sometimes deaths are produced by some persons or groups of persons in distant, usually affluent, nations. Sometimes such persons and groups of persons violate not only some persons' alleged right not to be allowed to die but also their more fundamental right not to be killed.

We tend to imagine violations of the right not to be killed in terms of the killings so frequently discussed in the United States today: confrontations between individuals where one directly, violently and intentionally brings about the other's death. As the lifeboat situations have shown, there are other ways in which we can kill one another. In any case, we do not restrict our vision to the typical mugger or murderer context. *B* may violate *A*'s right not to be killed even when

(a) *B* does not act alone.
(b) *A*'s death is not immediate.
(c) It is not certain whether *A* or another will die in consequence of *B*'s action.
(d) *B* does not intend *A*'s death.

---

[3] Cf. Singer, 'Famine, affluence, and morality', 232. I am in agreement with many of the points which Singer makes, but am interested in arguing that we must have some famine policy from a much weaker set of premises. Singer uses some consequentialist premises: starvation is bad; we ought to prevent bad things when we can do so without worse consequences; hence we ought to prevent starvation whether it is nearby or far off and whether others are doing so or not. The argument of this chapter does not depend on a particular theory about the grounds of obligation, but should be a corollary of any non-bizarre ethical theory which has any room for a notion of rights.

The following set of examples illustrates these points about killings:

(aa) *A* is beaten by a gang consisting of *B, C, D,* etc. No one assailant single-handedly killed him, yet his right not to be killed was violated by all who took part.

(bb) *A* is poisoned slowly by daily doses. The final dose, like earlier ones, was not by itself lethal. But the poisoner still violated *A*'s right not to be killed.

(cc) *B* plays Russian roulette with *A, C, D, E, F* and *G,* firing a revolver at each once, when he knows that one firing in six will be lethal. If *A* is shot and dies, then *B* has violated his right not to be killed.

(dd) Henry II asks who will rid him of the turbulent priest, and his supporters kill Becket. It is reasonably clear that Henry did not intend Becket's death, even though he in part brought it about, as he later admitted.

These explications of the right not to be killed are not too controversial taken individually, and I would suggest that their conjunction is also uncontroversial. Even when *A*'s death is the result of the acts of many persons and is not an immediate consequence of their deeds, nor even a certain consequence, and is not intended by them, *A*'s right not to be killed may be violated.

First class versus steerage on lifeboat Earth

If we imagine a lifeboat in which special quarters are provided for the (recently) first-class passengers, and on which the food and water for all passengers are stowed in those quarters, then we have a fair, if crude, model of the present human situation on lifeboat Earth. For even on the assumption that there is at present sufficient for all to survive, some have control over the means of survival and so, indirectly, over others' survival. Sometimes the exercise of control can lead, even on a well-equipped lifeboat, to the starvation and death of some of those who lack control. On an ill-equipped lifeboat some must die in any case and, as we have already seen, though some of these deaths may be killings, some of them may be justifiable killings. Corresponding situations can, do and will arise on lifeboat Earth, and it is to these that we should turn our attention, covering both the presumed present situation of global sufficiency of the means of survival and the expected future situation of global insufficiency.

Sufficiency situations

Aboard a well-equipped lifeboat any distribution of food and water which leads to a death is a killing and not just a case of permitting a death. For the acts of those who distribute the food and water are the causes of a death which would not have occurred had those agents either had no causal influence or had done other acts. By contrast, a person whom they leave in the water to drown is merely allowed to die, for his death would have taken place (other things being equal) had those agents had no causal influence, though it could have been prevented had they rescued him.[4] The distinction between killing and allowing to die, as here construed, does not depend on any claims about the other rights of persons who are killed. The death of the short-changed passenger of example (1B) violated his property rights as well as his right not to be killed, but the reason the death was classifiable as a killing depended on the part which the acts of the other passengers had in causing it. If we suppose that a stowaway on a lifeboat has no right to food and water and is denied them, then clearly his property rights have not been violated. Even so, by the above definitions he is killed rather than allowed to die. For if the other passengers had either had no causal influence or done otherwise, his death would not have occurred. Their actions – in this case distributing food only to those entitled to it – caused the stowaway's death. Their acts would be justifiable only if property rights can sometimes override the right not to be killed.

Many would claim that the situation on lifeboat Earth is not analogous to that on ordinary lifeboats, since it is not evident that we all have a claim, let alone an equal claim, on the earth's resources. Perhaps some of us are stowaways. I shall not here assume that we do all have some claim on the earth's resources, even though I think it plausible to suppose that we do. I shall assume that even if persons have unequal property rights and some people own nothing, it does not follow that B's exercise of his property rights can override A's right not to be killed.[5] Where our activities lead to others' deaths which would not have occurred had we either done something else or had no causal influence, no claim that the activities were within our economic rights would suffice to show that we did not kill.

---

[4] This way of distinguishing killing from allowing dying does not rely on distinguishing 'negative' from 'positive' acts. Such attempts seem unpromising since any act has multiple descriptions of which some will be negative and others positive. If a clear distinction is to be made between killing and letting die, it must hinge on the *difference* which an act makes for a person's survival, rather than on the description under which the agent acts.

[5] The point may appear rather arbitrary, given that I have not rested my case on one theory of the grounds of obligation. But I believe that almost any such theory will show a right not to be killed to override a property right. Perhaps this is why Locke's theory can seem odd: in moving from a right of self-preservation to a justification of unequal property rights, he finds himself gradually having to reinterpret all rights as property rights, thus coming to see us as the owners of our persons.

It is not far-fetched to think that at present the economic activity of some groups of persons leads to others' deaths. I shall choose a couple of examples of the sort of activity which can do so, but I do not think that these examples do more than begin a list of cases of killing by economic activities. Neither of these examples depends on questioning the existence of unequal property rights; they assume only that such rights do not override a right not to be killed. Neither example is one for which it is plausible to think that the killing could be justified as undertaken in self-defence.

Case one might be called the *foreign investment* situation. A group of investors may form a company which invests abroad – perhaps in a plantation or in a mine – and so manage their affairs that a high level of profits is repatriated, while the wages for the labourers are so minimal that their survival rate is lowered, that is, their expectation of life is lower than it might have been had the company not invested there. In such a case the investors and company management do not act alone, do not cause immediate deaths, and do not know in advance who will die; it is also likely that they intend no deaths. But by their involvement in the economy of an underdeveloped area they cannot claim, as can another company which has no investments there, that they are 'doing nothing'. On the contrary, they are setting the policies which determine the living standards which determine the survival rate. When persons die because of the lowered standard of living established by a firm or a number of firms which dominate a local economy and either limit persons to employment on their terms or lower the other prospects for employment by damaging traditional economic structures, and these firms could either pay higher wages or stay out of the area altogether, then those who establish these policies are violating some persons' rights not to be killed. Foreign investment which *raises* living standards, even to a still abysmal level, could not be held to kill, for it causes no additional deaths, unless there are special circumstances, as in the following example.

Even when a company investing in an underdeveloped country establishes high wages and benefits and raises the expectation of life for its workers, it often manages to combine these payments with high profitability only by having achieved a tax-exempt status. In such cases the company is being subsidised by the general tax revenue of the underdeveloped economy.[6] It makes no contribution to the infrastructure – e.g. roads

---

[6] These points were quite widely endorsed during early postwar decades in claims that underdeveloped economies are 'produced' by developed ones. Cf. P. A. Baron, *The Political Economy of Growth* (New York: Monthly Review Press, 1957), especially ch. 5 'On the roots of backwardness'; or A. G. Frank, *Capitalism and Underdevelopment in Latin America* (New York: Monthly Review Press, 1967).

and harbours and airports – from which it benefits. In this way many underdeveloped economies have come to include developed enclaves whose development is achieved in part at the expense of the poorer majority. In such cases, government and company policy combine to produce a high wage sector at the expense of a low wage sector; in consequence, some of the persons in the low wage sector, who would not otherwise have died, may die. These persons, whoever they may be, are killed and not merely allowed to die. Such killings may sometimes be justifiable – perhaps, if they are outnumbered by lives saved through having a developed sector – but they are killings nonetheless, since the victims might have survived if not burdened by transfer payments to the developed sector. But, one may say, the management of such a corporation and its investors should be distinguished more sharply. Even if the management chooses a level of wages, and consequently of survival, the investors usually know nothing of this. But the investors, even if ignorant, are responsible for company policy. They may often fail to exercise control, but by law they have control. They choose to invest in a company with certain foreign investments; they profit from it; they can, and others cannot, affect company policy in fundamental ways. To be sure, the investors are not murderers – they do not intend to bring about the deaths of any persons; nor do the company managers usually intend any of the deaths company policies cause. Even so, investors and management acting together with the sorts of results just described do violate some persons' rights not to be killed and usually cannot justify such killings either as required for self-defence or as unavoidable.

Case two, where even under sufficiency conditions some persons' economic activities result in the deaths of other persons, might be called the *commodity pricing* case. Underdeveloped countries often depend heavily on the price level of a few commodities. So a sharp drop in the world price of coffee or sugar or cocoa may spell ruin and lowered survival rates for whole regions. Yet such drops in price levels are not in all cases due to factors beyond human control. Where they are the result of action by investors, brokers or government agencies, these persons and bodies are choosing policies which will kill some people. Once again, to be sure, the killing is not single-handed, it is not instantaneous, the killers cannot foresee exactly who will die, and they may not intend anybody to die.

Because of the economic interdependence of different countries, deaths can also be caused by rises in the prices of various commodities. For example, the present near-famine in the Sahelian region of Africa and in the Indian subcontinent is attributed by agronomists partly to climatic shifts and partly to the increased prices of oil and hence of fertiliser, wheat and other grains.

The recent doubling in international prices of essential foodstuffs will, of necessity, be reflected in higher death rates among the world's lowest income groups, who lack the income to increase their food expenditures proportionately, but live on diets near the subsistence level to begin with.[7]

Of course, not all of those who die will be killed. Those who die of drought will merely be allowed to die, and some of those who die because less has been grown with less fertiliser will also die because of forces beyond the control of any human agency. But to the extent that the raising of oil prices is an achievement of Arab diplomacy and oil company management rather than a windfall, the consequent deaths are killings. Some of them may perhaps be justifiable killings (perhaps if outnumbered by lives saved within the Arab world by industrialisation), but are killings nonetheless.

Even on a sufficiently equipped earth some persons are killed by others' distribution decisions. The causal chains leading to death-producing distributions are often extremely complex. Where they can be perceived with reasonable clarity we ought, if we take seriously the right not to be killed and seek not merely to avoid killing others but to prevent third parties from doing so, to support policies which reduce deaths. For example – and these are only examples – we should support certain sorts of aid policies rather than others; we should oppose certain sorts of foreign investment; we should oppose certain sorts of commodity speculation, and perhaps support certain sorts of price support agreements for some commodities (e.g. those which try to maintain high prices for products on whose sale poverty-stricken economies depend).

If we take the view that we have no duty to enforce the rights of others, then we cannot draw so general a conclusion about our duty to support various economic policies which might avoid some unjustifiable killings. But we might still find that we should take action of certain sorts either because our own lives are threatened by certain economic activities of others or because our own economic activities threaten others' lives. Only if we knew that we were not part of any system of activities causing unjustifiable deaths could we have no duties to support policies which seek to avoid such deaths. Modern economic causal chains are so complex

---

[7] For typical claims about food availability in the 1970s, see Lester R. Brown and Erik P. Eckholm, 'The empty breadbasket', and N. Borlaug and R. Ewell, 'The shrinking margin', both in *Ceres* (FAO Review on Development), March–April 1974.

that it is likely that only those who are economically isolated and self-sufficient could know that they are part of no such systems of activities. Persons who believe that they are involved in some death-producing activities will have some of the same duties as those who think they have a duty to enforce others' rights not to be killed.

Scarcity situations

The last section showed that sometimes, even in sufficiency situations, some might be killed by the way in which others arranged the distribution of the means of subsistence. Of far more importance in the long run is the true lifeboat situation: the situation of scarcity. We face a situation in which not everyone who is born can live out the normal span of human life and, further, in which we must expect today's normal life-span to be shortened. The date at which serious scarcity will begin is not generally agreed upon, but even the more optimistic prophets place it no more than decades away.[8] Its arrival will depend on factors such as the rate of technological invention and innovation, especially in agriculture and pollution control, and the success of programs to limit human fertility.

Such predictions may be viewed as exonerating us from complicity in famine deaths. If famine is inevitable, then while we may have to choose whom to save, the deaths of those whom we do not or cannot save cannot be seen as killings for which we bear any responsibility. For these deaths would have occurred even if we had no causal influence. The decisions to be made may be excruciatingly difficult, but at least we can comfort ourselves that we did not produce or contribute to the famine.

However, this comforting view of famine predictions neglects the fact that these predictions are contingent upon certain assumptions about what people will do in the pre-famine period. Famine is said to be inevitable *if* people do not curb their fertility, alter their consumption patterns and avoid pollution and consequent ecological catastrophes. It is the policies of the present which will produce, defer or avoid famine. Hence if famine comes, the deaths that occur will be results of decisions made earlier. Only if we take no part in systems or activities which lead to famine situations can we view ourselves as choosing whom to save rather than whom to kill

---

[8] For further 1970s discussions of the time and extent of famine see, for example, P. R. Ehrlich, *The Population Bomb*, rev. edn (New York: Ballantine Books, 1971); R. L. Heilbroner, *An Inquiry into the Human Prospect* (New York: W. W. Norton, 1974); and *Scientific American*, September 1974, especially R. Freedman and B. Berelson, 'The human population'; P. Demeny, 'The populations of the underdeveloped countries'; and R. Revelle, 'Food and population'.

when famine comes. In an economically interdependent world there are few ·people who can look on the approach of famine as a natural disaster from which they may kindly rescue some, but for whose arrival they bear no responsibility. We cannot stoically regard particular famine deaths as unavoidable if we have contributed to the emergence and extent of famine.

If we bear some responsibility for the advent of famine, then any decision on distributing the risk of famine is a decision whom to kill. Even a decision to rely on natural selection as a famine policy is choosing a policy for killing – for under a different famine policy different persons might have survived, and under different pre-famine policies there might have been no famine or a less severe famine. The choice of a particular famine policy may be justifiable on the grounds that once we have let it get to that point there is not enough to go around, and somebody must go, as on an ill-equipped lifeboat. Even so, the famine policy chosen will not be a policy of saving some but not all persons from an unavoidable predicament.

Persons cannot, of course, make famine policies individually. Famine and pre-famine policies are and will be made by governments individually and collectively and perhaps also by some voluntary organisations. It may even prove politically impossible to have a coherent famine or pre-famine policy for the whole world; if so, we shall have to settle for partial and piecemeal policies. But each person who is in a position to support or oppose such policies, whether global or local, has to decide which to support and which to oppose. Even for individual persons, inaction and inattention are often a decision – a decision to support the famine and pre-famine policies, of the status quo, whether or not they are 'hands off' policies. There are large numbers of ways in which private citizens may affect such policies. They do so in supporting or opposing legislation affecting aid and foreign investment, in supporting or opposing certain sorts of charities or groups such as Zero Population Growth, in promoting or opposing ecologically conservative technology and lifestyles. Hence we have individually the onus of avoiding killing. For even though we

(a)   do not kill single-handedly those who die of famine
(b)   do not kill instantaneously those who die of famine
(c)   do not know which individuals will die as the result of the pre-famine and famine policies we support (unless we support something like a genocidal famine policy)
(d)   do not intend any famine deaths

we nonetheless kill and do not merely allow to die. For as the result of our actions in concert with others, some will die who might have survived had we either acted otherwise or had no causal influence.

Famine policies and pre-famine policies

Various principles can be suggested on which famine and pre-famine policies might reasonably be based. I shall list some of these, more with the aim of setting out the range of possible decisions than with the aim of stating a justification for selecting some people for survival. One very general policy might be that of adopting whichever more specific policies will lead to the fewest deaths. An example would be going along with the consequences of natural selection in the way in which the allocation of medical care in situations of great shortage does, that is, the criteria for relief would be a high chance of survival if relief is given and a low chance otherwise – the worst risks would be abandoned. (This decision is analogous to picking the ill man as the victim on the lifeboat in (2A).) However, the policy of minimizing deaths is indeterminate, unless a certain time horizon is specified. For the policies which maximise survival in the short run – e.g. preventive medicine and minimal living standards – may also maximise population increase and lead to greater ultimate catastrophe.[9]

Another general policy would be to try to find further grounds which can justify overriding a person's right not to be killed. Famine policies adopted on these grounds might permit others to kill those who will forgo their right not to be killed (voluntary euthanasia, including healthy would-be suicides) or to kill those whom others find dependent and exceptionally burdensome, e.g. the unwanted sick or aged or unborn or newborn (involuntary euthanasia, abortion and infanticide). Such policies might be justified by claims that the right not to be killed may be overridden in famine situations if the owner of the right consents or if securing the right is exceptionally burdensome. Any combination of such policies is a policy of killing some and protecting others. Those who are killed may not have their right not to be killed violated without reason; those who set and support famine policies and pre-famine policies will not be able to claim that they do not kill, but if they reason carefully they may be able to claim that they do not do so without justification.

From this vantage point it can be seen why it is not relevant to restrict the right of self-defence to a right to defend oneself against those who threaten one's life but do not do so innocently. Such a restriction may make a great difference to one's view of abortion in cases where the mother's life is threatened, but it does not make much difference when famine is the issue. Those who might be chosen as likely victims of any

[9] See *Scientific American*, September 1974, especially A. J. Coale, 'The history of the human population'.

famine policy will probably be innocent of contributing to the famine, or
at least no guiltier than others; hence the innocence of the victims is an
insufficient ground for rejecting a policy. Indeed it is hard to point a finger
at the guilty in famine situations. Are they the hoarders of grain? The
parents of large families? Inefficient farmers? Our own generation?

In a sense we are all innocent threats to one another's safety in scarcity
situations, for the bread one person eats might save another's life. If there
were fewer people competing for resources, commodity prices would fall
and starvation deaths be reduced. Hence famine deaths in scarcity situations might be justified on grounds of the minimal right of self-defence as
well as on grounds of the unavoidability of some deaths and the reasonableness of the policies for selecting victims. For each famine death leaves
fewer survivors competing for whatever resources there are, and the most
endangered among the survivors might have died – had not others done so.
So a policy which kills some may be justified on the grounds that the most
endangered survivors could have been defended in no other way.

Global scarcity is not here yet. But its imminence has certain implications for today. If all persons have a right not to be killed and a corollary
duty not to kill others, then we are bound to adopt pre-famine policies
which ensure that famine is postponed as long as possible and is minim-
ised. And a duty to try to postpone the advent and minimise the severity of
famine is a duty on the one hand to minimise the number of persons there
will be and on the other to maximise the means of subsistence.[10] For if we
do not adopt pre-famine policies with these aims we shall have to adopt
more drastic famine policies sooner.

So if we take the right not to be killed seriously, we should consider and
support not only some famine policy for future use but also a population
and resources policy for present use. There has been a certain amount of
philosophical discussion of population policies.[11] From the point of view of
the present argument it has two defects. First, it is for the most part
conducted within a utilitarian framework and focuses on problems such
as the different population policies required by maximising the total and
the average utility of a population. Secondly this literature tends to look at
a scarcity of resources as affecting the quality of lives but not their very

---

[10] The failure of 'right to life' groups to pursue these goals seriously casts doubt upon their
   commitment to the preservation of human lives. Why are they active in so few of the contexts
   where human lives are endangered?
[11] For example, J. J. C. Smart, *An Outline of a System of Utilitarian Ethics* (Melbourne University Press,
   1961), 18, 44ff.; and Jan Narveson, 'Moral problems of population', *Monist* 57 (1973), 62–86;
   'Utilitarianism and new generations', *Mind* 76 (1967), 62–72.

possibility. It is more concerned with the question, 'How many people should we add?' than with the question, 'How few people could we lose?' There are, of course, many interesting questions about population policies which are not relevant to famine. But here I shall consider only population and resource policies determined on the principle of postponing and minimising famine, for these are policies which might be based on the claim that persons have a right not to be killed, so that we have a duty to avoid or postpone situations in which we shall have to override this right.

Such population policies might, depending upon judgements about the likely degree of scarcity, range from the mild to the draconian. I list some examples. A mild population policy might emphasise family planning, perhaps moving in the direction of fiscal incentives or measures which stress not people's rights but their duties to control their bodies. Even a mild policy would require a lot in terms both of invention (e.g. the development of contraceptives suitable for use in poverty-stricken conditions) and of innovation (e.g. social policies which reduce the incentives and pressures to have a large family).[12] More draconian policies would enforce population limitation – for example, by mandatory sterilisation after a certain number of children were born or by reducing public health expenditures in places with high net reproduction rates to prevent death rates from declining until birth rates do so. A policy of completely eliminating all further births (e.g. by universal sterilisation) is also one which would meet the requirement of postponing famine, since extinct species do not suffer famine. I have not in this argument used any premises which show that a complete elimination of births would be wrong, but other premises might give reasons for thinking that it is wrong to enforce sterilisation or better to have some persons rather than no persons. In any case the political aspects of introducing famine policies make it likely that this most austere of population policies would not be considered. There is a corresponding range of resource policies. At the milder end are the various conservation and pollution control measures now being practised or discussed. At the tougher end of the spectrum are complete rationing of energy and materials consumption. If the aim of a resources policy is to avoid killing those who are born, any adequate policy may require both invention (e.g. solar energy technology and better waste retrieval techniques) and innovation (e.g. introducing new technology in such a way

---

[12] Cf. Mahmood Mamdani, *The Myth of Population Control* (New York: Monthly Review Press, 1972), for evidence that high fertility can be based on rational choice rather than ignorance or incompetence.

that its benefits are not quickly absorbed by increasing population, as has happened with the green revolution in some places).

At all events, if we think that people have a right not to be killed, we cannot fail to face up to its long-range implications. This one right by itself provides ground for activism on many fronts. In scarcity situations which we help produce, the defeasibility of the right not to be killed is important, for there cannot be any absolute duty not to kill persons in such situations but only a commitment to kill only for reasons. Such a commitment requires consideration of the condition or quality of life which is to qualify for survival. Moral philosophers are reluctant to face up to this problem; soon it will be staring us in the face.

CHAPTER 2

Rights, obligations and world hunger[1]

Hunger and famine

Many of the facts of world hunger and poverty towards the end of the twentieth century were widely known, among them the following:

1 World population was over 5 billion and rising rapidly. It would exceed 6 billion by the end of the century.

2 In many poor countries, investment and growth were concentrated in an urbanised modern sector, and the benefits reached a minority.

3 In many poor countries, the number of destitute and landless increased even when there was economic growth.

4 In many African countries, harvests had been falling and dependence on imported grain was growing.

5 The rich countries of the 'North' had surpluses of grain that went to poorer countries, most of it being sold.

6 The rural poor of the Third World were sometimes harmed by grain imports, which were distributed in towns, so depriving peasants of customers for their crops. These peasants then migrated to shantytowns.

And then there was Ethiopia. Famines are not unexpected natural catastrophes, but simply the harshest extreme of hunger. We know well enough where in the world poverty and hunger are constantly bad enough for minor difficulties to escalate into famine. Ethiopia had had earlier famines. We know which regions in Africa, Asia and (to a lesser degree) Latin America are vulnerable. Famine is the tip of the iceberg of hunger. It is the

---

[1] 'Rights, obligations and world hunger' in F. Jimenez (ed.), *Poverty and Social Justice: Critical Perspectives: A Pilgrimage toward Our Own Humanity* (Tempe, AZ: Bilingual Press, 1987), 86–100. It has been lightly edited, mainly by changing some tenses, cutting time sensitive references and minimal updating of terminology. However, it was published as and remains a 'manifesto' piece, and does not offer exhaustive arguments.

29

bit that is publicised and to which we react; but the greater part of the suffering is less lurid and better hidden.

Most hungry people are not migrating listlessly or waiting for the arrival of relief supplies. They are leading their normal lives with their normal economic, social and familial situations, earning and growing what they normally earn or grow, yet are always poor and often hungry. These normal conditions are less spectacular than famine, but affect far more people. We are tempted to set famine aside from endemic hunger and poverty. We often blame natural catastrophes, such as floods, drought, blight or cold for destroying crops and producing famine. But harsh circumstances cause famines only when social and economic structures are too fragile to absorb such natural shocks. Californians know that desert climates need not lead to famines. Minnesotans know that a ferocious winter need not be reflected in countless annual deaths from cold. Yet both regions would have catastrophic annual mortality if they lacked appropriate social and economic structures. Many natural catastrophes produce human catastrophes only when social structures are inadequate.

Focus on action

We could list the facts of world hunger, poverty and famine endlessly. But facts alone do not tell us what to do. What surely matters is action. Which action we advocate depends partly on our perception of the facts, and this perception depends partly on the ethical outlook we adopt. Both our perception of problems and our prescriptions for action reflect our ethical theory. Ethical theories are not elegant trimmings that decorate our reasoning about practical problems. They determine our entire focus. They lead us to see certain facts and principles as salient and others as insubstantial. They focus our action – or our inertia.

Here I shall consider three theories of what ought to be done about hunger and famine. Two are widely known and discussed in the English-speaking world. The third, though in many ways older and more familiar, now receives rather less public and philosophical attention. I shall criticise the two prevailing approaches and recommend the third.

The first approach sees human happiness and well-being as the standard for assessing action, and its most common modern version is utilitarianism. For utilitarians, all ethical requirements are basically a matter of beneficence to others. The second approach takes respect for human rights as basic and interprets the central issues of world hunger as matters of justice, to be secured by respecting rights. The third approach takes fulfilment of human obligations or duties as basic and insists that these include both obligations of justice and obligations of help or beneficence to others, and above all to others in need. Since no famine policy or development strategy would be adequate if it guided only individual action, all three of these positions point to ways in which public and institutional policies as well as individual action might be undertaken.

Measuring and maximising happiness

The central idea of all ethical reasoning that focuses on consequences or results is that action is right if it produces good results. The specifically utilitarian version of this approach assesses the goodness of results by their contribution to total human happiness: the best results are those that maximise human happiness. This position is very familiar to many people because restricted versions of it are incorporated in economic theory and in business practice, and often used in daily decision making. It leads naturally to the question: What will maximise human happiness?

This seems such a simple question, but has been given many unclear answers. Even discussions of hunger and famine, where the means to greater happiness may seem obvious, jangle with disagreements between utilitarian writers. The Australian philosopher Peter Singer[2] used simple economic considerations to argue that any serious utilitarian should undertake radical redistribution of his or her possessions and income to the poor. Standard marginalist considerations suggest that we can increase happiness by transferring resources from the rich to the poor. Any unhappiness caused by the loss of a luxury – such as a car – will be more than outweighed by the happiness produced by using the same funds to buy essential food for the hungry. He was immediately opposed by Garrett Hardin[3] who drew on the thought of the early nineteenth-century economist and population theorist Thomas Malthus to argue that providing food to the poor only fuels population increase, producing more people than can be fed and leading eventually to devastating famine and maximal misery.

It is an urgent practical question whether utilitarians can resolve these disagreements. The founder of utilitarianism, the late eighteenth-century radical philosopher and polemicist Jeremy Bentham, thought we could do

[2] Singer, 'Famine, affluence, and morality'.
[3] Garrett Hardin, 'Lifeboat ethics: the case against helping the poor' in W. H. Aiken and H. LaFollete (eds.), *World Hunger and Moral Obligation* (Englewood Cliffs, NJ: Prentice-Hall, 1977), 11–21.

so with scientific rigour: it was only a matter of measuring and aggregating seven dimensions of human happiness. To help us he provided a pithy mnemonic verse in his *Introduction to the Principles of Morals and Legislation:*

> *Intense, long, certain, speedy, fruitful, pure,—*
> *Such marks* in *pleasures* and in *pains* endure.
> Such pleasures seek if *private* be thy end:
> If it be *public* wide let them *extend*.[4]

But we know that this metric approach is inadequate rather than scientific. Despite the recurrent optimism of some economists and decision theorists about measuring *happiness*, we know we cannot generally predict or measure or aggregate happiness with any precision.

Accuracy, precision and needs

Yet we can, it seems, often make approximate judgements of human happiness. And perhaps that is enough. After all, we do not need great precision, but only reasonable (even if vague) accuracy. We know that hunger and destitution mean misery and that enough to eat ends that sort of misery. Do we need to know more?

   If we are to be utilitarians, we do need to know a lot more. We need not only to know what general result to aim at, but to work out what means to take. Since very small changes in actions and policies may vastly alter results, precise comparisons of many results are indispensable. Examples of some unsuspected results of intended beneficence make the point vivid. Some food aid policies have actually harmed those whom they were intended to benefit, or have benefited those who were not in the first place the poorest. (This is not to say that food aid is dispensable – especially in cases of famine – but it is never enough to end misery, and it can be damaging if misdirected.) Some aid policies aimed at raising standards of life, for example by encouraging farmers to grow cash crops, have damaged the livelihood of subsistence farmers, and harmed the poorest. The benefits of aid are often diverted to those who are not in the greatest need, and sometimes to those who are the most corrupt. The ubiquity of corruption also shows how essential it is for utilitarians to make precise rather than vague judgements about how to increase human

---

[4] Jeremy Bentham, *An Introduction to the Principles of Morals and Legislation* (1823) in *A Fragment on Government with an Introduction to the Principles of Morals and Legislation*, ed. Wilfrid Harrison (Oxford: Basil Blackwell, 1967), 151.

happiness. Benevolent intentions are quite easy to identify; but beneficent policies cannot be identified if we cannot predict and compare results precisely.

To do their calculations, utilitarians need not only precise measurements of happiness, but precise predictions of the results policies produce. They need the sort of comprehensive and predictive social science to which many researchers have aspired, but which they have not attained. At present we cannot resolve even very basic disagreements between rival utilitarians. We cannot show whether happiness is maximised by attending to nearby desires where we can intervene personally (even if these are desires that reflect no needs), or by concentrating all our help on the neediest. Indeed, we often know too little even to predict which public policies will benefit the poor most.

And if utilitarians developed the precise methods of prediction and calculation that they lack, the results might not endorse help for the poor. Utilitarian thinking assigns no special importance to human need. Happiness produced by meeting the desires of those around us – even their desires for unneeded goods – may count as much as, or more than, happiness produced by ending real misery. All that matters is which desire is more intense. If the neediest are so weakened and apathetic that they no longer have strong desires, or have preferences that are adapted to their realities, their need may count less rather than more in a utilitarian calculus. Moreover we know that charity that begins at home, where others' desires are evident to us, can find so much to do there that it often ends at home, too. Unless needs are given a certain priority in ethical thinking, they may be neglected.

Meanwhile, utilitarian thinking unavoidably leaves many dilemmas unclarified and unresolved. Was it beneficent, and so right, to negotiate massive development loans, although soaring interest rates meant that much of some poor countries' export earnings were swallowed by interest payments? The present rich countries developed during a period of lower and more stable interest rates: they now control the ground rules of a world economy that may not provide that context of opportunity for remaining poor countries. Has it been happiness maximising to provide development loans for poor countries in these conditions? Might happiness have been greater if they had relied more on lesser but indigenous sources of investment? Or would the cost of slower growth have been a larger total of human misery that could have been avoided by accepting higher interest rates? These are bitter questions, and I do not know the answers in general, or for particular countries. I raise them to illustrate the difficulty of relying

34 Hunger across boundaries

on predictions and calculations about maximal happiness in determining what ought to be done and what it would be wrong to do.

The human rights movement

The difficulties of utilitarian thinking may seem to arise from its ambitious scope. Utilitarianism tries to encompass the whole of morality under a single principle, and to select acts and policies that are not only right, but best or optimal. One alternative might be to aim for rather less. This might be done by looking at principles for evaluating acts and rejecting those that are wrong, rather than adopting grand proposals to aim to identify just those acts and policies that provide optimal results.

The most common contemporary embodiment of this approach is provided by the human rights movement. The rhetoric of rights is all around us. Its sources are well known, and include the grand eighteenth-century documents, such as Tom Paine's *The Rights of Man*, and the Declarations of Rights of the US and French revolutions. More recently concern for human rights has been based on the post-World War II search for foundations for a new international order, and the prominent role of the *Universal Declaration of Human Rights* of 1948. In subsequent decades the human rights movement gained global influence, so that the standard ethical requirement in human affairs now construes justice as a matter of respect for rights.

Liberty rights and social or 'welfare' rights

Within discussions of rights there has been persistent disagreement about the list of rights that justice comprises. In general terms, some right-wing proponents of rights assert that there are only rights to liberty, hence that we have only the core responding obligations not to interfere with others' liberty. Other proponents of rights assert that there are also certain social or 'welfare' rights, hence certain positive obligations to help and assist others. Those who think that all rights are liberty rights point to supposed rights to life, liberty and the pursuit of happiness, including the right to unregulated economic activity. On this view it is unjust to interfere with or restrict others' exercise of democratic political rights or (full) capitalist economic rights. Those who think that there are also social or 'welfare' rights point to rights to food, health care or welfare payments. Since rights to unregulated economic activity are incompatible with these, they reject unrestricted economic rights.

These disagreements cannot be settled by appeal to documents. The United Nations documents were a political compromise and resolutely confer *all* sorts of rights. Proponents of liberty rights therefore think that these documents advocate some spurious rights, which are neither part of nor compatible with justice. However, it is worth remembering that this political compromise has in fact been accepted by nearly all governments, who therefore prima facie have institutionalised treaty obligations to enact both liberty and social or 'welfare' rights.

Human rights and human needs

It matters hugely for the destitute which interpretation of rights is accepted as the authoritative guide to policies and decisions. If human rights were all of them liberty rights, then justice to the poor and hungry would be achieved by laissez-faire policies: provided liberties were not curtailed, justice would be served. This position can be harsh, since it sees the economic effects of individual and corporate action that does not violate liberties as no injustice, even if this devastates the economy on which many depend, and thereby many lives, and provides no safety net of social or 'welfare' rights. Hardship that arises when interest rates or commodity prices are volatile is not unjust, provided no liberties have been violated. But if human rights include certain social and economic rights, including 'welfare' rights, justice will require that some of these needs be met. For example, if there are rights to food or to subsistence, then it is unjust not to meet these needs, and unjust not to regulate economic activities that will prevent their being met. However, any claim to social or 'welfare' rights will be no more than rhetoric unless the counterpart obligations are both justified and allocated to individuals and institutions that can discharge them. And here many advocates of human rights are evasive about the real demands of the rights they favour. It is a significant and non-trivial matter that there is no human obligations movement.

Rights, liberty and autonomy

These disputes cannot be settled without showing which rights there are. The eighteenth-century pioneers often claimed that certain rights were self-evident. This claim now seems brazen, and in any case cannot settle disputes between the advocates of different sets of rights. One widely used line of argument aimed at settling these disputes takes it that human rights constitute collectively the largest possible realisation either of human *liberty* or of human *autonomy*. However, even if we could justify assuming that (some conception of) liberty or autonomy is the most fundamental of moral concerns, the two point to quite divergent claims about what rights there are. Unsurprisingly, advocates of these claims often disagree about the proper list, or the proper interpretation of human rights.

Those who think that what is fundamental is liberty, understood as mere, 'negative' non-interference by others, allow only for liberty rights. The idea of a consistent partitioning of human liberty would collapse as soon as we add rights to receive help or services, for the obligations that make these social or 'welfare' rights a reality will be incompatible with various rights of action that basic liberty rights are intended to protect. If we have duties to provide food for all who need it, we cannot have unrestricted rights to do what we choose with any food we own. At best certain societies may use their liberty rights to set up institutionalised rights to certain benefits – e.g. to education, welfare, health care – as has been done in most economically advanced states. But an institutionalised right is not a natural or human right. The social or 'welfare' rights institutionalised in developed countries have no bearing on the hunger and poverty in states where such rights have not been institutionalised.

Those who think that it is autonomy (or dignity, in some versions) rather than mere non-interference that is fundamental insist that there are some social or 'welfare' rights to goods and services, such as a right to subsistence. For without adequate nutrition and shelter, human autonomy is destroyed, and liberty rights themselves would be pointless. But the advocates of subsistence rights have so far produced no convincing arguments to show who should bear obligations to feed others. Yet this is the question that matters most if 'rights to subsistence' are to meet human needs.

Rights and charity

Some advocates of human rights, in particular those who take a libertarian standpoint, suggest that we should not worry too much if theories of rights neglect human needs. We should remember that justice is not the whole of ethics, which also includes wider duties such as those of beneficence or charity. The thought that the needs of the poor can be met by charity appeals to many people. But it is an unconvincing one in the context of a theory of human rights. The rights perspective itself undercuts the status of charity, all too often seeing it not as any sort of obligation, but as something that we are free to do or to omit, or even (and less plausibly) as a matter of supererogation rather than of obligation. Such a view of help for the needy may be comfortable for the 'haves' of this world, since it suggests that they go beyond duty and do something especially good if they help others at all. But it is damaging and depressing for the 'have-nots' who cannot claim help of anybody, since it is not a matter of right. They can just hope that help will happen; and usually what happens will be witheringly inadequate.

Human agency, rights and obligations

Justice need not be understood in the terms either of the human rights movement or of the utilitarian view of justice as just one contribution among others to human happiness. One way of taking a different approach is to see obligations or duties rather than rights as fundamental. This has been a standard approach to ethical questions, both before and throughout the Christian tradition. Rights are eighteenth-century upstarts in moral discourse, as is the elevation of individual happiness to be the arbiter of moral judgement. Both these approaches see human beings in a somewhat passive way. This is plain enough in the utilitarian picture of human beings as bearers of pains and pleasures. But it is less obvious that men and women are seen as passive by theories of rights. On the contrary, the turn to rights is sometimes defended on the grounds that it assigns a more active role to the powerless, who are to see themselves as wronged claimants rather than as the humble petitioners of more traditional, feudal pictures.

It is true that the human rights movement sees human beings as *more* active than they are in utilitarian theories, or in theories that celebrate charity. But it still does not see them fully as agents. Claimants are active insofar as they agitate for *others* to act. When we claim liberty rights, our first demand is that *others* act, so yielding us a space or opportunity in which we may or may not act. When we claim social or 'welfare' rights, we need not picture ourselves as acting at all, but must see *others* who bear the corresponding obligations as acting. By contrast, when we see obligations as basic, we address those who can produce or refuse changes – the very audience that the rights perspective addresses only indirectly.

The French philosopher Simone Weil, writing during the Second World War, put the point this way in *The Need for Roots*:

> The notion of obligations comes before that of rights, which is subordinate and relative to the former. A right is not effectual by itself, but only in relation to the obligation to which it corresponds, the effective exercise of a

right springing not from the individual who possesses it, but from other men who consider themselves as being under a certain obligation towards him.[5]

We do not know what a right amounts to until we know *who* has *an* obligation to do *what* for *whom* under *which* circumstances. When we try to be definite about rights, we always have to talk about obligations. The fundamental difficulty with the rhetoric of rights is that it addresses only part – the less powerful part – of the relevant audience. This rhetoric may have results where the poor are not wholly powerless; but where they are, claiming rights provides meagre pickings. When the poor are powerless, it is the powerful who must be convinced that they have certain obligations – whether or not the beneficiaries claim the performance of these obligations as their right. The first concern of an ethical theory that focuses on action should therefore be to justify obligations, rather than rights.

Obligations of justice

A theory of obligations can help deliberation about world hunger only if it is possible to show what obligations human beings have. The effort to show this without reliance on theological assumptions was made in the eighteenth century by Immanuel Kant. Kant's work is sometimes seen as one more theory of human rights. This may be because he based his argument for human obligations on a construction analogous to that used in thinking of human rights as a partitioning of maximal human liberty or autonomy. For he asks what principles of action could consistently be shared by all agents. The root idea behind such a system of principles is that human obligations are obligations never to act in ways in which others cannot in principle also act. The fundamental principles of action must be shareable, rather than principles available only to a privileged few. Kant's method of determining the principles of obligation cannot be applied to the superficial detail of action: we evidently cannot eat the very grain another eats or have everyone share the same roof. But we can try to see that the deep principles of our lives and of our institutions are shareable by all, and then work out the implications of these deep principles for particular situations.

The Kantian construction can reach some interesting conclusions about human obligations. One obligation of justice that it vindicates is that of

[5] Simone Weil, *The Need for Roots* (New York: Harper & Row, 1952), 3.

non-coercion. For a fundamental principle of coercion *cannot* be shared by all, since those who are coerced will be prevented from acting, and so cannot share this principle of action. Coercion, we might say with Kant, is not *universalisable*. This argument alone does not tell us what non-coercion requires in particular situations. Clearly it rules out many things that respect for liberty rights rules out. For example, a principle of non-coercion rules out killing, maiming, assaulting and threatening others. This range of obligations not to coerce is as important for the well-fed as for the hungry. But other aspects of non-coercion are peculiarly important for the hungry. Those who aim to act on a principle of non-coercion must take account of the fact that it is always rather easy to coerce those who are weak or vulnerable by activities that would not coerce richer or more powerful people.

Avoiding coercion is not just a matter of avoiding a short list of interferences in others' action, as rights approaches would have us imagine. Avoiding coercion means making sure that in our dealings with others we leave them room either to accept or to refuse the offers and suggestions made. This shows why an emphasis on obligations not to coerce is particularly telling in evaluating our dealings with the poor and vulnerable: They are more easily coerced. We can make them 'offers they cannot refuse' with the greatest of ease.[6] Proposals that might be genuine offers among equals, which others can accept or reject, can be threatening and unrefusable for the needy and vulnerable. Those who are vulnerable may be harmed in ways that threaten life by standard commercial or legal procedures, such as business deals that locate dangerous industrial processes where people live, or exact stiff political concessions for investment or for what passes as aid, or that set harsh commercial conditions on 'aid', such as mandating unneeded imports from a 'donor' nation.

Arrangements of these sorts can coerce even when they use the outward forms of commercial bargaining and legality. These forms of bargaining are designed for use between agents of roughly equal power. They may not be enough to protect the powerless. Hence both individuals and agencies such as corporations and national governments (both of the North and of the South) and aid agencies must meet exacting standards if they are not to coerce the vulnerable in ordinary legal, diplomatic and commercial dealings. Economic or material justice cannot be achieved without avoiding institutionalised as well as individual forms of coercion.

---

[6] I subsequently looked more closely at these 'offers': see 'Which are the offers *you* can't refuse?' in R. G. Frey and Christopher Morris (eds.), *Violence, Terrorism and Justice* (Cambridge University Press, 1991); republished in my *Bounds of Justice*.

A second fundamental obligation of justice is that of avoiding deception. A principle of deception, too, is not universalisable, because victims of deception, like victims of coercion, are in principle precluded from sharing the perpetrator's principle of action, which is kept hidden from them. However, since the obligation of non-deception is relevant to all public and political life, and not solely for dealings that affect the poor, the hungry and the vulnerable (although they are more easily deceived), I shall not explore its implications here.

Obligations: emergency relief, development and respect

In a framework that treats rights as fundamental, the whole of our moral obligations are brought under the heading of justice. But an obligations approach of the Kantian type can also be used to justify obligations that are not obligations of justice and whose performance cannot be claimed as rights. Some types of action cannot be done for all others, so they cannot be a universal obligation or have corresponding rights. Yet they also are not contingent on any special relationship, so they cannot be a matter of special, institutional obligation. Yet they can be a matter of obligation. A theory of obligation, unlike a theory of rights, can allow for 'imperfect' obligations, which are not allocated to specified recipients, so cannot be claimed.

This provides a further way in which an appreciation of need can enter into a theory of human obligations. We know that others in need are vulnerable and not self-sufficient. It follows that, even if they are not coerced, they may be unable to act, and so unable to become or remain autonomous agents who could act on principles that can be universally shared. Hence, if our fundamental commitment is to treat others as agents who could adopt the very principles that we act on, then we must be committed equally to strategies and policies that enable them to become and to remain agents. If we do anything less, we do not view others as doers like ourselves. However, nobody and no agent can do everything to sustain the autonomy of all others. Hence obligations to help are not and cannot be obligations to meet all needs; they can be obligations not to base our lives on principles that are not indifferent to or neglectful of others' need, nor of what it actually takes to sustain their agency. In some situations such 'imperfect' obligations may require specific and arduous action. The fact that we cannot help everyone only shows that we have no obligation to help everyone, and not that we have no obligation to help anyone.

If we are not indifferent or neglectful of the requirements for sustaining others' autonomy we will, I suggest, find ourselves committed not only to justice but to various further principles in our action towards the poor and vulnerable. First we will be committed to material help that sustains agency, by helping people over the threshold of poverty below which possibilities for autonomous action are absent or meagre. Since sustained and systematic help is needed if vulnerability and dependence are not to recur endlessly, this implies a commitment to development policies as well as to emergency food aid.

Unreliable aid does not secure autonomy. But nor, of course, can withholding food aid in emergencies secure autonomy. Since human needs are recurrent, food aid is not enough. Food is eaten and is gone; help can secure others' agency only if it constructs social and economic institutions that can meet human needs on a sustained basis. This means that help to the poorest and most vulnerable must seek sustainable production to make sure that when a given cycle of consumption is past, more is in the pipeline. Development of the relevant sort evidently not only is an economic matter, it also includes the development of human skills and capabilities by appropriate education and institutional changes that help poor and vulnerable people to gain some control over their lives.

Since the basis of these obligations to help is the claim that principles of action must be shareable by all, the pursuit of development must not itself reduce or damage others' capacities for agency. It must not fail to respect those who are helped. Their desires and views must be sought, and their participation respected. Agency is not fostered if the poor experience 'donor' agencies as new oppressors. Others' autonomy is not sustained if they are left feeling that they have been the victims of good works.

Conclusions and afterthoughts

The theory of obligations just sketched is surprisingly familiar to most of us. It is not distant from pictures of human obligation that we find in the Christian tradition and in other religious traditions, and it is present in the idiom of much of our social life. Many aid agencies are fond of quoting a Chinese proverb that runs: 'Give a man a fish and you feed him for a day; teach him to fish and you feed him for life.' Although this position is traditional and familiar, the favoured ethical theories of today do not endorse it. Utilitarian perspectives endorse the pursuit of happiness without specific concern to meet needs; human rights perspectives often fail to allocate obligations to help those in need. It therefore seems appropriate to end this sketch with some polemical questions rather than a feeling of reassurance. How and why have we allowed uncertain images of maximal happiness and self-centred visions of claiming human rights to distort our understanding of central ethical notions such as justice, beneficence and respect for human agents? Why have so many people been sure that our obligations to others are a matter of not interfering in their concerns – of doing nothing?

If human obligations are based on the requirements for respecting and securing one another's agency, then we may find another of Simone Weil's remarks to the point:

> The obligation is only performed if the respect is effectively expressed in a real, not a fictitious, way; and this can only be done through the medium of Man's earthly needs ... On this point, the human conscience has never varied. Thousands of years ago, the Egyptians believed that no soul could justify itself after death unless it could say, 'I have never let anyone suffer from hunger.' All Christians know they are liable to hear Christ say to them one day, 'I was an hungered, and ye gave me no meat.' Everyone looks on progress as being, in the first place, a transition to a state of human society in which people will not suffer from hunger.[7]

To make that transition is indeed no longer a matter of feeding the beggar at the gate. Modern opportunities are broader and demand political as well as – perhaps more than – merely individual action. Of course, no individual can do everything. But this will daunt only those who are riveted by an exclusively individual conception of human endeavour and success. If we remember that many human activities and successes are not individual, we need not be daunted. We can conclude that no individual and no institution is prevented from making those decisions within their power in ways that help fulfil rather than spurn obligations to the hungry.

---

[7] Weil, *The Need for Roots*, 6.

CHAPTER 3

Rights to compensation[1]

Legal and fundamental rights to compensation

Rights to compensation have been much invoked and much disputed in liberal debates. Some argue that a fundamental (natural, human or moral) right to compensation should be recognised and that doing so would transform many lives. For example, special treatment in education or employment might be owed in compensation for past denials of equal opportunity in developed societies; special consideration for Third World countries in aid and trade terms might be owed in compensation for the injustices of the colonial past.

We can make ready sense of the idea of *legal* rights to compensation. Legal rights to compensation provide (some) recompense for damage suffered. The damage for which compensation is given may or may not be produced by wrongdoing; it may also be negligent or accidental or due to natural causes. In law, compensation is not always contingent upon the victim having suffered harm caused by others' wrongdoing, or on saddling wrongdoers with the costs of compensation. Insurance policies standardly cover damage due to accident and neglect. Legal rights to compensation may provide payments to victims of violent crime, to those whose property is requisitioned or damaged, to victims of libel or malpractice, and to victims of natural disasters such as floods or earthquakes. Legal rights to compensation are a standard way of dealing with the predicament of those who are harmed, whether the harm is due to others' (criminal) action, their own negligence or natural catastrophe. Nor do they show that there are *fundamental rights* to compensation. Legal rights to compensation may lack moral grounding; and if they are morally grounded, they may be backed not by fundamental rights to compensation, but by other

[1] 'Rights to compensation', *Social Philosophy and Policy* 5 (1987), 73–87. The text has been abbreviated and updated in minor ways.

background claims or institutions. However, fundamental rights to compensation are also widely invoked. Surprisingly, some *libertarians* (*laissez-faire liberals*)[2] and less surprisingly many *welfare liberals* (*social justice liberals*) have embarked on this journey, while disagreeing sharply about where it ends.

Since the 1970s discussion of rights to compensation has often concentrated on cases where poverty and discrimination are said to have reduced the educational or employment prospects of specific social groups, for example women and racial minorities in developed countries. The proposed remedies, often more discussed than implemented, included various educational and employment measures that are thought of as compensating for a previously unjust distribution of various sorts of opportunities. Rights to compensation have been justified – or disputed – as ways of compensating for past wrongdoing.

Subsequently international measures of compensatory justice became a focus of debate. A central question has been whether compensation is owed to the descendants of those wronged during and following the European invasion of the non-European world.[3] The present victims of past European expansion are often held to include the descendants of those once enslaved (e.g. black citizens of the USA), the descendants of those who became marginalised minorities in their own countries (e.g. Australian Aborigines, Maoris, Native Americans in Canada and the USA), and the descendants of those who underwent generations of colonial rule, but were not displaced by European settlers (e.g. the present citizens of ex-colonies). However the arguments for *rights* to compensation are widely disputed.

Restitution, punishment and compensation

Compensation is always a secondary response to some previous damage. Many liberals of various persuasions hold that only damage arising from violations of rights that constitute *injury* provides a basis for a *right* to compensation. Loss or damage that is self-inflicted, due to natural events, or to actions that violate no rights, will not be due to injury, and unless

[2] Most strikingly, Nozick in his *Anarchy, State, and Utopia*.
[3] Early philosophical discussions include George Sher, 'Ancient wrongs and modern rights', *Philosophy and Public Affairs* 10 (Winter 1981), 3–17; and David Lyons, 'The new Indian claims and original rights to land', *Social Theory and Practice* 4 (1977), 249–72.

there are specific legal or social arrangements to provide for payments in such cases, those who suffer harms will be owed nothing by others, who have done them no injury. (Some refuse to call those whose loss or damage does not result from injury by others *victims*.)

Before anything can be shown about *rights* to compensation, it is necessary to consider what compensation is and how it differs from other forms of rectificatory justice. For even when rights have been violated, compensation is only one of several forms of rectificatory justice. Wrong-doing can also be rectified by forms of *restitution*, such as restoration, apology, forgiveness or acceptance, and by forms of *punishment* ranging from ostracism and censure, through capital and corporal punishment, to modern regimes of incarceration, other (partial) losses of liberty, and varied modes of social control and supervision. There is much to be said about each form of rectificatory justice. I shall deal with restitution and punishment cursorily, and then say more about compensation and rights to compensation.

Restitution seeks to restore situations to those that obtained before wrong was done. It is a response not so much to offenders and victims, as to the ruptured relationship between them. Literal restoration – of national independence or boundaries, of usurped status or property, of affections – is usually incomplete. Even after restoration, not everything is restored, although the outcome may be taken symbolically as constituting complete restitution. Some modes of restitution are entirely symbolic: apology, forgiveness and acceptance do not undo wrongs, but (at their best) they expunge them.

Restitution cannot be vicarious. That which has been lost, or its symbolic equivalent, must be restored by those who did wrong, or by their heirs or representatives, to those who suffered wrong, or to their heirs or representatives. The restoration of the Stuart monarchy in England and Scotland in 1660 could not replace Charles I on his throne: he had been executed. It could place his heir, whom royalists recognised as the true king, on that throne. It was not done by the Parliament that had removed Charles I from his throne, but by later leaders who had been on both sides during the interregnum. It did not restore the full range of powers that Charles I had claimed, but it restored many of them. As restorations go, this was a rather complete one, by which the rightful king was restored to his rightful throne. The symbolic adequacy of what was done was accepted by all concerned, as was necessary if it was to be seen as a restoration: no good giving Charles II some other throne, or his kingdoms some other king. Another example of symbolic adequacy is the public restoration to aboriginal groups in Australia of ancestral hunting grounds or sacred places, of which they had been wrongly deprived. Restitution could not have been achieved by transferring an equivalent acreage, or a sum of money, or by aboriginal peoples purchasing their lost lands.

Symbolic restitution does not require that the *particular* lost possession or status or relationship be restored (which may be impossible). It requires that particular wrongdoers, or their mutually acknowledged heirs or representatives, acknowledge their offence, and that this be accepted by those whom they wronged, or their mutually acknowledged heirs or representatives. Nothing is achieved if somebody other than the wrongdoer 'apologises' or if someone other than the victim 'accepts' or 'forgives'. Restitution may be the most profound response to past violations of rights, and the only one that genuinely wipes out wrongs. However, it is least available and least adequate in public affairs.

Nevertheless, symbolic restitution is sometimes achieved in public life, when representatives of past wrongdoers have accepted responsibility for wrongs done by their predecessors. For example, in 1990 the President of the Federal Republic of German apologised on behalf of the German state (in international law the successor state to the Third Reich) to the (then still extant) Czechoslovak state for the Nazi invasion and annexation of Czechoslovakia in 1938/39, and the Czechoslovak President, Vaclav Havel, apologised for the Czechoslovak expulsion of Germans after the war. No boundaries were changed, no artefacts were handed over: the point was to try to restore relationships by mutually acknowledging the past and the faults on both sides. A similarly symbolic acknowledgement of state wrongdoing took place when the Chilean Committee of National Reconciliation, in a situation where no individual wrongdoer could be named or punished (there was an amnesty) recognised the wrongs that had been done. This was done by taking a solemn and official record of injuries inflicted by the state and its (necessarily anonymised) officials and operatives, based on the testimony of those wronged: this public acknowledgement of the depositions, of the honour and innocence of those killed and tortured, and of the wrongs done to them, made some symbolic restitution. It named the victims but not the perpetrators, and while it does not attribute guilt to individuals it sent the incriminating evidence it could gather to the courts.[4]

---

[4] The English translation of the Committee's Report can be found at www.usip.org/sites/default/files/resources/collections/truth_commissions/Chile90-Report/Chile90-Report.pdf.

Punishment has generally been a more prominent theme than restitution in discussions of rectificatory justice. Like restitution, punishment cannot justly be vicarious: however, it is a response not to ruptured moral relations, but solely to past offences. There are, of course, many ways of punishing. Ostracism, though little discussed, has been rather widely used and advocated (consider the role of Siberia and lesser forms of rustication in modern states, or the total exile 'from the world' that Arendt's hypothetical judgement on Eichmann proposed). Censure too plays a slight role in modern theories of punishment, while capital punishment and corporal discipline are mostly rejected in favour of forms of social control such as incarceration, supervision, fines and other (partial) restrictions of liberty. Controversies about the forms punishment may take have tended to dominate discussions of rectificatory justice. There are widely differing views of the importance of retribution for the wrong done, of deterrence of further wrongs, and of protection for possible victims of future wrongs.

Compensation is a further, distinct approach to rectifying past wrongdoing and the harm inflicted. Compensation responds neither to ruptured moral relationships nor to offenders, but to those who have suffered harms. It is a distinctive form of rectificatory justice, because it *must* be vicarious in one respect, and *may* be vicarious in a second respect.

Victims are compensated when somebody offers them an *equivalent*, but *non-identical* (hence *vicarious*) substitute for their loss or damage; moreover this equivalent may be provided *vicariously*, i.e. by those who did not cause the loss or damage (for example the taxpayers of a later generation). Compensation differs from restitution in that it does not restore what a victim has lost: somebody who restores a kidnapped child to its parent, or a stolen car to its owner, does not compensate, but makes (possibly incomplete) restitution. Compensation also differs from punishment. Punishment seeks to rectify wrongdoing by focusing on the perpetrators, and often pays scant attention to the victims, or to any previous relationship between wrongdoer and victim.

These brief remarks about restitution, punishment and compensation may suggest not only that they are distinct, but that each would have a place in a complete account of rectificatory justice, which would need to consider both what it takes to restore antecedent relations between wrongdoer and victim, and how both wrongdoer and victim should be treated. Further reflection suggests, however, that adequate restitution may preempt both punishment and compensation. Once a wrong is expunged, there is nothing to punish and nothing to compensate for. Adequate restitution may consist in the literal restoration of that which was wrongly taken, or in symbolic restitution and symbolic punishment that 'makes amends'. When restitution succeeds, what may be offered as amends is not a form of compensation. It is not a material equivalent, and it could not have been provided by just anybody; it is a symbolic offering from wrongdoer to victim (or their mutually acknowledged successors) that restores the previous relationship, thereby making both compensation and punishment redundant, even offensive.

Compensatory proposals are therefore quite independent of proposals for punishing those who may have injured or discriminated against others. The perpetrators may, after all, be dead or unknown. Victims of misfortune or of injury can supposedly be compensated even when nobody knows who did them wrong, and nobody can be justly punished.

These general points take no stand on *rights to* compensation, which are much disputed. For example, some laissez-faire liberals are dubious about rights to compensation except where those who inflicted wrong are identifiable, so can be required to compensate for the injuries they inflicted. On such views rights to compensation are symmetrical with rights to punish, and justifiable compensation requires an injuring as well as an injured party. On the other hand, some welfare or social liberals, while agreeing that justifiable compensation must compensate specifically for harm caused by injury, deny that obligations to compensate must fall on those who inflicted the specific injury, and argue that harms caused by certain social practices create right to compensation, even in cases where it is difficult or impossible to identify the wrongdoers.

Punishment and compensation in Locke and Nozick

These distinctions provide a context for considering Nozick's appeal to rights to compensation in the early chapters of *Anarchy, State, and Utopia.* Although Nozick describes his enterprise as 'Lockean', it is strikingly different in starting point and argument from Locke's *Second Treatise of Government.*[5] Locke's wider framework is theological: he sees human beings as free agents, subject to natural law, and human obligations rather than human rights as morally fundamental. He argues that human beings comply imperfectly with natural law, and that the only just way to improve compliance is by a system of enforcement that is non-capricious. But if punishment were in the hands of individuals, the results would be

[5] John Locke, *Second Treatise of Government* (1689) in *Two Treatises of Government*, ed. Peter Laslett (Cambridge University Press, 1960).

capricious and unjust. So the enforcement of natural law by punishment must be socialised. The political order is justified as the best way of enforcing natural law. Locke's picture centres on free agents and what they ought to do, and not on bearers of rights and what ought to be done or omitted for them. His perspective is one of agency, not of recipience; he is concerned in the first instance with securing the performance of obligations, rather than with the rights that will be respected if obligations are fulfilled. Compensation is only a subsidiary concern.

When Locke looks at wrongdoing from the victim's perspective, he speaks not of *compensation* but of *reparation*. He thinks that (unlike rights to punish) rights to exact reparation should be held by 'the damnified person', who may recover from the offender 'as much as may make satisfaction for the harm he hath suffered'.[6] This right to reparation is a right to an equivalent of the damage, not to an equivalent of the offence. Locke does not here assume that there is any general measure of moral value, but more modestly that there is a certain range of injuries where the damage caused, rather than the injury itself, can be compensated for by providing an equivalent.

There is a sharp contrast between the limited role Locke assigned to compensation and the central role Nozick accorded it. On Nozick's account there can be compensation not merely for *damage* inflicted by wrongdoing, but also in certain circumstances for wrongdoing itself, that is, for *action* that violates rights. This point is the basis of his claim that certain violations of rights are permissible, *provided that they are compensated for*. Surprisingly, rather than maintaining that action that violates rights is forbidden and action that does not violate them permissible, Nozick asked what should be done about risky action that *may* violate rights. In particular, what should be done about the private enforcement of justice? He agreed with Locke that private justice is risky, and likely to violate rights. Then he argued[7] that risky punitive action may be forbidden *only* if compensation for this restriction of liberty rights is provided. An emerging state may legitimately monopolise the legitimate use of force by forbidding the use of risky procedures of private justice, provided that it compensates those whose (supposed) rights to punish are violated. This argument has been subject to many criticisms: I shall look only at one.

Nozick's position is a curious one for any rights theorist – let alone for a libertarian – since it appears to concede that rights can be weighed in terms of some more fundamental measure of value, and so that they are not after

[6] *Ibid.* ch. II, paras. 10 and 11, 273–4.   [7] Nozick, *Anarchy, State, and Utopia*, ch. 4.

all ethically fundamental.[8] Nozick got into this position because he tried to splice a broadly utilitarian view of human psychology and action with a theory of rights. He had to view actions as having a value or utility in order to think them compensable, yet he also insisted that rights are fundamental side constraints on the pursuit of goals, including utility. R. P. Wolff made the point aptly when he accused Nozick of combining

> a model that was developed as a theoretical elaboration of utilitarianism and a moral theory antithetical to the intrusive paternalism of utilitarianism[9]

and claimed that Nozick,

> given his extremely strong theory of individual rights, side constraints and so forth ... ought in all consistency to come to the conclusion that *no* unconsented-to-boundary-crossings (i.e., rights violations) are permissible, regardless of compensation.[10]

Nozick's reliance on compensation for rights violations has been the object of some detailed criticism. Here I have only noted the fundamental implausibility of the undertaking. This is sufficient reason for scepticism about introducing fundamental rights to compensation into a position that seeks to justify a minimal state.

I now turn to wider uses to which supposed rights to compensation have been pressed by non-libertarian rights theorists. Surely, one may think, rights theorists must take account of the uncertainty of human action and so must take some line on whether it is wrong to prohibit action that merely *risks* rights violation. However, a more coherent way for a libertarian rights theorist to take account of uncertainty is not to assume a metric for valuing actions that is independent of rights, but to insert probabilistic considerations into contexts of deliberation where what is at stake is whether *in particular circumstances* doing thus or so would or would not constitute a violation of rights. This is not to deny that rights theories should be – but often are not – based on an adequate theory of action.

---

[8] Cf. Jeffrey Paul, 'The withering of Nozick's minimal state' in Jeffrey Paul (ed.), *Reading Nozick: Essays on Anarchy, State, and Utopia* (Totowa, NJ: Rowman & Littlefield, 1981), 68–76; and Robert Paul Wolff, 'Robert Nozick's derivation of the minimal state', in *ibid.*, 77–106.

[9] Wolff, 'Robert Nozick's derivation', 86. Nozick's uneasy hovering between two ethical theories is also apparent in a second major use he makes of the notion of compensation, in his interpretation of the Lockean proviso that just appropriation must leave 'enough and as good' for others. Cf. *Anarchy, State, and Utopia*, ch. 7, and criticism of the argument in Cheyney C. Ryan, 'Yours, mine and ours: property rights and individual liberty', *Ethics* 87 (1977), 126–41.

[10] Wolff, 'Robert Nozick's derivation', 87.

Rights to compensation for ancient and distant wrongs

The justice of various proposed rights to compensation is frequently disputed. The problem is not (or not only) that compensatory arrangements are hard to implement. Institutions *could* perhaps be set up to provide compensation to the 'damnified persons' for (aspects of) past wrongs, and even for harms not produced by wrongs. Procedures *could* be devised to assess the magnitude of harm suffered, to establish who wronged whom, to work out how much compensation is owed, and to assign burdens of compensation.

Nor is the problem with compensation for past wrongs reducible to Nozick's problem of trying to splice a metric of value with a theory of fundamental rights. Compensation for past violations *could* be thought of (Lockeanly) as owed in recompense only for the harm or damage done by violating a right (for which some value equivalent *could* be worked out), and not as a way of making violation of rights permissible. However, even if compensation is only for the damage done in violating another's rights, claims to compensation would have to show that continuing loss or harm resulted from past injury. This is all too often impossible where harms have been caused by ancient or distant wrongs.

So it is not surprising that many discussions of rights to compensation for past wrongs have focused on wrongs that are *not particularly ancient or distant*, such as ongoing or recent violations of equal opportunity, and have advocated remedies such as compensatory educational and preferential hiring policies. But matters are far harder when we consider the more ancient and distant wrongs that might be important in discussing justice across borders. The wrongs of colonialism and slavery raise profoundly disturbing questions that are extremely hard to answer. Is everybody who descends (in part) from those who were once enslaved or colonised still being harmed by those now ancient and distant misdeeds? Can we offer a clear enough account of the causation of current harms to tell where compensation is owed? Can we show who ought to do the compensating?

There is no doubt that those who were enslaved, invaded and dispossessed during the period of European expansion were both injured and seriously harmed. Anybody would judge these injuries gross violations of rights. The Africans who were deported into slavery in the New World, and the indigenous peoples who were excluded from lands where they formerly hunted or herded, or whose rulers handed over a sovereignty of which they had little conception to distant powers, were greatly wronged. In spite of a surface veneer of commercial and political negotiation, the

European penetration of the non-European world, like many other great historic changes, violated many rights.

If these wrongs were being inflicted today, they would count as great crimes and would raise clear demands both for punishment for wrongdoers and for compensation for victims. But with the passage of time causal links are harder to ascertain. Although it is little over a century since Conrad wrote *Heart of Darkness*, and little over half a century since most of the colonial empires were disbanded, both the perpetrators and the victims of most of these wrongs are dead, and the impact on succeeding generations ramifies in complex ways.

Nobody doubts that varied effects of ancient wrongs continue, but we need to know more than that if we are to work out who ought to compensate whom. The present international order and the forms of life of both the European and non-European worlds would be unimaginably different had the era of European expansion not taken place. Indeed, we may be reasonably sure that no present person would exist had the massive movements of population and transformations of ways of life of the European expansion not taken place. The people of the possible world in which everyone stayed put were never born. If none of us would exist but for the period of European expansion, for what loss produced by that expansion might any of us owe or be owed compensation?[11] May not some of those whose ancestors were greatly wronged now enjoy advantages? May some whose ancestors wronged others now suffer disadvantages? Compensation is required for present harm caused by past wrongdoing, not simply for current disadvantage *however caused*. Unless we can trace the causal pathways, we cannot tell who has gained from ancestral wrongdoing, and should now shoulder the costs of compensating those whose present disadvantage was caused by past wrongdoing.

It may therefore make more sense for liberals – of all persuasions – to argue for a distributive – or redistributive – account of aspects of justice, which seeks action to redress present disadvantage, *whatever its origins*. If it is impossible to determine who suffered as a result of whose wrongdoing, the advantages of a compensatory approach are limited. If we cannot now reliably tell which of our contemporaries are disadvantaged because some of their ancestors were the victims of ancient wrong, while others are disadvantaged for other reasons, appeals to rights to compensation may not be as useful as their proponents hope.

---

[11] Cf. Derek Parfit, *Reasons and Persons* (Oxford: Clarendon Press, 1984), 351ff., especially 361.

A sideways look at rights, victims and compensation

The disputes between laissez-faire and welfare or social liberals have become part of the staple fare of contemporary political and public debate, and can be conducted at every level, from the most refined and theoretical to the gutter press and the bar. Here I propose to duck rather than resolve them. I will offer three reasons for ducking, and then try to approach the topic circumspectly to see whether some progress can be made from another angle.

The first reason for ducking is common prudence. Well-trodden terrain is usually muddy and offers few footholds. The second reason is that I suspect that the deep issues between laissez-faire and welfare or social liberals lie buried in their divergent conceptions of human nature and freedom, but that these issues lie well below the surface of their debates and cannot be readily grasped in a discussion of supposed rights to compensation. The third reason is that it seems to me that it might be more interesting at this juncture to consider what *unites* contemporary liberals of all sorts, and in particular some of the reasons why the intrinsically minor issue of rights to compensation should have been of such interest to both, and the locus of many of their disputes.

Theories of rights are not the only ethical and political positions that make principles of action basic and reject the views that anything whatsoever may be traded for advantage. Theories of obligation, too, view principles of action as constraints that are not to be breached for gains in utility. Yet many recent liberal discussions proceed as if treating rights rather than obligations as fundamental were no more than a matter of a preference for one rather than another of two equivalent vocabularies. Yet appeals to rights are mere rhetoric unless somebody bears the correlative obligations. Indeed, one way of putting the reservations that laissez-faire rights theorists have about appeals to rights to compensation for the descendants of slaves and dispossessed indigenous peoples is that there can be no such rights unless we show who holds the correlative obligations, which cannot easily be done when the harms suffered are ancient, systemic and multifactorial rather than attributable to wrongful action by identifiable agents inflicted on identifiable victims. If the preference for theories of rights over theories of obligations were only a matter of choice between idioms, there might be little reason to prefer theories of obligation. But the two perspectives are not equivalent. I offer two reasons.

First, theories of rights and of obligations are not even extensionally equivalent. While it is true that there cannot be rights (i.e. claim rights:

I leave aside 'mere' liberties) without correlative obligations, there can well
be obligations without correlative rights. In traditional ethical thinking
(including Christian, Natural Law, Kantian, not to mention Utilitarian
thinking) those obligations were called *imperfect obligations*. The term *imperfect* did not mean that they were not really obligations, or that they were
optional, but that they were incomplete, since it was not specified *for whom*
each particular bearer of such obligations must fulfil the obligation. Consequently performance of imperfect obligations could not be claimed as a
matter of right. The importance of Locke's use of a natural law rather than a
natural rights framework is that he does not leave out imperfect obligations:
although his main concern is with justice, he starts from a standpoint where
'the great maxims of justice and of charity'[12] are coordinate.

By contrast, contemporary liberal thinking marginalises imperfect obligations. Many exclude all but justice from their ethical perspective, and
take pride in being 'agnostic about the good for man'. This confronts
liberals with a dilemma. Either they must show that what were traditionally thought imperfect obligations are really perfect obligations and
required for justice, so have counterpart rights. This is the view taken by
many 'welfare' liberals – up to a point. Or they must take the *laissez-faire
liberal* view and classify much that was traditionally regarded as a serious
matter of obligation as a matter merely of individual preference or style,
whose neglect might at worst be 'naughty' or 'not decent'. Such trivialising
terms reveal a theoretical perspective that lacks the resources to distinguish
between trivia that are indeed a matter of style or individual preference,
obligatory action that is not a matter of respect for rights, and genuine
cases of supererogatory, saintly or heroic action.

A reduced ethical vision is not the only cost of preferring the perspective
of rights to that of obligations. A second considerable cost is that a recipient's rather than an agent's view of human life is made central. When we
ask about rights we no doubt assume that there are agents, but our first
concern is with entitlements, with what ought to be received from or
accorded by others. When we ask about obligations we begin by asking
what ought to be done.

There are dangers in giving priority to asking what people may be owed,
and what others may owe us. It invites a conception of oneself and others
above all as recipients and victims, rather than as doers or citizens; it

[12] Locke, *Second Treatise of Government*, ch. I, para. 5, 270. See Onora O'Neill, 'The great maxims
    of justice and of charity' in *Constructions of Reason: Explorations of Kant's Practical Philosophy*
    (Cambridge University Press, 1989), 219–33.

distracts attention from capacities for acting. Anybody can recognise the appeal of Kennedy's challenge: 'Ask not what your country can do for you, but what you can do for your country.' The thought can be put more abstractly by asking 'What can or should we do?', and putting the recipient's question 'What can or should others do for us?' in second place.

The prominence of rights to compensation in contemporary debates about human rights reflects the recipients' view of ethical relations that is central to all theories of rights. It is when we see ourselves as passive, and in particular when we fear harm and injury from others, that we begin by pointing to what we are owed, and so make questions of rights our first concern. Treating rights as fundamental gives prominence to the perspective of victims, and lends itself all too readily to an emphasis on the form of rectificatory justice of most concern to victims, namely compensation.

Compensation can be institutionalised whether or not the harm suffered constitutes an injury inflicted by identifiable agents. There are after all schemes to compensate farmers for the havoc caused by drought, and victims of criminal injuries for their suffering. In the first case there is no offender; in the second case the offender may remain unknown; in neither case is the cost of compensation borne by the offender. An ethical outlook which takes a passive or victim's perspective is one in which it is easy to take harm suffered as sufficient grounds for compensation, whether or not the harm constitutes an injury, whether or not any wrongdoers can be identified, and whether or not costs of compensation are to be borne by those who inflicted injury. One way of reading the objections laissez-faire liberals have made to certain sorts of compensatory schemes and the enthusiasm they have lavished on others is that they reject, at least in part, the victim's perspective within which it can seem unimportant where compensation comes from. It is one thing for utilitarians to take no account of injury or wrongdoing in the assignment of duties to aid: it is well known that utilitarian accounts of rectificatory justice are resolutely forward looking, and ahistorical. But rights theorists, and in particular those of them who invoke rights to compensation, cannot consistently be casual about these matters.

Laissez-faire liberals do not entirely reject the perspective of recipience. Like 'welfare' liberals, they see rights rather than obligations as fundamental. Their first question is 'What am I owed?' rather than 'What ought I do?' One frequent move in the construction of such accounts of rights is to try to identify the largest set of liberties that can consistently be accorded to all. Yet it is puzzling that laissez-faire liberals remain so confident, in the face of serious and competent criticism and evidence, that individuals can be the sorts of agents their ethical theory requires. The source of their confidence, I suggest, may be that when one looks at ethical relations primarily from the perspective of recipience, the actual capacities and incapacities of those required to act, like their part in prior wrong-doing, remain very much in the background. A focus on what should be received has enabled many liberals, including some laissez-faire liberals, to be casual about the sources of compensation.

All of this would be beside the point if liberals had no choice but to rest their arguments on the perspective of recipience, and to view human obligations as inferences from human rights. However, the reverse is closer to the truth. Given that there is no metric for action, there can be no way of ranking alternative sets of liberties or more broadly of rights, that can be shared by all as greater or smaller. Attempts to identify the most extensive liberty compatible with like liberty for all, or the maximal set of rights that can be universally held, fail because both formulae are radically indeter-minate. By contrast, attempts to state what principles of action can universally be adopted and what obligations these imply are not indeter-minate. A shift from the perspective of rights and recipience to that of obligation and agency does not disable us from talking about human rights: it provides them with firmer foundations. The perspective of rights is not suppressed but *aufgehoben* in the perspective of obligation.

Third, since theories of obligation work from a perspective of agency, they have to take account of (rather than to assume away) the partial, interdependent and socially produced character of human agency. Rights theorists often come to grief over whether to treat certain sorts of harm, such as poverty and vulnerability, whose causation is complex and obscure, as injuries that demand compensation. But starting from the perspective of agency, the relief of poverty and vulnerability that damage agency itself may appear as a matter of fundamental obligations, rather than as some-thing that ought to be redressed if redress is required to compensate for earlier injury. This is particularly pertinent for discussing justice for the poor. It could make a great difference if we *began* by considering what we ought to do about poverty and need that disable agency itself, rather than arguing about whether or not we can stretch notions of compensation for violation of rights to cover the selective rectification of problems of poverty.

Finally, it seems to me, the underlying aspiration of a commitment to rights is better expressed through a focus on obligations, action and agents than by a preoccupation with rights, recipience and victims. That preoccu-pation makes too much of rights to compensation because those who see themselves and others primarily as rights-holders and potentially as victims understandably would like to have protection analogous to that available where legal rights to compensation have been established. But where the relevant perpetrators are not identifiable, no appeal to rights to compensation can provide that comfort.

PART II

Justifications across boundaries

CHAPTER 4

Justice and boundaries[1]

Boundaries in political philosophy

Boundaries creep into political philosophy without us noticing. For example, within the liberal tradition of political discourse a theory of justice is typically deployed to give some account of universal rights and of the limits of legitimate state powers, yet before we know it we are talking about the powers not of the state but of the *states*. As soon as we have states, we also, of course, have boundaries or borders between states, yet these new arrivals are hardly noticeable until somebody raises a question about the just location of boundaries. At that point familiar discussions about notions of self-determination and about the status of a right to secession get going – without prior consideration of the nature or justice of boundaries. Yet it seems to me that it might be worth reflecting on the justice of boundaries before we start asking which boundaries there may or should justly be. My reflections on the matter are quite incomplete, but are guided by a couple of ideas, which it may be as well to state explicitly before I start out on what will otherwise certainly seem a meandering and wilful path – and may still seem wayward even with these signposts. The first idea is that traditional arguments about state and nation ought to be relevant, but that we must be very careful not to accept the terms of those traditional debates uncritically. The second idea is that there ought to be at least some link between discussions of the scope of ethical principles and the justification of boundaries.

If we look at the current debates in political philosophy it may seem that the problem of justifying boundaries could arise only for those who advocate universal principles – many of them liberals of one sort or another – and would not even arise for communitarians, relativists and other historicists, who will always look at matters from some determinate

---

[1] 'Justice and boundaries' in Chris Brown (ed.), *Political Restructuring in Europe: Ethical Perspectives* (London: Routledge, 1994), 69–89.

location, hence from within and as legitimately limited by some set of boundaries. I think the supposed myopia of communitarian and kindred positions provides little insight. It is true that for communitarians boundaries are, so to speak, only visible from the inside. That is perhaps why some of them are drawn to the metaphor of horizon, rather than boundary: horizons are limits that we neither reach nor cross, as we do boundaries, but which we may enlarge or shrink. Where some actual boundary is taken to be the horizon of thought, what lies beyond that pale must be either incomprehensible to insiders, or no concern of theirs. In this case the legitimacy not merely of boundaries but of certain actual boundaries has been built into the very account of political discourse – even of all discourse. An attempt to think away boundaries that are constitutive can only disorient all discourse. Yet any attempt to vindicate boundaries from 'within' cannot take seriously – indeed may not be able to acknowledge – either the predicaments of those who are excluded, or the alternatives for those who have been included. A ruthless relativism may suppress these concerns, at costs so high and implausible that I shall leave them unexplored.[2]

Today I want to leave aside the particular difficulties of taking any type of communitarian – or more broadly relativist – view of boundaries and to see how boundaries are overlooked within those sorts of political philosophy that argue for some version of moral cosmopolitanism, yet largely reject forms of institutional cosmopolitanism.[3] What, for example, justifies Rawls's assumption that justice for a society 'conceived for the time being as a closed system isolated from other societies' can serve as the paradigm

---

[2] Wittgensteinians and communitarians have both treated boundaries as constitutive of ethical discourse. Sophisticated examples of the two approaches were provided by Peter Winch, *Ethics and Action* (London: Routledge & Kegan Paul, 1972) and Michael Walzer, *Spheres of Justice: A Defence of Pluralism and Equality* (Oxford: Martin Robertson, 1983), and have been developed by many others. For further references and for criticisms of the two ways of limiting the reach of ethical discourse see Onora O'Neill, 'The power of example' in *Constructions of Reason*, 165–86, as well as 'Ethical reasoning and ideological pluralism', *Ethics* 98 (1988), 705–22, and pp. 79–88 below.

[3] For this distinction see Charles Beitz, 'Cosmopolitan liberalism and the states system' in Brown, *Political Restructuring in Europe*, 123–36; Beitz's discussion of Rawls's handling of boundaries and international justice in his *Political Theory and International Relations* (Princeton University Press, 1979, rev. 1999) is also instructive on this theme. Many writers, especially those with Hegelian tendencies, and particularly after the revolutions of 1989, but by no means only they, began to mount explicit attacks on institutional cosmopolitanism, and to re-engage with arguments for the indispensability of concepts of nation and national identity in political philosophy. See, for example, D. N. McCormick, 'Nation and nationalism' in his *Legal Right and Social Democracy* (Oxford: Clarendon Press, 1982), ch. 13, and more recently 'Is nationalism philosophically credible?' in William Twining (ed.), *Issues of Self-determination* (Aberdeen University Press, 1990); and Alasdair Macintyre, 'Is patriotism a virtue?', Lindley Lecture (Department of Philosophy, University of Kansas, Lawrence, 1984). However, very little of this writing addressed the tangled connection between (national) identity and territoriality which is the theme of this chapter.

for all justice?[4] How convincingly did Nozick get from the assumption that individuals have rights, which will need enforcing, to the claim not merely that only a minimal state is just, but that there may justly be a plurality of such minimal states, although this will curtail the rights of those outside their 'own' state?[5] More generally, how can those who argue for universal principles of justice, or for human rights, endorse structures that entail that the rights people actually have depend on where they are, or more precisely on which place recognises them as citizen rather than as alien? Would not a consistent account of universal principles of justice reject as unjust the differentiated restrictions on rights that boundaries must entail? These themes seem to me as topical as they are murky: perhaps fittingly, the topic of boundaries has no very clear boundaries of its own. So I start by considering a jamboree of arguments, some of which have been around for a long time, but many of which seem to me not to answer questions they have been intended to address. In the last part of the chapter I shall go on to a more systematic, but rather general, account of the scope of justice and suggest a way of looking at borders which at least has definite implications, and may have advantages.

States, territories and identities

It is often said that a plurality of political units, hence of states, is needed for justice, because world government would concentrate power too much, and so endanger the very considerations – e.g. order, freedom, other rights – that are thought to legitimate government. The division of powers on a global scale is then said to be just because it is needed to safeguard us from global tyranny, just as a domestic division of powers safeguards us from lesser tyrannies.

This argument takes us a certain distance, but fails to show that the appropriate form of global division of powers is a division into territorially defined states, whose boundaries limit all government functions and all citizens' rights at a single spatial demarcation. After all, the division of powers that people have in mind as important when they put forward the same argument for the constitutions of particular states is not a division into distinct territories. Moreover, it does not look as if a system of

[4] John Rawls, *A Theory of Justice* (Cambridge, MA: Harvard University Press, 1971), 8. For Rawls's account of international justice see 378–82, and for comments on the works by Beitz cited above see and Thomas Pogge, *Realizing Rawls* (New York: Columbia University Press, 1990).
[5] Nozick, *Anarchy, State, and Utopia*.

territorially defined sovereign states is a particularly good way of avoiding tyranny, even if it does avoid global tyranny. Sovereign states often abuse their citizens, and there are dangerously few restraints on the methods they use to settle their disputes with other sovereign states. The arguments that were brought against absolutist, undivided conceptions of 'internal' sovereignty during the Enlightenment, above all in the many criticisms of Hobbes, may be matched by contemporary criticism of exaggerated 'realist' insistence on the need for absolute 'external' sovereignty. Excess concentration of power within states is dangerous; so is excess independence of states from one another. The vast effort that goes into the construction of regional and international structures and organisations testifies that a division into territorially defined sovereign states has long been seen as a risky and imperfect way of avoiding the tyranny of world government.

A modified argument in favour of a plurality of territorially defined states might be this. Although a territorially demarcated division of powers is not by itself a safeguard against tyranny, it is a component of any set of institutions which provides an adequate safeguard.[6] At least some powers of government have to be exercised across contiguous and spatially limited territories. We may think of police powers and public services. We may think that we do not want a world police force or a world sewage system. Neither would be alert to local needs; both would concentrate excess powers. However, this argument also can be turned in two other ways. In the first place, there are a lot of territorially based functions of government that we have reason to want globally coordinated. We want global regulation of air waves, air traffic control, drug traffic and environmental standards. So we have reason to hope that even police forces and waste disposal policies are coordinated across state boundaries. Secondly, even when we think that some government functions, or at least some aspects of those functions, are best exercised within territorial demarcations, still we would need an argument to show why all demarcations should coincide for a vast range of distinct functions: for it is only by superimposing the demarcations for many intrinsically distinguishable matters that we arrive at a world of bounded states. A diversity of territorial limitations would not otherwise add up to a system of states that control a single set of boundaries. The evident link between territoriality and some tasks of government does not then provide clear reasons for establishing or maintaining a plurality of sovereign states, which will circumscribe all the functions of

---

[6] Even here there are exceptions: former Pakistan; island states.

government at a single set of territorial boundaries. Would it not make more sense to start with functional rather than territorial divisions of the tasks of government? And if we did so, would not the optimal territorial arrangements probably differ for different types of governmental function? It seems unlikely that any straightforwardly functional or instrumental argument would lead from an account of the ends of government or of just government (e.g. order, freedom, other rights) to a vindication of a system of territorially defined sovereign states. Of course, there may be other ways in which such an argument might be constructed.[7]

At this point some of the less radical arguments deployed by the communitarians and their predecessors are tempting. For it may be said that territory isn't really the basic issue. What makes it just to limit all government powers at the boundaries of territorial states is a deeper argument that starts from claims about nations, peoples or communities, that is, from what are now often called identities. It is because groups of people recognise one another as members of one community, and recognise certain others as outsiders, that they can legitimately aim to establish states, which are divided from other states, hence from other nations and communities, by definite borders. Within those borders they can then do things in their own way and preserve and develop their own traditions; beyond them they make either no claims, or claims of a different and more questionable sort – including hostile, irredentist and imperialist claims. Such arguments are typically strengthened by pointing out that a feeling of affiliation to nations or communities is not a mere matter of preference, but the basis of the very sense of self and identity of the persons so linked. Hence the romance of the nation-state, and more everyday stories of community life.

There are difficulties in linking this romance with the banalities of boundaries and territories. The most fundamental of these is that membership of communities is usually neither inclusive nor exclusive within any given territory. That is to say that a given community will often share a territory with others whom it does not regard, or who do not regard themselves, as members, and that many who are regarded as members by themselves and by others will also be regarded as members of other communities both by themselves and by others. Both problems are recalcitrant.

---

[7] See Thomas Baldwin, 'Territoriality' in Hyman Gross and Ross Harrison (eds.), *Jurisprudence: Cambridge Essays* (Oxford: Clarendon Press, 1992), 207–30, for a stimulating exploration of the links – and the surprising missing links – between statehood and territoriality.

Consider first the case of those who are not regarded as (full) members, but live in the same territory as some well-defined nation or community. There may, of course, be ways of forcing on such people some outsider status – they may be physically displaced (e.g. expelled, 'resettled', pushed on to reservations) or socially marginalised (e.g. ghettoised or assigned a more or less uncomfortable minority status). Alternatively there may be ways of subjecting outsiders to policies of cultural, social and religious assimilation and incorporation which would destroy or damage not them, but their differing sense of identity. However, if the basic argument in favour of the justice of boundaries and a plurality of states appeals to the importance of nationality or community for a sense of identity, it can hardly be just either to displace or marginalise, or to assimilate, those whose sense of identity is other: if identities matter, minority identities matter.

Secondly, there are many members of most communities who sense themselves to be simultaneously members of other communities. Sometimes a dual identity is assumed to be obviously coherent and unproblematic – at least by most people. This is often the case with dual identities of which one is thought to fall within the other – for example, provincial and national, national and regional identities. Many people today take it that there is now no problem in being Breton and French, or Scots and British, or Irish and European – although there are people who see a problem in each of these dual identities. Yet in our century certain other intrinsically no less plausible combinations of senses of identity have become problematic. Notoriously to remain German and Jewish became impossible. In other cases it is a matter of pressure and context. To be Irish and British is unproblematic in Britain but became problematic in Ireland. (In the United States I was once told that it was a contradiction to be Irish and Protestant, and by implication that nobody could have the identity that I had lifelong taken myself to have.) If membership of a community is essential to somebody's sense of identity, it is clearly a grave injury if they are required to give up either all or part of what they are, or if what they are is not recognised by others.

Arguments about these matters are sometimes well muddied by adding the vocabularies of nation or community on to those of state and citizenship. For if we take it that to be a citizen is *ipso facto* to be a member of 'the community', then the problem of non-members living within the same territory can ostensibly be made invisible, if citizenship is available to all inhabitants. Notoriously minorities are often unconvinced by this failure to recognise who or what they are. By the same magic, the problem of membership of multiple communities can also be made to vanish, by treating citizenship as settling who is a member of the which community. In this way questions of identity can be and have been obscured in much public debate.

However, there are good reasons to distinguish the legal and political notions of state and citizenship from the social and cultural categories of community membership or national affiliation or identity. In particular, those who hope to use notions of community or nation or people as a basis for arguing for a plurality of states – nation-states – divided by boundaries, cannot define these notions themselves in terms of the state-based notions of citizenship, on pain of undercutting their hoped-for justification.

Another, and more robust, way of handling the problems of outsiders and dual membership can be read out of Rousseau, who writes that he would wish to be a member of a state whose antique origins are lost in 'the darkness of time',[8] and whose citizens see themselves as a single community with a common good. He looked more to the traditional world of Swiss peasant life than to the conflict-ridden realities of the Geneva he purportedly admired to assure himself that such communities were possible, and knew well enough that his wish was not satisfied by any actual community. There are few if any communities so homogeneous that all their members identify with a single conception of the common good, hence few for which any General Will can be defined. Rousseau's General Will is not the will of the actual inhabitants of any historical state, some of whom may lack full allegiance to any given conception of that community and its good, while others have multiple allegiances or identities, but the will of 'corrected' citizens who have been 'forced to be free', and who now correctly identify with the community – or, putting the matter bluntly, identify with the corrected community. This is why Rousseau's Sovereign, the embodiment of the General Will 'merely by virtue of what it is, is always what it should be'.[9]

Realigning territories and identities

Since such wished-for homogeneous communities do not exist, Rousseau, followed by many others, considers how they may be created by a

---

[8] Jean-Jacques Rousseau, Dedication to 'Discourse on the origins of inequality' in *A Discourse on Inequality*, trans. Maurice Cranston (Harmondsworth: Penguin Books, 1984), 59.
[9] Jean-Jacques Rousseau, *The Social Contract*, trans. G. D. H. Cole (London: Dent, 1913), book I, ch. vii.

combination of nostalgic and utopian strategies. Nostalgic looking back to an archaic earlier time of supposed homogeneous community – Swiss peasants wisely settling affairs of state under an oak (!) – allegedly legitimates a certain view of who now counts as a community member, and who as an outsider, as alien, as non-member. Utopian looking forward points to a future in which a process of nation-building will have reformed everybody within certain boundaries, by imposing a single sense of identity, a single national allegiance in which all will the common good. Later nationalists often follow Rousseau in combining nostalgic and utopian elements: a mythical past is to be one of the tools for forging a united future, which is then (mis)conceived of as a 'return to roots'. In this way people who live within actual state borders, who are seldom homogeneous, and nearly always include some (or many) who do not share the majority identity and others who have multiple identities, are to be forced to be free.

Some results of implementing such strategies can be seen in at least partly benign forms in the constitution of a previously missing sense of national identity in some actual states (rather obviously the United States; less obviously the Republic of Ireland), and in largely malign form in the totalitarian versions inculcated in Nazi Germany, and in rather different ways in Eastern Europe under formerly existing socialism.[10] The weight placed on mythical past and on desired future may vary greatly. Historicist conceptions of nationality stress origins more; Rousseauian and Kantian discussions of civil religion and ethical commonwealth and contemporary discussions of 'constitutional patriotism' view community and identity as task rather than either as origin or as fate.[11]

However, once we begin to think of national or community identity as something to be constituted rather than as a given reality, appeals to (national) identity to vindicate state boundaries look a great deal less impressive. Any given appeal may be countered by pointing out other

---

[10] For these examples see Oliver MacDonagh, *States of Mind: A Study of Anglo-Irish Conflict 1780–1980* (London: Allen & Unwin, 1982), and Vaclav Havel's essay 'The power of the powerless' in *Living in Truth*, ed. Jan Vladislav (London: Faber & Faber, 1986). MacDonagh's work will surprise those who imagine that Irish nationalism, the model for many later nationalist movements, is of great antiquity; Havel's essay captures the daily face of the attempted reformation of sense of identity under 'really existing' socialism.

[11] On civil religion, see both *The Social Contract* and Immanuel Kant, *Religion within the Limits of Reason Alone*, trans. Theodore M. Green and Hoyt H. Hudson (New York: Harper & Row, 1960); on constitutional patriotism and related themes see Jürgen Habermas, 'Ist der Herzschlag der Revolution zum Stillstand gekommen?' in *Die Ideen von 1798 in der deutschen Rezeption*, ed. Forum fur Philosophie Bad Homburg (Frankfurt: Suhrkamp, 1989); and also Ulrich K. Preuss, *Revolution, Fortschritt und Verfassung: zu einem neuen Verfassungsverstiindnis* (Berlin: Wagenbach, 1990).

possible conceptions of (national) identity. If the elements and scope of a (national or community) sense of identity are not given but constructed, then it is always an open question whether they should not have been, or now be, differently constructed, and whether those who do not like the status quo should be urged – or, if we follow Rousseau, forced – to change their sense of identity rather than to challenge existing boundaries. A nationalism that appeals to processes of identity formation in order to create a homogeneous nation has no simple answer to those who urge assimilation into other identities. Looked at in this way, nationalism and assimilationism, secession and imperialism, historicism and civil religion, are just different programmes for identity formation, that urge people to construct or fasten on differing accounts of shared origins or on differing visions of shared destinies, which could then be used to 'justify' differing boundaries.

The flimsiness of all such appeals to national or other identity as justification for maintaining or changing territorial demarcations and boundaries is often obscured by relying once again on hybrid concepts such as those of the 'nation-state' or 'community of citizens', whose proper use tacitly presupposes the very alignment of identity and territory that is in question. If the social conceptions of nation, tribe, community or people are to do the work of justifying territorial borders between political units, they must not be redefined in terms that presuppose these boundaries. Such definitional strategies undercut the aim of vindicating territorial boundaries or changes in boundaries by appeals to national and other identities.

Another approach to the disparities between territorial realities and actual conceptions of (national) identity accepts that a single sense of identity is rarely found in all who share a given territory, and aims to align the two by permitting or requiring those with the 'wrong' sense of identity to change not their share of identity but their location. As a strategy this has a lot to be said against it, because it is always unjust and often impossible. Policies of forced relocation are hugely unjust; policies of supposedly 'voluntary' transfer are often driven by fear. Moreover, any proposed alignment of identity to territory by relocation is not merely unjust but impossible when sense of identity itself is bound to territory, so that the two are not detachable. The same territories may be integral to the actual sense of identity of groups with differing, even antagonistic, conceptions of their own identity – witness the Palestinian/Israeli problem and many of the struggles in former Yugoslavia. To give up the homeland may amount to giving up a sense of identity.

A yet more general reason for doubting any strategy for justifying territorial boundaries by appeal either to the present or to some revised pattern of senses of identity or allegiance is this. The concepts by which people define who they are – in which they articulate their sense of identity – are all of them concepts without sharp borders, and hence cannot provide a basis for sharp demarcations such as political borders between states. Most concepts not merely permit borderline cases but are strictly boundaryless, in that their sense is given by a pair or larger number of contrasts, rather than by the existence of a well-defined set of items of which the concept is true.[12] Although we have clear ideas of what it means to be red as opposed to yellow, or a child as opposed to an adult, or Irish as opposed to British, this is not because anybody can form the sets that contain all and only those items that are red, or are children or are Irish. Our understanding of national and community identity is always framed in terms of boundaryless concepts – so cannot provide an adequate basis for fixing sharp borders. These considerations also suggest why our understanding of national identity is so often given in terms of certain contrasts: we identify who counts as a fellow-countryman only insofar as we identify others as foreigners or even as enemies. When furthest from home we greet as compatriots others with whom we have tenuous links; when closest to home we may see those from the next valley as foreign.

This scattering of arguments has looked back in an unsystematic way over various chapters of political philosophy, in which appeals to national identity have been thought to have some justifying role in explaining why there must or may justly be a plurality of territorially bounded states. I think that the arguments are not individually impressive. An adequate approach to these issues would reject both the fiction that all government functions for some group have to be confined within common territorial limits, and the myth that the world does or ought to be made to consist of homogeneous nations lodged in mutually exclusive territories with well-defined boundaries.

Legitimate boundaries without myths

I want now to try to say something a bit more positive, if rather modest, by sketching some arguments for the legitimacy of a plurality of political units, hence of boundaries, without invoking these particular myths and

---

[12] Mark Sainsbury, 'Concepts without boundaries', Inaugural Lecture (Philosophy Department, King's College London, 1990).

fictions. Before I do this I would like to head off one misunderstanding. It is not part of my argument to suggest that a sense of national (or tribal, religious, cultural or community) identity is a myth or illegitimate or unimportant. All too clearly these matters are not mythical, surely they are important, and presumably they can be appropriately appealed to for some purposes. The failure of the arguments just surveyed suggests only that the various types of identity that are or could become important to people don't provide promising starting points for justifying a system of arranging political power by division into mutually excluding nation-states that jointly exhaust all territories. Nationality and other sorts of community may be very important even if they have little to do with the legitimacy of political boundaries. I also think it clear that securing a national state may sometimes be *instrumentally* important in securing justice for some – we have only to think of the predicament of the minorities who fear oppression, or suffer expulsion. But equally securing a national state for some can be instrumental in bringing injustice to others – we have only to think of the nationalities problems of the former USSR, former Yugoslavia or parts of the Middle East.

The question of the legitimacy of boundaries can hardly be raised unless we take some view of the scope of principles of justice. Questions of scope are not settled by showing that principles of justice are universal principles: for a principle to be universal is only for it to hold for all cases in some domain. It is the definition of that domain which would settle issues of scope. A universal principle might, for example, hold for all inhabitants of a certain area, or for all human beings, or for all members of a certain class, or for all adult males. In many contemporary debates the issue of the scope of principles of justice – and more generally of morality – is treated as the question of establishing the moral status or standing of those entitled to just treatment. Most of these debates take it for granted that all adult, normal human beings have this standing – they count, for example, as persons or as holders of rights – and then move on to ask who and what else have moral standing. Debates have raged about the moral standing and claims of foetuses, of children, of the terminally ill, of animals and of numerous other cases. These debates are familiar and extraordinarily repetitive. One reason why they are so repetitive may be that most of the protagonists are looking for an essentialist answer: they hope to identify some essential property or set of properties that confers person-hood or moral standing. Yet they are often wholly unwilling to argue for any of those metaphysical positions that could establish essentialist claims. This is particularly clear in the endlessly rehearsed abortion debates.

The so-called 'right to life' groups may not have found any metaphysical arguments that convince their opponents of their essentialist claims, but they have lured those opponents onto essentialist terrain, which those who defend no metaphysical essentialism find both slippery and sloping.

For reasons that I will not go into here, I doubt whether we can show that any property or set of properties is either necessary or sufficient for moral standing. Yet if we cannot, it seems that we will have no clear view of the scope of principles of justice, or of other moral principles, so will hardly be in a position to start thinking about how this might be relevant to the status of political boundaries. Unless both the scope and the content of justice are fixed, it may remain obscure whether boundaries obstruct justice, or whether they are indispensable elements of its institutional embodiment. If we do not know the scope of justice, how can we either vindicate or criticise the practice of differentiating rights or justice on a territorial basis? Indeed, how could we even come to any view of the relativist and communitarian strategies of interpreting the boundaries of actual communities as the boundaries of justice?[13]

An alternative way of approaching the question of the scope of justice might be to take it as a practical rather than a theoretical question. That is to say, we could give up the search for a theoretical demarcation of spheres of justice that requires essentialist claims or sharp demarcations where none is available, and note that we need an account of the scope of justice in contexts of action where there is a potential for conflict. A practical account of the scope of justice can perhaps be premised not on the metaphysics of the person, but on the assumptions to which agents are already committed whenever they act in circumstances where justice can be an issue. To see that a practical approach to the scope of justice might be very different from a general, theoretical approach we need only consider the practically unimportant case of justice to previous generations. Since we cannot affect any but surviving predecessors, there is no practical need to identify a limit to the scope of justice to predecessors. It does not matter from *a practical point of view* at what point our remotest predecessors acquired moral standing (we do not need to know whether Neanderthal men and women were right holders). Yet if there were a comprehensive, 'perspectiveless' account of the scope of justice we could expect it to distinguish predecessors who had moral standing from those who did not. From a practical point of view *nothing* need be said or

---

[13] See the references in note 2.

assumed about such cases. Seen from such a theoretical perspective, a practical account of moral standing might be judged to have gaps: yet these notional gaps may be wholly irrelevant to action.

However, a practical approach to questions of scope will offer no advantage if it too needs some account of the metaphysics of the person to provide the criterion of moral standing. This demand may perhaps be avoided by working not from any view of the nature of persons, but from an account of the circumstances of action, or more narrowly from the circumstances of justice.

Hume provided the classical version[14] of these circumstances when he identified moderate scarcity and confined generosity as the key elements of the circumstances of justice. Rawls offered[15] a rather more extensive account that combines objective and subjective circumstances of justice. Hume and Rawls use these premises as part of an account of the content as well as the scope of principles of justice. For present purposes my concern is only with their scope.[16] For this purpose it may in fact be sufficient to take a weaker view of the circumstances of justice than either Hume or Rawls proposes, and to view them simply as the circumstances that hold when a plurality of finite agents share a world, in the sense that they could affect one another. Each of these elements of the circumstances of justice needs brief comment and vindication.

To be part of a plurality of agents who share a world is a significant circumstance of justice because it excludes the case of pseudo-pluralities, among whom conflict would be impossible, hence justice without a task. Circumstances of justice are absent among bodily distinct beings who are so coordinated, whether by instinct or by pre-established harmony, that conflict, and so also the mediation of conflict by principles of justice, are pre-empted. The circumstances of justice are always also circumstances of possible injustice. The classical formulation of this thought is Aristotle's criticism of Plato: 'if unification advances beyond a certain point, the city will not be a city at all':[17] here the political virtue, justice, would be without point. Circumstances of justice are circumstances in which

---

[14] David Hume, *A Treatise of Human Nature*, ed. L. A. Selby Bigge, revised 1958 (London: Routledge & Kegan Paul), 494–5.
[15] *A Theory of Justice*, 126–30.
[16] I believe that a non-metaphysical approach can provide the basis of an account of the content of principles of justice, but will leave this large claim dangling in mid-air: here I assume only that we can establish some universal principles of justice, but leave it open which ones we can establish.
[17] Aristotle, *Politics*, 1261a.

conflict between agents is possible, and may be avoidable or at least regulable by just institutions. This view assumes no strong form of individualism, but only that conflict and the mediation of conflict by whatever means have a place only among pluralities of at least partially distinct agents.

Finitude is a second distinct element of any circumstances of justice. Taken strictly, plurality already entails some sorts of finitude: there cannot be pluralities all of whose members enjoy unlimited dimensions, possessions or powers. However, finitude forms a distinct element of the circumstances of justice because it is important not to introduce false assumptions about the powers of the agents who compose a given plurality. Fictions of idealised self-sufficiency or rationality or of idealised cognitive or physical powers, that might in principle be found in some pluralities of finite agents, but to which the members of human pluralities do not measure up, are often used but seldom (if ever) justified in the construction of theories of justice. Human action, and thereby also human justice, as they can actually exist, are predicated not on mere plurality, but on a plurality of mutually vulnerable beings who never achieve more than limited and specific forms of rationality, independence and self-sufficiency.

Finitude and plurality are necessary conditions for questions of justice to arise, but they are not sufficient. A plurality of finite agents who were not connected to one another could not come into conflict. Their action would therefore never be predicated on claims about the action or collaboration of those unknown others. For example, the inhabitants of Viking Dublin and their contemporaries in Peru neither knew of nor affected one another's lives. Their actions were in no way predicated on assumptions about one another's capacity to act. It would be absurd to ask whether they dealt with one another either justly or unjustly. Although a set consisting of a plurality of finite agents can be formed by taking Dubliners and Peruvians of that time, circumstances of justice would not obtain between members of the conjoined sub-sets because they did not share a world. By 'sharing a world', I mean to invoke not any presumption of close community, let alone Hannah Arendt's particularly strong understanding of this phrase, but only the relation that holds when agents premise action – whether cooperative or hostile or neither – on their assumptions about the competent agency either of nearby or of distant others.

Where all three elements of the circumstances of justice – plurality, finitude and sharing a world – obtain, injustice can arise and issues of justice can be raised. It is clear that these circumstances are not confined within the boundaries of states, or within the more indeterminate boundaries of nations or of communities. Although the most familiar case of a world shared by a plurality of finite agents is that of a community whose members interact a great deal, interaction now hardly ever stops at political or at other boundaries. Action-at-a-social-distance is a commonplace on which we constantly rely in the modern world. In saying that we rely on it we are saying only that we presuppose its possibility, in that we predicate our plans, policies and individual acts on such interaction. We trade, we broadcast, we travel, we negotiate, and above all we communicate with distant others. For practical purposes we are already committed to viewing numerous distant and unknown others as agents like ourselves. Hence if we think that there are ethical principles – principles of justice – whose scope includes all with whom we interact, we cannot exclude distant others. Although the notions of 'global community' or 'global society' may be no more than a sentimental rhetoric of cosmopolitanism, the weaker relation of sharing a world with distant others is one that agents today cannot consistently deny.

And yet these realities are often denied. 'Idealised' conceptions of sovereignty and self-sufficiency, or on the other hand of community and unity, are used as strategies by which the scope of justice can be surreptitiously set in preferred ways. By idealising sovereignty and independence we obscure our *connectedness* to certain others and the fact that we share a world with them; by idealising community and unity we obscure the *distinctness* of certain others and overlook plurality. In either case, claims of justice are ruled out of order. Between them these strategies can be and have been used both to exclude some ('enemies', 'foreigners') from (full) moral concern, and to deny the separateness of others ('our own', 'dependants') and so play down the full demands of justice between insiders.

In the circumstances of action that we actually find and rely on in the contemporary world, neither sort of idealisation is either attained or approximated. Foreigners and other 'outsiders' are not others with whom we do not, let alone cannot, interact and share a world. Compatriots, intimates and kin, with whom we may share much, do not form an 'ideal' united community that pre-empts plurality and the need for justice. In all these cases we have to do with a plurality of finite beings who assume they share a world with others, and who cannot then define the limits of justice to exclude those others of whom they make these assumptions. Others cannot consistently be discounted, once they are already relied upon as distinct yet connected agents.

Given our present actual commitments and involvements in acting, we cannot then coherently argue that moral concern, and least of all that justice, stops either at boundaries of states, or at social boundaries of other sorts. Anyone who makes such moves in our world evidently shifts ground illegitimately. If we assume that 'foreigners' are people with whom it is possible to trade, translate and negotiate, who can be expected to carry complex and intelligent roles, we cannot rescind the imputations of agency, rationality, competence and so on, to which we are committed, midway in the argument. If in other cases we take these to be legitimate bases of moral concern, we must do the same in these cases. Hence even a minimal conception of the circumstances of justice as those of an agent who lives among a plurality of finite others who are taken to share the same world has strong and expansive implications for the scope of justice in the contemporary world, and in particular strong implications for nearly all contemporaries, whose plans and practices are in fact predicated on sharing a world with so many others.

Justice across borders

The practical implication of these thoughts for the justice of state boundaries is not, however, that only a world without state boundaries could be a just world. Such a world state would concentrate power, and the common reasons given for fearing world government and its colossal concentration of powers seem to me serious reasons. The reasons for thinking that justice is helped by bonds of sentiment between citizens, and can be destroyed by lack of all such bonds, are also strong. The evidence that those bonds are easier to forge when a sense of identity is shared is also considerable.

However, while boundaries may be necessary for justice, boundaries are often impediments to justice. In saying this I do not mean that they are drawn at the wrong places. It is not in itself unjust that some nations find themselves divided by state boundaries (e.g. postwar Germany), or that others find themselves sharing a state with people they come not to regard as part of their own nation (Serbs and Croats). Given the non-coincidence of national and other identities with territory, such outcomes are unavoidable, and in themselves no injustice. There cannot be rights to live in homogeneous, territorially bounded nation-states, and those who imagine that a right to self-determination can or must be interpreted in this way embark on dangerous self-deception. The way in which boundaries can be unjust is rather that they can be used to discount the claims to justice of those on the far side of some boundary either in whole or in part. (They can also become part of an institutional framework for inflicting injustice on insiders – witness the case of East Germany.)

The more interesting case is that of boundaries which systematically inflict injustices on outsiders. The case can be sketched by contrasting two hypothetical states, for which we need make no assumptions about the presence or absence of a homogeneous national identity. If the boundaries are just, the two states will acknowledge that those beyond their boundaries too have claims to just treatment, and in so far as their action affects those beyond the boundaries they will seek to do them no injustice. If the boundaries are unjust, the policies and practices of at least one state will impinge on those who live in the other, in ways that do the other injustice. Typically this will be justified – it will not be seen as injustice – under the heading of 'not interfering in the internal affairs of another sovereign state', or of 'lack of responsibilities towards non-citizens'. However, once the legitimacy of treating actual state boundaries as limits of justice has been called into question, an appeal to sovereignty or to assumed lack of responsibilities to non-citizens cannot automatically counter appeals to justice. For in this context the appeal to sovereignty or to lack of responsibilities is simply the appeal to use state borders to limit the scope of justice, even when there are other considerations to show that the scope of justice ought not to be restricted in this way. This is not to say that justice demands the complete abrogation of sovereignty or the abolition of states – but it does demand an interpretation of sovereignty that does not constitute an arbitrary limit to the scope of justice.

If these considerations are convincing, they may have very significant and complex implications for justifiable interventions in the case of human rights violations beyond state boundaries, for the justice of legislation that selectively restricts boundary crossing, whether for asylum, travel, migration, abode, work, settlement or to take up citizenship,[18] and for the justice of an economic order predicated on transnational economic interaction that lacks both transnational powers of taxation and transnational institutions to relieve poverty. An account of just borders that takes proper account of these issues need not deny the importance of nations and of national identity: but it must deny that they create claims to bounded states which exercise absolute internal or external sovereignty.

---

[18] On some of these issues see Brian Barry and Robert E. Goodin (eds.), *Free Movement: Ethical Issues in the Transnational Migration of People and of Money* (Hemel Hempstead: Harvester Wheatsheaf, 1992).

The legitimate claims of nations cannot be to impermeable boundaries, which limit justice to those beyond them, but at most to a political order within which nations and other communities of identity can secure, celebrate and hand on their specific ways of life and senses of identity.[19]

---

[19] See the works by D. N. McCormick, cited in note 2 above, and Iso Camartin, *Von Sils-Maria aus Betrachtet: ein Blick von dem Dach Europas* (Frankfurt: Suhrkamp, 1991). Securing national and other identities through policies that respect minorities and their cultures is neither a soft nor a minimal option, especially where national identity has been inflated into aspiration to sovereignty over territory that others share; but it is a political goal which is compatible with the realities of intermingled nations.

CHAPTER 5

Ethical reasoning and ideological pluralism[1]

A crisis in liberal thinking?

Many of the ways of thought that Europe has exported claim universal applicability: that was perhaps one reason why they travelled well.[2] Christianity was the first universal mode of thought that Europe exported; science, technology, and the ideology of markets have been among the hardiest travellers. European political ideologies mostly share the universal aspirations of their Christian ancestry and have also travelled well. Liberalism and socialism have colonised large parts of the world. Both claim universal scope and propose accounts of progress and justice that do not stop at national or other boundaries. From the start, human rights and proletarian revolution (in varied and contested forms) were thought of as human and not merely as national goals.

At present nearly all liberal and socialist political practice takes place within and in subordination to the boundaries and categories of states and of national interest. This restriction is often seen by liberals and socialists as a transitional stage, which will (or at least ought to) be followed by a new international order in which the goals of liberal or socialist thought are no longer subordinated to national or other boundaries and interests.

---

[1] 'Ethical reasoning and ideological pluralism,' first published in *Ethics* 98 (1988), 705–22. The text has been minimally edited by updating tenses and temporal references.

[2] It is neither a sufficient reason – theories may claim universal scope yet be very generally rejected – nor a necessary one, since a theory need not claim universal scope to be widely accepted (outcasts may even accept ideologies that cast them out). However, there cannot be good reasons for those whose standing is denied by an account of practical reasoning to accept that reasoning: theories can be vindicated only to those whose standing they accept. If we have no transcendent vindication of the authority of reason, practical reasoning claims that universal scope can be vindicated only by showing that it is accessible and cogent without restriction of audience. Hence justifiable universal scope and universal accessibility of ethical or political reasoning are intimately linked. See the papers in Part I of Onora O'Neill, *Constructing Authorities: Reason, Politics and Interpretation in Kant's Philosophy* (Cambridge University Press, 2015).

Some writing by liberals and their critics questions liberalism's long-standing internationalist commitments. It suggests that the subordination of social and political categories to those of states and especially of nation-states and nationalism (or to other and perhaps narrower loyalties) is ineliminable, and even that liberalism's claim to universal justification and application is unfounded. I shall look at some of these suspicions and ask whether they can be dispelled or whether they must be recognised as limitations of liberal thinking. I shall not discuss parallel issues within socialist thinking.

Many challenges to liberal universalism are directed against 'deonto-logical liberalism' and its claim to identify universal, invariant principles of justice that should have global reach. This universality, which has traditionally been part of the appeal of liberal thinking, is now sometimes cited as evidence of its inadequate and abstract conception of morality and its reliance on conceptions of the human subject that abstract from social and historical context. Many such criticisms revive and rework the charges of empty formalism that Hegel first levelled against Kantian *Moralität*.

The criticisms have come from many quarters.[3] Sandel has argued that Rawlsian liberal thinking assumes an implausibly abstract account of human subjects and fails to take seriously their actual historical identities and the ways in which these depend on specific communities.[4] Walzer insists that distributive justice presupposes a political community but regards 'the international community' as merely hypothetical and casts questions of international or global justice as questions about member-ship in and exclusion from particular political communities.[5] Williams argues that 'the morality system' that lies behind liberal political thinking, is 'under too much pressure on the subject of the voluntary' in that, once again, it assumes too abstract a view of human agency.[6] Macintyre articulates the patriot's claim that 'liberal morality' is a permanent source of danger because of the way 'it renders our social and moral ties too

---

[3] Including the work of Michael Sandel, Michael Walzer, Bernard Williams, Alasdair Macintyre, Charles Taylor and Richard Rorty, who have all queried abstract moral theory (*Moralität*) and stressed the importance of the norms of actual communities (*Sittlichkeit*). See in particular the discussion by Taylor in his *Hegel* (Cambridge University Press, 1975), chs. 14 and 15; excerpted in Michael Sandel (ed.), *Liberalism and Its Critics* (Oxford: Basil Blackwell, 1984), 177–99.

[4] Michael Sandel, *Liberalism and the Limits of Justice* (Cambridge University Press, 1982).

[5] Walzer, *Spheres of Justice*.

[6] Bernard Williams, *Ethics and the Limits of Philosophy* (London: Fontana, 1985), 194.

open to dissolution by rational criticism'.[7] These writers share a muted Hegelianism. They hold that appeals to *Moralität* cannot convince, since the audiences for political debate consist not of abstract individuals who respond to abstract reasoning, but of particular men and women whose identities are constituted by their participation in particular institutions, traditions and nations, who are alive to reasoning only when it is conducted within these terms. They think that *Sittlichkeit* cannot be assumed away: it provides the context and the horizon of ethical reasoning and there is both peril and impotence in pretending otherwise.

These criticisms of deontological liberalism were not ignored by leading liberal thinkers. Rawls in particular challenged his critics' reading of his work. They read *A Theory of Justice* as advocating principles that would be chosen rationally under fair procedures, where fairness is defined by (a certain sort of) abstraction from actual social conditions. They take it that Rawls is committed to universal and invariant principles (at least for 'circumstances of justice').

In the 1980 Dewey lecture 'Kantian constructivism in moral theory', and in his 1985 'Justice as fairness: political not metaphysical',[8] Rawls emphasises a different articulation of his work. There he seeks to avoid 'claims to universal truth or about the essential nature and identity of persons'[9] and states: 'Justice as fairness is a political conception of justice because it starts from within a certain political tradition.'[10] He thinks this unavoidable if political theorising is to convince: 'Justification is addressed to others who disagree with us, and therefore it must always proceed from some consensus, that is, from premises that we and others publicly recognise as true.'[11] The conception of the person on which his argument rests is not the abstract individualism with which Sandel and others have charged him, but a conception of persons as citizens[12] of a modern democratic polity, who (while they may disagree about the good)[13] accept the original position as a 'device of representation'[14] that accurately captures their ideal of a fair system of cooperation between citizens who so disagree. Far from deriving a justification of democratic citizenship from metaphysical foundations, Rawls in his later work invited readers to see

---

[7] Macintyre, 'Is patriotism a virtue?' and in Derek Matravers and Jonathan E. Pike (eds.), *Debates in Contemporary Political Philosophy: An Anthology* (London: Routledge, 2003).

[8] John Rawls, 'Kantian constructivism in moral theory', *Journal of Philosophy* 77 (1980), 515–72, and 'Justice as fairness: political not metaphysical', *Philosophy and Public Affairs* 14 (1985), 223–51.

[9] Rawls, 'Justice as fairness', 223. Cf. Comments in Charles Beitz, 'Cosmopolitan ideals and national sentiment', *Journal of Philosophy* 80 (1983), 591–600.

[10] Rawls, 'Justice as fairness', 225.   [11] *Ibid.*, 229.   [12] *Ibid.*, 234.   [13] *Ibid.*, 245ff.

[14] *Ibid.*, 236.

A Theory of Justice as providing a recursive vindication of those principles of justice we would acknowledge if we drew deeply on our underlying conceptions of free and equal citizenship. The vindication of justice is not to be seen as addressing others who, unlike 'us', do not start with such ideals of citizenship; it has nothing to say to those others.

Rawls is not, of course, aiming to vindicate a conception of justice by embedding it in the *Sittlichkeit* of a particular community. However, he denies that justice can be vindicated in complete abstraction from the specific ideals of 'our' community. The defenders of *Sittlichkeit* should surely welcome this reading of Rawls's enterprise: even if it is not the reading which they have given themselves, it offers much that they demand.

Moreover there is textual evidence as well as Rawls's authority behind his 'political' reading of *A Theory of Justice*. The very title of the book disclaims knowledge of *the* theory of justice. The method of reflective equilibrium uses 'our considered moral intuitions' as one consideration for determining principles of justice. If we are the actual inhabitants, indeed citizens, of particular nation-states, 'our' particular loyalties, in particular 'our' recognition of some as fellow citizens and others as aliens, will legitimately be reflected in 'our' considered judgements, and so in the principles of justice to which 'we' would assent even in original positions. Whether or not there was a change in Rawls's position, it is clear that he came to defend a modest liberalism, whose internationalist commitments (if any) can be defended only to those who are already liberals of a certain sort. A liberalism that is grounded in intuitions that may be unique to 'our' *Sittlichkeit*, and that are certainly absent in many *Sittlichkeiten*, will also be bounded by those intuitions. It is less likely to impose an 'overload of obligations'; it may sit cosily with many of 'our' ideals – or prejudices.[15]

Although Rawls held that the historical circumstances of liberal justice are given by the ineradicable ethical pluralism of modernity, he takes it that this pluralism has not destroyed the bonds or the boundaries of societies. Principles of justice are always 'our' principles of justice. Liberal principles reflect and articulate an ideal that is part of 'our' institutions, 'our' traditions, and (for those who are Rawls's compatriots) 'our' nation: in short, of 'our' *Sittlichkeit*. Rawlsian methods will lead to a liberal conception of justice only where (as perhaps in the United States)

---

[15] Utilitarian liberals are widely held to face an 'overload of obligations' problem; see James Fishkin, *The Limits of Obligation* (Yale University Press, 1982). If deontological liberalism makes demands that go beyond state boundaries it too appears to ask 'too much' (e.g., that 'we' secure worldwide human rights and economic progress). A retreat to liberalism without those commitments would avoid 'excessive' moral demands and the hypocrisy or adventurism they could generate.

considered moral judgements incorporate more or less liberal ideals. MacIntyre's speculation that the United States is 'a country and a culture whose *Sittlichkeit* just is *Moralität*[16] is aptly illustrated by the emphasis Rawls came to place on his own work.

However, not everybody's *Sittlichkeit* is or includes or even is compatible with *Moralität*. Principles of justice that are justified as the principles that citizens would adopt as providing the best articulation of their ideal of citizenship may seem quite beside the point to those who do not think of themselves or of (some or all) others as citizens. Rawls's particular principles of justice will also be rejected by those whose political vision incorporates a more determinate image of citizenship that cannot be combined with diverse *Sittlichkeiten*.[17] The audience who will take seriously the liberal principles of justice that Rawlsian citizens would choose will be restricted. Rawlsian principles of justice will provide no basis for communicating criticisms of their political institutions or practices to those in non-liberal societies, unless their members share 'our' conceptions of citizenship and of fair procedures of cooperation.[18]

The internationalist (let alone global) commitments and implications of liberalism are damaged if they are vindicated by reference to an aspect of the *Sittlichkeit* of a specific tradition. When claims to universal scope are (supposedly) vindicated in terms that *could not* be made universally accessible, liberal internationalism is uncomfortably based on intellectual imperialism. The uses to which liberal thought was put by critics of apartheid, or is put by Amnesty International or by the human rights movement, cannot convince those whom they criticise if liberal thinking lacks vindication that stretches beyond the boundaries of 'our' shared conception of citizenship, and cannot impose liberal principles on others without embracing forms of (at least ideological) imperialism or paternalism that liberalism itself shuns.

---

[16] Macintyre, 'Is patriotism a virtue?', 19. This speculation might be taken either as the thought that *Moralität* is the only *common* culture of the United States, which has many subcultures of distinctive *Sittlichkeit*, or more strongly as the thought that it is the only *Sittlichkeit* of the United States and has marginalised or corrupted other more traditional loyalties.

[17] For example, it might not fit Rousseau's vision of citizens who are not only free but fit to be free because they share 'those austere morals and that noble courage' that can emerge only in 'a happy and peaceful commonwealth of which the history was lost, so to speak, in the darkness of time': Rousseau, Dedication, 59.

[18] In *A Theory of Justice* (115) Rawls retains a shadowy conception of 'natural' duties that 'hold between persons irrespective of their institutional relationships' as a basis for obligations that cross institutional, ideological, national or generational boundaries. However, since 'the principles of natural duty are derived from a contractarian point of view', they too judge actions that cross boundaries from a liberal standpoint that some will reject.

Edmund Burke criticised the revolutionaries of France for appealing to abstract rights, rather than to the determinate historical rights and liberties of Frenchmen, and liberalisms that are grounded in *Sittlichkeit* must echo Burke and eschew claims about justice that stretch beyond borders. Liberalism that renounces claims to travel will seem pretty harmless to many illiberal regimes.

Abstraction, idealisation and ethical pluralism

Many liberals will be reluctant either to shed their internationalist aspirations or to justify them in terms of premises that are accepted only within certain boundaries. They will look for ways to meet or avoid the criticisms raised by the defenders of *Sittlichkeit* and by Rawls's self-interpretation in his later writings. Various moves are possible.

One move is to distance liberal thinking from specifically deontological starting points and to lean on utilitarian liberalism. Utilitarian reasoning has few inhibitions about crossing national and ideological boundaries.[19] However, utilitarian starting points do not appeal to all liberals. Despite J. S. Mill's optimism about the close fit between utilitarian foundations and liberal conclusions, utilitarian reasoning is widely thought unable to explain why rights should be taken as overriding, why majorities should not tyrannise minorities, and in general why some lives should not be used and used up as means to happiness enjoyed in other lives. Liberals therefore have good reasons to take specifically deontological liberalism seriously.

A second response to the neo-Hegelian criticisms of liberalism would be to ignore them and view Rawls as mistaken in adapting liberalism to meet these criticisms, and insist that deontological liberals should simply stick to their universalist claims. This view is held by many libertarian liberals, who are prepared to insist that universal human rights and their implications for international or global justice are the core of liberalism, which is compromised by offering a 'political' grounding for liberal thinking. Libertarian liberals indeed do not avoid claims about international or global justice, which some of them think mandate freedom of trade and migration, or the

---

[19] There are many utilitarian approaches to nuclear issues, and many discussions of economic development and hunger; the best known include Peter Singer, 'Famine, affluence and morality', and his *Practical Ethics* (Cambridge University Press, 1979). The assumptions that utilitarian thinking has to make to reach across national and ideological boundaries are questionable; see O'Neill, *Faces of Hunger*, chs. 4 and 5.

dismantling of bilateral and multilateral aid schemes. This reassertion of liberalism's internationalist aspirations would be powerful if those who make it could show how such abstract reasoning is to convince those who do not start from liberal, let alone libertarian, premises.[20]

A third approach would try to answer rather than avoid the criticisms of deontological liberalism that have been raised by the defenders of *Sittlichkeit*. Among the questions they have posed are the following. Why should principles on which hypothetical abstract rational beings agree be binding for actual, partially rational beings? Is the thinking of such abstracted individuals of the least relevance to 'us' – or to any other actual men and women with particular and diverse histories, loyalties and aspirations? Are 'we' not on unsure ground in claiming that abstracted beings would choose any principles of cooperation at all? More generally, does not the move to abstract reasoning escape from historical and cultural limitations at the cost of becoming inaccessible to its possible audiences, each of which finds itself and its thinking constituted and bounded by a particular history and tradition? If so, will not abstract reasoning be irrelevant to many, and politically impotent? Why should we take seriously reasoning that offers an exaggerated, phony choice between utter hypocrisy and revolutionary changes in action and policies? A major appeal of deontological liberalism has been the charge that utilitarian liberalism fails to take the separateness of persons seriously enough. But does the choosing of abstractly rational beings fail to take the connectedness of persons seriously enough? These are serious criticisms that cannot be brushed aside. We may begin a response to them by considering what a move to abstract reasoning is, what its part in the liberal tradition has been, and whether it is avoidable.

Abstraction or idealisation?

Abstraction, taken literally, is a matter of selective omission, of leaving out some predicates from descriptions and theories. Selective omission can hardly be objected to. It is unavoidable. No use of language can be fully determinate. Abstraction is a precondition for logic, for scientific reasoning, and for many highly respected (and lucrative) forms of practical reasoning, such as legal and commercial reasoning. Abstraction is also needed if we are to reason in ways that can be taken seriously by others who disagree with us. By abstracting we may succeed in reasoning in ways

[20] Cf. Onora O'Neill, 'The most extensive liberty', *Proceedings of the Aristotelian Society* n.s. 80 (1979–80), 45–59.

that are detachable from commitment to the full detail of our own beliefs. The less abstract our reasoning, the greater the likelihood that it hinges on premises that others will dispute and that its conclusions will seem obscure or irrelevant to those others.

With so much going for abstract reasoning, it seems harder to explain why abstraction has been so criticised than it is to explain its appeal. Anybody who wants to appeal beyond past institutions and categories of discourse now established and to reach a wide or universal audience is bound to use and advocate reasoning that abstracts from features of the current scene. Abstraction is neither the invention of liberal theorists nor is it something unique to European intellectual traditions. It is basic to all use of language and theory, and it is indispensable to all communication that succeeds in the face of disagreement. Yet the abstract reasoning of Enlightenment political thought met immediate opposition. Complaints about deontological liberalism's abstraction have been made from its beginning. There are not many points on which Bentham, Burke, Hegeland Marx agree, but they are at one in condemning the abstraction of deontological liberalism, which was known to all of them in the form of appeals to the Rights of Man, and to Hegel and Marx also in the form of Kant's theory of obligations. Why should an aspect of reasoning that is in principle unavoidable, that lies at the core of highly esteemed modes of thought, and that is a precondition of reaching a wide audience have met quick and fierce condemnation both from early critics of 'enlightened ideas' and among our contemporaries?

Some of these objections, considered carefully, are not strictly objections to abstraction but objections to relying on idealised conceptions of agency. An idealised account or theory not merely omits certain predicates that are true of the matter to be considered but adds predicates that are false of the matter to be considered. Idealisation requires abstraction, but they are not the same thing. The omission of some predicate, F, is not tantamount to the addition of the predicate $\sim F$. 'Omission' of a predicate in abstracting merely means that nothing is allowed to rest on the predicate's being satisfied or not satisfied. By contrast, when we idealise, we add a predicate to a theory, and the theory applies only where that predicate is satisfied. Abstract but non-idealised accounts of agents and their reasoning can apply to agents of diverse *Sittlichkeit*; idealised accounts of agents and their reasoning not merely do not refer to the varying historical and cultural characteristics of particular agents, but apply only to idealised, hypothetical agents whose cognitive and volitional features may be missing in all actual human agents. Typically, idealised models of human agency assume various superhuman capacities, such as complete transitively ordered preferences, complete knowledge of the options available and their outcomes, and unwavering powers of calculation; on occasion they include embellishments such as transparent self-knowledge and archangelic insight into others' preferences.

Such models of man may be thought to idealise in two senses. They do not merely posit perfected versions of capacities that human agents have only in part; they also standardly take perfect versions of those capacities as setting ideals for human action. Rational economic man, ideal moral spectators, utilitarian legislators and their ilk are seen not merely as theoretical models of varying interest but as models that are exemplary for human conduct. Appeals to the choice procedures of idealised agents may offer a good model for practice in domains of life where we might want those capacities highly developed, such as shopping or betting. In domains of life where we do not expect or aim for idealised choosing, appeals to such ideals may be irrelevant and even harmful. Nobody would aim to design a health service for ideal rational patients or hope to find an ideal rational lover. (If this does not convince, remember that 'ideal rational lover' is to be construed as an ideally rational being who also (but only when rationality requires it) is a lover – not as an ideal lover who happens to be rational.) There are contexts where we judge idealised rational behaviour closer to subhuman than superhuman.

Many of the complaints levelled at abstraction in ethical and political reasoning are in fact complaints about reliance on idealised conceptions of agency. These complaints may be particularly pertinent to the models of rational choice preferred in utilitarian liberal writing. Proponents of deontological liberalism (by and large) make fewer idealising claims about human agency and rationality. Rawls in particular aimed to appeal to abstract, but not to idealised, views of rational choosing. He described the original position is a 'device of representation' to be deployed by actual citizens in their deliberations. The distinctive feature of those in the original position is not that they order their preferences better or know more or calculate differently from ordinary mortals, but that they have fewer preferences and know less (in particular less about themselves and their prospects). They cannot calculate their self-interest in any detail and so supposedly end up settling for equal liberty and the highest available floor for the distribution of other goods.

However, the abstraction on which Rawls relies is not an abstraction that could be made from every configuration of capacities to choose and to act. It is rather a specific abstraction from the choosing of those who share a certain conception of citizenship, and cannot be abstracted from the capacities of those whose identity is in no way structured by that ideal. For the 'insiders' of a certain liberal tradition, Rawls's model may be an abstraction; for 'outsiders' it is an implausible idealisation. In the background of Rawls's thinking, and in that of other deontological liberals, is an ideal of human identity and choosing that is notably independent of the institutional and ideological context that actual reasoners inhabit. The ideal of citizenship that informs such reasoning prizes the mutual independence of citizens: it is the ideal of making *Moralität* not merely the only shared culture but ultimately the only public culture.

An appeal to a certain ideal of citizenship is not to be seen as an attempt to tie liberal thought to a homogeneous *Sittlichkeit*. Rawls holds that only an account of justice that abstracts from ideological diversity is appropriate for a pluralistic society in which no agreement is to be found or expected on basic ethical issues. The expulsion of *Sittlichkeit* from a theory of justice is unavoidable in societies which are not ideologically homogeneous. Yearnings for a more determinate view of citizenship are at best nostalgia; at worst they fuse citizenship with nationality or culture and license forms of racism, hostility or exclusion. Although Rawls's deontological liberalism is not embedded in a highly specific *Sittlichkeit*, it faces up to the national, ideological and social divisions of the modern world. He denies that we can have an objective account of the good for man, insists that the right is prior to the good, and holds that we can vindicate principles of justice even if unable to agree about the good for man. Even those who are not wholly agnostic about the good for man – who think that *Moralität* does not drive out *Sittlichkeit* – see in deontological liberalism specifically a political theory, a theory of justice, and not a complete theory of morality. They construe abstraction from determinate accounts of the good for man as a strength rather than a failing. Their critics suspect that, in making a certain ideal of mutually independent citizenship the basis of a theory of justice, many sorts of *Sittlichkeit* are expelled not merely from a certain conception of justice but from human life.

Sittlichkeit versus justice beyond borders

The aspiration that lies behind the move to abstraction in liberal thinking is clear enough. Abstraction is the move that political thinking has to make in order to adjust to the absence of homogeneous community and culture. Without (considerable) abstraction, there is no communication with those of differing culture and no account of justice that can be made accessible to diverse audiences; in short, there is nothing that is universally relevant. It is beside the point to complain that an abstract liberal account of justice fails to take community seriously enough, since it is predicated on the view that in modern times a serious conception of justice cannot presuppose community. However, it is a different matter if liberal thinking not merely abstracts but surreptitiously introduces a specific, idealised conception of agents and their capacities to choose. Such idealisations may be alien to many and will render liberal reasoning inaccessible to those whose *Sittlichkeit* does not include or is incompatible with that ideal of citizenship. Abstraction enables us to reach audiences who disagree with us (in part); idealisation disables us from convincing audiences who do not fit or share the ideal.

Liberal accounts of international, let alone global, justice face an acute dilemma here. Liberals traditionally hoped to establish a conception of justice that was not anchored in any particular *Sittlichkeit*, so they did not view national or ideological boundaries as either boundary or horizon. They aspired to criticise the political practice of societies that are anchored in other traditions and to make this criticism accessible to its targets. Yet if their conception of justice in fact idealises (aspects of) a particular type of *Sittlichkeit*, rather than abstracting what is common to all human choosing, any internationalist or global aspirations may be no more than a mask for cultural or national imperialism. Those whose *Sittlichkeit* is not compatible with specifically liberal ideals of mutually independent citizenship will find liberal arguments irrelevant and unconvincing. Marx's claims in 'On the Jewish question' are apt here: merely political (i.e. liberal) emancipation is incompatible with certain modes of *Sittlichkeit*; it marginalises old ways of thought and life by construing them as merely private affairs. Those whose *Sittlichkeit* is relegated to a 'merely private' status by liberal standards of justice reasonably complain. They think appeals to liberal justice and human rights threaten established and cherished conceptions of the human good. Is there anything liberals can say that should convince those who reject ideals of mutually independent citizenship that liberal principles of justice should be taken seriously?

One move that is open to liberals who acknowledge that their principles of justice are rooted in a culturally specific ideal of mutually independent citizenship is to point out how widely this liberal ideal is *in fact* now understood and shared. Liberalism, they might agree, would have had limited appeal at the end of the sixteenth century when a vast diversity of forms of *Sittlichkeit* that were incompatible with mutually independent citizenship could be found in various parts of the world. At the end of the twentieth century things have changed. Liberal ideals have penetrated far and wide. No doubt this penetration was produced by political and commercial forces that were often unjust, judged by liberal standards. The colonial empires and the economic dependency that outlives them were built on injustices. However, their results include a wide comprehension and even acceptance of the discourses of liberal democracy, market relations and human rights, which can now be used to advocate liberal principles to a worldwide audience. The present wide accessibility of liberal principles of justice was produced by violence that liberals would condemn; all the same, it has given those principles wide appeal.

This appeal to the *de facto* accessibility of liberal ideas is not a comfortable position for those liberals who want to claim that their ideas have global implications and can be vindicated in terms that will be cogent to all. No retrospective justification is conferred on the European destruction of other modes of *Sittlichkeit* by showing that the European legacy (Christian and socialist as well as liberal) exported and imposed standards which now prevail and make liberalism (or Christianity or socialism) a widely accessible and accepted political ideology. Any such 'justification' would license all successful ideological changes, including illiberal ones. The fact that imposed beliefs are later accepted by those on whom they have been imposed, and by their descendants, is no justification either for those ideas or for their imposition. The retrospective view of one whose consciousness has been changed shows only that it has been changed, not that is has been raised; that certain beliefs have been made accessible, not that they have been justified.

Liberals disagree on these issues. Some more Hegelian liberals may link accessibility and justification closely. They may think that justification can only be relative to *Sittlichkeit* and that if the colonial era has inscribed liberal ideals into many forms of *Sittlichkeit*, these must now provide the context and horizon for justification. Liberalism's claims can and must be grounded in its historically achieved dominance. The most deeply Hegelian liberals may construe the emergence and spread of liberal modes of thought as the self-unfolding of spirit and see their present wide accessibility and acceptance as their justification.

Other liberals will insist that liberal principles cannot be adequately justified in terms of standards that do not appeal beyond the circles in which they are already inscribed. They will remind us that not everybody has had liberal ideals inserted into their forms of *Sittlichkeit*. They will insist that if justification is simply anchored in whatever modes of *Sittlichkeit* have developed, then the wide audience that liberal reasoning now finds is tribute only to the power with which liberalism has been disseminated and not to any special cogency in liberal thinking. Adequate justification, they will claim, is not anchored in *Sittlichkeit*: 'ought' cannot be derived from 'is'.

Rawlsian constructivism aims to occupy a middle ground. A conception of justification that appeals to 'our' shared ideals accepts that justification addresses a restricted audience and depends on (aspects of) the political, social and ideological realities that make some but not other modes of reasoning accessible. Although Rawls did not vindicate his theory of justice by embedding it deeply in a determinate form of *Sittlichkeit*, he anchored the justification as well as the accessibility of liberal principles of justice in (limited) aspects of the ideals of a certain *Sittlichkeit*. Principles of justice that are justified by constructivist methods that invoke culturally specific ideals will lack justification where those ideals are not shared.

Abstract principles and determinate deliberation

Liberals apparently pay a heavy price in meeting the charges made by the critics of deontological liberalism. Can they avoid paying it? Could they vindicate and deploy liberal principles of justice without either offering a transcendent metaphysical justification of those principles or resting their case on the sharing of an ideal of mutually independent citizenship? (They need not renounce that ideal, but they would have to argue for it rather than presuppose it as the ground of liberal principles.) Are such arguments possible? If liberals do not appeal to the ideals of particular sorts of *Sittlichkeit*, will they not have to rely on the highly abstracted modes of reasoning that both Rawls and the critics of deontological liberalism suspect make liberal reasoning inaccessible, and so without practical import or convincing justification? How can abstract reasoning be made accessible or justified to those who inhabit varying modes of *Sittlichkeit*? Can it be used to vindicate an ideal of mutually independent citizenship? Or is this ideal peculiar to certain political cultures? Is political culture rather than superior abstract reasoning the secret of the wide accessibility of Rawlsian liberalism in the United States, and perhaps a reason why it has not always travelled well beyond the United States?

If those whose *Sittlichkeiten* differ were trapped in mutually impenetrable and incomprehensible discourses, abstracting from any mode of discourse would get one no nearer to any other. However, the actual situation of those whose *Sittlichkeiten* differ is not like this. Typically those whose lives are cast in differing terms are able to follow or to learn how to follow the terms in which others' lives are cast in large part and for large stretches. They may follow and dispute others' categories and their implications rather than see others' discourse as beyond the pale of comprehension. It is because they understand others (if incompletely) that they can be in dispute. The image of radical conceptual isolation depends on an exaggerated picture of differing ways of thought as closed and complete.[21] Ways of thought and life are often (perhaps always) neither. Their boundaries are ill defined; they are porous to and often receptive of elements from disparate ways of life and thought. We are not so much speakers of one of a range of mutually untranslatable languages as we are multilingual. Those who think that modes of *Sittlichkeit* have determinate and uncrossable boundaries take an idealised view of communities, ideologies and nations.

If the boundaries of modes of thought and of communities are indefinite and variable, we can perhaps follow or learn to follow initially alien ways of thought. The first question in looking for the justification for principles of justice need not be 'What agreement can we presuppose?' but rather 'What understanding and what agreement can we construct?'[22] The difference between the two questions is apparent when one reflects on the interpretation of the 'we' assumed in each. If one is concerned with presupposable agreement, the 'we' must be taken rather strictly. Liberal debates must be understood as confined to those who already agree on much – for example, on an ideal of citizenship – and they can be made more widely accessible only by imposing a conception of justice that embodies that ideal. (If understanding stops at boundaries, fundamental ideas can travel only when they conquer.) Yet, if liberal conceptions of justice rule out unconsented-to interventions, they cannot justly be imposed. If, on the other hand, one is concerned with the agreement that can be achieved, 'we' may have no unique interpretation and need not be defined by reference to any shared ideal or outlook. In this case the preliminaries for moving towards the vindication of liberal conceptions of justice are quite different.

Consider some of these preliminaries. Suppose that we view the circumstances of justice much as Rawls does, and join him in seeing ethical pluralism as (in part) constitutive of modern circumstances of justice. Rawls also saw ethical agreement on a certain ideal of citizenship as the basis for determining principles of justice. This is not strictly inconsistent,

---

[21] Cf. Ernest Gellner, *Nations and Nationalism* (Oxford: Basil Blackwell, 1983).

[22] The term 'construct' is used both to refer to processes of negotiation, debate and politics and to suggest the project of a constructivist approach to practical reasoning.

since ethical pluralism does not rule out selective agreement, but there is an evident tension. A plurality of human beings between whom there were deep differences of outlook could no more presuppose shared ideals of citizenship to guide them to principles of justice than they could appeal to pre-established harmony. Rawls relied on the separation of the right from the good to underpin his appeal to selective sharing of ideals against a background of ethical pluralism. As we have seen, this separation, and the corollary subordination of *Sittlichkeit* to *Moralität*, is a central criticism made against deontological liberalism.

Liberals who reject Rawls's move must look for *achievable* rather than *presupposed* agreement. They can begin by asking what can be done by those who find themselves confronted with the pluralism that is constitutive of modern circumstances of justice, yet seek to vindicate principles with universal scope. They cannot (without rejecting the search for such principles) appeal to a specific ideal of citizenship or to other non-universal features of human choosers: hence they must seek abstract but non-idealised principles of justice. However, if their reasoning is not to be inaccessible to many audiences, they must also find ways of deliberating that connect these abstract principles of justice to the more specific and accessible categories of discourse of particular communities. This means that liberal reasoning that both answers the critics of deontological liberalism and retains internationalist let alone global commitments would have to address the charge of abstraction in both of these ways.

A search for abstract but non-idealised principles that could be justified beyond the circles where liberalism is already accepted would have to show that the most basic principles of liberal thought were not political in so narrow a sense as Rawls assumes. Rawls takes it that liberalism must assume not only the ideological pluralism that constitutes the circumstances of justice but also a specifically liberal ideal of citizens as mutually independent. It is the second of these that introduces idealisation, rather than mere abstraction, into his theory and makes it questionable for those who do not share this ideal. However, idealisation may be avoidable. Liberals could perhaps seek to generate principles of justice simply from an abstract account of the modern circumstances of justice and seek to vindicate rather than assume ideals of mutual independence or other specifically liberal ideals.

The modern circumstances of justice include ethical diversity, and the fact that people have variously constituted capacities to reason and to act, and varying forms and degrees of independence from one another and from the institutions and practices that constitute their *Sittlichkeit*.

Plurality without coordination is the classic condition in which the problems both of order and of justice arise, and modern plurality is more demanding because we cannot assume a homogeneous *Sittlichkeit* either within or beyond boundaries. Principles of justice are redundant where there is only a single agent, or where a pre-established harmony (a well-entrenched total ideology?) coordinates agents. It is of no practical concern if liberal thinking cannot arrive at principles that cover these debased cases, where (by hypothesis) conflict cannot arise. What is decisive for the liberal enterprise is whether modern circumstances of justice can provide the ground for principles of justice without additional appeals to ideals that are part of some but not of other sorts of *Sittlichkeit* and without requiring recourse to an apparently unavailable objective account of the good for man.

If modern circumstances of justice include the plurality not just of agents but of ideologies, any principles of justice which can be vindicated beyond the boundaries of a specific mode of *Sittlichkeit* must be shareable by outsiders as well as insiders. However, if a plurality is to share principles, acting on those principles must leave everybody's agency intact. Those whose agency is destroyed or subverted or bypassed or undermined cannot act on any principles, a fortiori cannot share the same principles as others. Either modern circumstances of justice do not obtain, or (if they do) any universal principles will be only those that rule out destroying, subverting, bypassing or undermining others' (no doubt far from ideal) capacities to reason and to act. In more familiar terms, the principles of justice must *at least* include principles of avoiding coercion and deception, since these are principles of destroying or subverting others' agency.

Liberal thinking that started in this way might, it seems, avoid appealing to idealisations that subvert or undermine the supposed universality of scope and vindication of Rawlsian principles of justice. However, would it not immediately be accused of the abstraction with which Kantian thinking has often been charged? Is there any practical benefit in establishing very abstract principles of justice, such as 'Do not coerce' and 'Do not deceive', if their determinate implications are obscure? On the other hand, if these determinate implications could be worked out, would they not be the same for all, regardless of circumstances? Will not abstraction from modern circumstances of justice lead us either to conclusions that are inaccessible so not action-guiding for those who have to act, or to demands for uniformity that are unresponsive to diverse circumstances? By sticking strictly to abstraction we appear to get abstract answers, but no guidance on what counts as coercive or deceptive in particular situations; and if that could be overcome, we would get principles that prescribed with rigid uniformity.

Does this show that a purely abstract liberalism is useless and that Rawls took the only available way forward for liberal thinking in tying it to the ideals of a minimal yet specific liberal *Sittlichkeit?* This conclusion deserves further scrutiny. We do not usually complain when principles fail to determine their own application. Rather it is thought the merit of principles that they cover many cases, and unavoidable that they are indeterminate. This is true even for the most ordinary principles for which no universal scope is claimed and which are deeply embedded in a given mode of *Sittlichkeit*. *Sittlichkeit* does not and cannot eliminate the need for deliberation, or the possibility of disagreement: it simply allows disagreements to be formulated and debated in mutually comprehensible and accepted ways. Surely one should not expect highly abstract principles of justice to be unlike more specific principles in that they alone entail their applications. Yet much criticism of deontological liberalism implicitly makes this demand. The demand leads to searches for highly specific criteria for the justice of particular arrangements and actions – such as informed consent that meets certain protocols, or forms of democratic legitimation. Such demands set implausible standards. The abstract principles of avoiding coercion and deception may have implications that vary greatly with circumstances. We have no reason to think that there is a unique interpretation of what constitutes coercion and deception in all circumstances: the boundaries for coercion and deception are always matters for deliberation.

Coercion is generally taken to be a matter either of force or of threat. Both force and threat can eclipse others' agency, and reliance on either disregards (even destroys) the separateness and hence the plurality (of agents and of ideologies) that is constitutive of modern circumstances of justice. What constitutes force or threat in particular circumstances will, however, depend on how others and their capacities to act are vulnerable. Force that overcomes a seven-stone weakling may not bother Superman. Threats that deter or control the weak or timid may be laughed off by others. There is (despite much effort expended) no prospect that liberals – or anyone else – will offer an account of what coerces that does not vary with agents' actual capacities to choose and to act. An account of what would coerce ideally rational beings is irrelevant to actual agents. Those who seek to threaten or to force others understand this all too well, and adjust their action to take advantage of their victims' vulnerabilities. They judge nicely which specific modes of intervention, or of (supposed) laissez-faire, will destroy or undermine others' capacities to act.

Similar points can be made about deception. The many possible ways of misleading others have in common that they seek to subvert and bypass others' agency, which is why reliance on deception is deeply destructive of modern (and indeed of other) circumstances of justice. What constitutes deception will, however, vary with victims' capacities and is always a matter for deliberation. A stratagem that dupes a child may amuse an adult; a lie that works on a victim whose desires it flatters and fulfils will be pointless with a sceptic who resists it. There is no prospect of finding an account of deception that does not have to be adjusted to the cognitive capacities and states of those who are to be deceived. It is irrelevant to point to procedures that would be adequate to avoid deceiving idealised rational beings. As deceivers have always known, successful deception too works on its victims' specific vulnerabilities.

If principles of non-coercion and non-deception have no unique interpretation, their application must use deliberation that takes account of actual conditions of action. Deontological liberalism cannot meet its critics' charges merely by sticking to abstraction and avoiding idealisation in selecting principles of justice. An abstract deontological liberalism cannot guide action or be accessible to agents of varying *Sittlichkeit* unless abstract principles can be connected to determinate judgements that take account of the actual characteristics and capacities of agents. A real commitment to abstraction rather than idealisation has to be supported by serious consideration of the move from abstract principles to actual judgements. However, the need for deliberation is not some peculiar liability of abstract liberal thinking. The move from abstract principle to determinate interpretation or judgement in a given context is part and parcel of all ethical reasoning (indeed of all practical reasoning) and so indispensable both within any mode of *Sittlichkeit* and between those of differing *Sittlichkeit*. When Socrates asked Cephalus what justice was, and was given the conventional Athenian answer that it is a matter of giving every man his own, he promptly asks whether this includes giving back a knife to its frenzied owner. Even within Athenian *Sittlichkeit* – our classic image of a community with shared ideals – principles do not entail their own applications.

Although the move from abstract principle to its determinate implications for a given context is indispensable, deontological liberals say little about it. This may be because idealised rather than merely abstract accounts of principles of justice have so often been preferred. Once idealised accounts of agency are deployed, the preferred ideals will invade all applications of principles of justice, and the indispensability of deliberation may be less obvious. For once we have it in mind that there is some unique criterion for non-coercion, or for informed consent, or for non-deception, it may seem unnecessary to talk about deliberation. Yet it is here, in debates about what it would take for determinate agents with specific modes of *Sittlichkeit* to act justly in specific situations, that the move from abstract principle to accessible and action-guiding judgements must be made.

Will it not also be here that liberal principles become hostage to received views? Will the categories and modes of discourse of a particular *Sittlichkeit* not shape, and perhaps corrupt, the process of deliberation in which liberal principles are applied? There are endless examples. An example that is revealing, because it misuses the ideal of mutually independent citizenship, is that of the 'treaty' of Waitangi, which was 'signed' by newly and barely literate Maori chiefs, who thereby (it was held) 'ceded' lands and sovereignty.[23] Here the outward forms of negotiation, consent and legal contract were used to achieve 'agreement' that is transparently an element of a coercive policy, and liberal principles were mockingly subordinated to imperial goals. Coercion and deception in public, including international, affairs are often less crude or obvious. Where some are far more powerful than others, it is easy for them to subvert or undercut the agency of the weak.[24] Such deception and coercion readily present the outward face of legal, diplomatic and commercial negotiation and mask injustice. Others' agency cannot be respected by inflicting on them modes of bargaining and negotiation which, while they would not undercut or subvert idealised agents, coerce or deceive those with limited rationality and power. It is always easy for the powerful to make the weak offers that they cannot refuse and to lead the ignorant to hold beliefs that they cannot test.

If abstract principles can so readily be assimilated to the policies of the powerful, what are they worth? They certainly are not and cannot be algorithms for action that generate determinate guidance for each situation. In this they do not differ from other principles, including those for which no universal scope is claimed. The procedures of deliberation by which situations are specified and described in one way and the specification then challenged and modified are more difficult when we are dealing with very abstract principles; but they are continuous with procedures by which specification and articulation of cases goes on within the most enclosed of *Sittlichkeiten*. From this we may conjecture that abstract

---

[23] D. F. McKenzie, 'The sociology of a text: orality and print literacy in early New Zealand', *The Library* 6th ser., 6 (1984), 333–65.

[24] I say nothing here about which agents carry the obligations for global justice, but it is a corollary of taking the contextualised view of agency that I have relied on here that they may include a range of institutions, groups and states, as well as individuals. See the chapters in Part III, below.

liberalism should view the need for deliberation not as intellectual defeat, but as an essential task.

The claim that some action would (or would not) constitute coercion or deception, or another form of injustice, in a given situation is often controversial. It is open to assessment, challenge and rejection. Nobody lives ensconced in a unique mode of ethical discourse that settles all questions. However, the very multiplicity of modes of discourse that distinguishes modern circumstances of justice allows not only for disagreement, but also for debate and for the possibility of finding reasons that convince others not merely within but across boundaries. Those who can follow and listen to a swirl of distinct discourses can also dispute which of them gives the most pertinent and complete account of matters. Ethical pluralism provides the context for conflict, but also allows for discussion and revision of descriptions and discourses between those who disagree. No doubt such discussions will be buffeted by powerful interests that advocate construing matters in one way rather than in another. Politics begins here, in debates about the terms of discussion themselves. If liberals are to advocate global justice they must not only articulate the wider implications of liberal political discourse but consider what view liberals should take of the ethics and the politics of discourse.

CHAPTER 6

Bounded and cosmopolitan justice[1]

The scope of justice

Since antiquity justice has been thought of as a political or civic virtue, more recently as belonging in a 'bounded society',[2] and often as a primary task of states.[3] All these views assume that justice requires or presupposes boundaries, which demarcate those who are to render and to receive justice from one another from others who are to be excluded. Yet the view that justice is intrinsically bounded sits ill with the many other claims that it is cosmopolitan, owed to all regardless of location or origin, race or gender, class or citizenship. The tension between moral cosmopolitanism and institutional anti-cosmopolitanism has been widely discussed, but there remains a lot of disagreement about its proper resolution.

Take, for example, the specific version of this thought that views justice as wholly internal to states. If we start with cosmopolitan principles, the justice of states will suffice only if we can show that any system of just states will itself be just. But this claim is highly implausible. We can certainly imagine a system of states that would be just provided that each state was just. For example, a set of just states without mutual influence or effects (imagine that they are located on different continents in a

---

[1] 'Bounded and cosmopolitan justice', *Review of International Studies* 26 (2000), 45–60; an earlier version under the title 'Civic and cosmopolitan justice' appeared as the Lindley Lecture for 2000, published by the Department of Philosophy of the University of Kansas.

[2] John Rawls relies on the idea of a *bounded* society throughout his work. References to his writings will use the following abbreviations: *A Theory of Justice*: *TJ*; 'Themes in Kant's moral philosophy' (1989) in Samuel Freeman (ed.), *Collected Papers of John Rawls* (Cambridge, MA: Harvard University Press, 1999), 497–528: *TKMP*; *Political Liberalism* (New York: Columbia University Press, 1993): *PL*; *The Law of Peoples* (Cambridge, MA: Harvard University Press, 1999): *LP*.

[3] It is not entirely clear which version of this view underlies the UN *Universal Declaration of Human Rights* of 1948: the text uses a range of non-equivalent terms, including *member states*, *peoples*, *nations* and *countries*.

pre-modern world or on different planets today) could be just, provided that each state was just. But the system of states in the various forms in which it has existed in recent centuries is not at all like this. The relations of domination and subordination between states always shape their pro-spects and powers, and the structures they can establish internally; the exclusions which state boundaries create may themselves be sources of injustice. The same line of thought suggests that it is implausible to think that societies, or cities, or communities, or other bounded entities provide the sole contexts of justice. Boundaries of whatever sorts are not unques-tionable presuppositions of thinking about justice, but institutions whose structure raises questions of justice.

Equally, commitment to cosmopolitan principles does not entail – although it also may not rule out – commitment to cosmopolitan political institutions, such as a world state, or a world federation. Principles are intrinsically indeterminate, and can be institutionalised in many distinct ways.[4] In some circumstances the best way to institutionalise a commit-ment to cosmopolitan justice might be to abolish certain sorts of bound-aries; in others it might not. The risk of cosmopolitan institutions is that they concentrate power, and that we have good reasons for ensuring that power is not concentrated at a global level, just as the political thinkers of the seventeenth and eighteenth centuries had good reasons for insisting on the separation of powers within states. On the other hand, the risk of anti-cosmopolitan institutions is that they may institutionalise justice in ways that groundlessly exclude some (or many) from its benefits – and its burdens.

In this chapter I contrast two views of justice beyond borders. Both are alert to the claims both of bounded contexts and of universal principles. The two positions are those proposed by Immanuel Kant in a number of works, in particular in his political writings of the 1780s and 1790s, and by John Rawls in his later work, and especially in *Political Liberalism* and in *The Law of Peoples*.

Rawlsian and Kantian views of justice are often thought of as quite similar: Rawls speaks of his own work as 'Kantian', and follows Kant in building his account of justice on a conception of 'public reason' that has certain affinities with Kant's conception of public reason. More

---

[4] Alan Gewirth, 'Ethical universalism and particularism', *Journal of Philosophy* 85 (1988), 283–302; Onora O'Neill, *Towards Justice and Virtue* (Cambridge University Press, 1996), and 'Principles, practical judgement and institutions' in *Bounds of Justice*, 50–64.

specifically, both Rawls and Kant advance what may be loosely called a *semi-cosmopolitan* view of just institutions: neither endorses a world state, but each thinks that justice requires more than can be delivered by states and their internal institutions. I shall say only a small amount about the specific institutional proposals for international justice that Rawls and Kant put forward, and will concentrate mainly on their respective starting points rather than their policy recommendations.

There are two reasons for choosing this focus. The first is that comparisons between proposals that address such different worlds may mislead. Kant's proposals were in their day a remarkable blend of political realism and radical thinking. Writing at a time when there were few republican states and no full democracies, he proposed a league of republican states that acknowledge obligations to their own citizens, as well as more limited obligations to the citizens of other (republican) states. By contrast, Rawls's proposals for justice across boundaries are quite conservative for our day. He wrote at a time when the United Nations and its organisations, the World Bank and varied institutions for adjudicating issues that cross boundaries, had all existed for some time, and suggested that international justice will require some institutions or other of roughly these sorts.[5] My second reason for saying only a limited amount about the specific institutions of justice across borders to which Kant and Rawls point is that others have already said a good deal.[6] But in my view too little has been said about the respective starting points of their thought about justice beyond borders; so it is to these that I shall turn. For reasons that will become clear, I shall discuss Rawls before Kant rather than sticking to the historical order.

---

[5] By contrast, some of his commentators have argued that Rawlsian conceptions of domestic justice should be applied globally: for example, that the difference principle should be applied to global distributive justice, or that fair equality of opportunity should be extended globally. See Beitz, *Political Theory and International Relations*; Pogge, *Realizing Rawls*, especially Part III; Andrew Kuper, 'Rawlsian global justice: beyond the law of peoples to a cosmopolitan law of persons', *Political Theory* 28 (2000), 640–74.

[6] See James Bohman and Matthias Lutz-Bachmann (eds.), *Perpetual Peace: Essays on Kant's Cosmopolitan Ideal* (Cambridge, MA: MIT Press, 1997), especially the essay by Jürgen Habermas, 'Kant's idea of perpetual peace, with the benefit of two hundred years' hindsight', 113–53; Katrin Flikschuh, *Kant and Modern Political Philosophy* (Cambridge University Press, 2000); Elisabeth Ellis, *Kant's Politics: Provisional Theory for an Uncertain World* (New Haven, CT: Yale University Press, 2005); Pauline Kleingeld, *Kant and Cosmopolitanism: The Philosophical Ideal of World Citizenship* (Cambridge University Press, 2012); Andrew Kuper, *Democracy beyond Borders: Justice and Representation in Global Institutions* (Oxford University Press, 2004); and Pogge, *Realizing Rawls* especially Part III.

Communitarians and justice beyond boundaries

Before turning to Rawls, it is useful to call to mind the communitarian views he opposes, in which the very principles of justice and the reasoning that is to support them are viewed as bounded. A merit of communitarian thought is that it incorporates a strong view of the basis of practical reasoning, which it views as legitimately formed and bounded by the categories, norms and practices of actual communities and their cultures. Although this move may seem arbitrary from the point of view of out-siders, it is anchored in a conception of human identity as shaped by the constitutive norms and practices of the communities and traditions of which a given individual is part, and so offers substantial premises for working out an account of justice and other normative issues appropriate to that community. These norms and practices are, to use a useful Hegelian phrase, seen as *nicht hintergehbar*: there is no going behind them. Since they are constitutive of the identity of the community or tradition, and so of its members' senses of identity, there is no deeper range of premises that could provide a basis for challenging these norms.

Communitarians are not unaware of the possibility that the constitutive norms of communities and traditions may change, indeed be changed by those within a community. They see the categories and values of commu-nities as open to revision in the light of its internal conceptual resources. Hence it is a mistake to think that communitarian reasoning is inevitably *conservative*. However, I believe that it would not be a mistake to think that reasoning that proceeds within the constraints set by the categories, norms and other resources of a community or tradition must inevitably be *ethnocentric* or *inward looking*. Communitarian reasoning is inevitably insiders' reasoning, and takes no account of the categories, the concerns or the views of outsiders. This does not, of course, mean that communi-tarians can have no view of the proper treatment of outsiders: they might be convinced of the merits of exclusion or of integration, of neglect or of assimilation, or perhaps (more worryingly) of marginalisation, colonisation or extermination.[7] However, they do not think that there could be reasoned dialogue with unassimilated outsiders, with whom neither cat-egories nor norms, nor therefore the means of reasoning, are shared.

---

[7] Communitarian reasoning has often been put forward by writers whose substantive political commitments are more or less liberal – but its potential is not adequately assessed unless account is taken of the fact that communitarianism is equally hospitable to substantive norms that are anti-liberal, excluding, separatist or even imperialist.

Although communitarians take a realistic view of the possibilities for change within any given tradition, I believe that they take an unrealistic view of the boundaries between traditions and communities. Political borders form highly variable filters; the cultural boundaries which communitarian reasoning is chiefly concerned with are yet more porous and malleable. Many people are inward with the categories and norms of a number of traditions; those who are not initially familiar with the thought of some community can often grasp a good deal about others' categories and norms, and therefore about their reasoning. (For contemporary evidence, consider the amazing spread of the rhetoric of rights!) Sense of identity is not invariably anchored in the actual norms and categories of a single community; even where it is, those who live by the ways of thought and life of a specific community may understand a fair range of outsiders. Like the rest of us, communitarians in fact hold that foreigners and other cultural outsiders are persons with whom we can communicate, if not perfectly, still a great deal, and that trade and translation, travel and collaboration are real possibilities. In my view these everyday assumptions undermine the plausibility of any communitarian conception of practical reason and show that it offers no convincing basis for reasoning either about domestic justice or about justice beyond boundaries.

However, reasoning that does not draw on culturally specific categories and norms will be considerably impoverished. It is not obvious what alternative premises for practical reasoning will be available. Once we allow that not all reasoning about justice can be based on the rich conceptual resources of a tradition or community, we must look for an alternative account of practical reason. One promising direction in which to look is to John Rawls's work, and in particular to his later work, in which he both advances and deploys a conception of practical reason as public reason that can address questions of justice.

Rawls on public reason

In *Political Liberalism* and in *The Law of Peoples*, Rawls explicitly rejects one underlying assumption of the communitarian project: 'pluralism is not seen as a disaster but rather as the natural outcome of human reason under enduring free institutions'.[8] If this is the case, it will not always be possible to identify constitutive categories and norms for the very units for which

---

[8] *PL* xxiv; cf. 47, 55; *LP* 31–2. See also the separate essay, 'The idea of public reason', included in *LP* 131–80.

Rawls thinks questions of justice primarily arise. Justice, as he sees it, has its context in a *bounded society*, a perpetually continuing scheme of cooperation that persons enter only by birth and leave only by death, and which is self-sufficient.[9] Within each bounded society, reasonable persons will not come to complete agreement about ethical matters and may be expected to form differing 'conceptions of the good'. However, being reasonable they may be expected to accept a form of reciprocity, namely to be 'ready to propose principles and standards as fair terms of co-operation and to abide by them willingly, given the assurance that others will likewise do so'.[10] Reasonable persons are committed to a conception of public reason, and prepared to work out the framework for the public social world they share and to construct the principles of justice by which they will live together, despite their irresolvable ethical disagreements. Public reason, as Rawls construes it, is 'citizens' reasoning in the public forum about constitutional essentials and basic questions of justice'.[11] Evidently this conception of public reason as reciprocity between fellow-citizens presupposes the constitutive institutions that define not just *citizenship* but more specifically *fellow-citizenship*: the bounded society and the constitutional basis of citizenship (including liberal rights and democracy in just societies, on Rawls's account). This essentially civic conception of public reason is coupled with what we might view as an associative conception of practical reasoning for narrower spheres (Rawls calls this 'non-public reason'; his thought is close to Kant's writing on 'private uses of reason').[12]

In short, although Rawls's conception of public reason in *Political Liberalism* does not assume the shared culture that communitarian reasoning presupposes, it does presuppose shared political arrangements, including boundaries, and (for just societies) liberal democracy and citizenship. It is a nice question whether the boundaries that are presupposed are – contrary to Rawls's claims about them – in fact state boundaries. On the one hand he claims only to presuppose a 'bounded society', on the other hand the assumption that nobody enters except by birth or leaves except by death suggests that Rawlsian bounded societies are well policed, that within their territories legitimate force is exercised, indeed presumably monopolised. And this is the Weberian definition of a state.

---

[9] This formulation is to be found throughout *TJ*; in later works the emphasis on bounded societies continues, but their liberal democracy and the citizenship of their members are increasingly emphasised; these shifts are corollaries of Rawls's shift to a 'political' conception of justification.

[10] *PL* 49, including the note.   [11] *PL* 10; cf. 212ff. and *LP* 132–3.

[12] For Rawls's views on non-public reasoning see *PL* 213ff., especially 220–2 and *LP* 134; for Kant's views on public and private reason, see below.

These issues are discussed in more detail in Rawls's *The Law of Peoples*. Here he argues that issues of justice beyond boundaries are to be approached by considering public reasoning as conducted by *peoples*. He rejects both the communitarian thought that the basis of reasoning is to be culturally defined (a community, a tradition), and the thought that the parties who consider justice beyond boundaries are to be thought of as individuals or as states.[13] Liberal peoples are considered as inhabiting their own territories, and as negotiating standards of international justice with other liberal peoples, as well as with those non-liberal peoples who have what Rawls calls a 'decent hierarchical society'. Rawls believes that the principles that would be mutually accepted will include those of non-aggression, non-intervention except in self-defence (and sparingly to end grave violations of human rights in other societies).[14] He also thinks that reasonable peoples are likely to agree on some version of the UN organisations, some form of World Bank and some form of global trade agreement.[15] Moreover, Rawls thinks that reasonable peoples have a duty of assistance to help heavily burdened societies to progress towards justice, but that the difference principle is not to be extended to global economic institutions.[16] Since the procedures of Rawlsian public reasoning are specified only in very general terms, it is reasonable to ask whether they would in fact lead to agreement on these specific arrangements. The claim that peoples will take this limited view of transnational economic justice depends crucially on Rawls's assumption that the 'bounded societies' of peoples are prior to justice. Otherwise it would be obscure why reasonable peoples would not agree to a more extended view of economic justice.

The conception of the state that Rawls rejects in *The Law of Peoples* is in my view indeed a pretty unpromising basis for any account of justice beyond boundaries. What he rejects is the realist conception of states as 'anxiously concerned with their power – their capacity (military, economic, diplomatic) – to influence others and always guided by their basic interests'.[17] However, this has always been an idealised, indeed ideologised, conception of the state; it is certainly not the only option. Others have thought that states themselves are capable of action that is not self-interested, and that they can and should be bound to justice in their dealings with other states.

---

[13] *PL* 18; *LP* 23–30.   [14] *LP* 35.   [15] *LP* 38.
[16] *LP* 115–19; for commentary sees Beitz, *Political Theory and International Relations*; Thomas Pogge, *Realizing Rawls*, and *World Poverty and Human Rights: Cosmopolitan Responsibilities and Reforms*, 2nd edn (Cambridge: Polity Press, 2002).
[17] *LP* 28.

Nevertheless, the conception of a 'people' on which Rawls builds his account of justice beyond boundaries is in fact remarkably *state-like*, in that it views peoples too as preoccupied by protection of territory and self-interest:

> Liberal peoples do, however, have their fundamental interests as permitted by their conceptions of right and justice. They seek to protect their territory, to ensure the security and safety of their citizens, and to preserve their free political institutions and the liberties and free culture of their civil society.[18]

Evidently Rawls conceives of peoples as territorially bounded and politically organised, and as able to appoint representatives[19] through whom they are to reason with other peoples about justice beyond boundaries. In short, peoples are conceived as having all the powers, capacities and features of states, and in addition the concern 'to preserve their free political institutions and the liberties and free culture of their civil society'. There is little here that distinguishes liberal peoples from liberal states. Rawls, however, holds that

> What distinguishes peoples from states – and this is crucial – is that just peoples are fully prepared to grant the very same proper respect and recognition to other peoples as equal.[20]

In Rawls's view, peoples can be reasonable, but states are wedded – or condemned – to rational self-interest.

The choice of *peoples* rather than *states* as the agents whose deliberations are basic to justice beyond boundaries is, I think, motivated in large part by an inaccurate assumption that states must be ideal typical structures that fit a certain Hobbesian or realist paradigm. Yet states *as we have actually known them* do not fit that paradigm.[21] The view that states and governments have limited powers, yet can adhere to fundamental principles, by which they modify the pursuit of rational self-interest, is central to the liberal tradition of political philosophy and to contemporary international politics. States *as they have really existed and exist* never had and

---

[18] *LP* 29. Note also the following: 'The point of the institution of property is that, unless a definite agent is given responsibility for maintaining an asset ... that asset tends to deteriorate. In this case the asset is the people's territory and its capacity to support them in perpetuity; and the agent is the people themselves as politically organised', *LP* 39.

[19] *LP* 32, 34.   [20] *LP* 35.

[21] Theorists of international relations acknowledge that many of the states we see around us fall far short of the realist paradigm of statehood: they speak of quasi-states and dependent states; and there are states that maintain strong internationalist and liberal commitments. Rawls acknowledges that realism about state action is false – yet seemingly accepts a realist conception of the state; see *LP* 46.

never have unlimited sovereignty, internal or external – although various theorists of sovereignty, proponents of strategic reasoning, hawks in powerful states and romantic nationalists without powerful states have made grandiose claims. States *as they currently exist* are committed by numerous treaty obligations to a limited conception of sovereignty and a degree of respect for human rights; and there is nothing contradictory about these commitments, although like other commitments they are sometimes not honoured. Peoples as *they may once have existed without state structures* lack bounded territories; peoples who negotiate with other peoples, who have boundaries, who keep outsiders out and who make agreements do so by using state and governmental structures.

It is not hard to see what leads Rawls to this distinctive view of the basis for thinking about international justice. Since he has proposed an account of public reason that focuses on the notion of reciprocity among agents, he has to determine who the relevant agents are, among whom reciprocity is to be achieved (or not achieved). Since he assumes the realist conception of the state, according to which states must act solely from self-interest, he reasonably concludes that states cannot be agents of justice who rely on Rawlsian public reason. By default, the reasonable agents who are to carry the burden of international negotiation and justice across boundaries are then identified as *peoples*. Yet in reality the only peoples who have well-defined and controlled boundaries and capacities to negotiate with outsiders on a sustained and potentially reasonable basis are peoples with states. There is something laborious about anchoring an account of reasoning in a conception of territorial agents not well exemplified in our world, and who (if they were exemplified) would acquire the political capacities Rawls imputes to them only by developing the very state and governmental structures from which he tries to detach his argument.

Kant: public reason as non-derivative

Rawls views his philosophy as in many ways Kantian, and makes frequent references to Kant in his writing on justice across boundaries. However, he also, and in my view rightly, distances his work from Kant's. In *The Law of Peoples* he writes:

> Since my presentation of the Law of Peoples is greatly indebted to Kant's idea of *foedus pacificum* and to so much in his thought, I should say the following: at no point are we deducing the principles of right and justice, or decency, or the principles of rationality, from a conception of practical

reason in the background. Rather, we are giving content to an idea of practical reason and three of its component parts, the ideas of reasonableness, decency and rationality. The criteria for these three normative ideas are not deduced, but enumerated and characterised in each case. Practical reasoning as such is simply reasoning about what to do, or reasoning about what institutions and policies are reasonable, decent, or rational and why. There is no list of necessary or sufficient conditions for each of these three ideas.[22]

As Rawls sees it, Kant's reliance on an account of practical reason has unacceptable metaphysical presuppositions.[23] Kant, by contrast, does seek to derive his account of justice from an account of practical reason. However, it is not obvious that Kant's conceptions of practical reason, of ethics, of justice or specifically of international justice *must* be derived from transcendental idealism under a strongly metaphysical interpretation. In particular, Kant's distinctive non-Rawlsian understanding of public reason provides relatively accessible arguments that do not draw on metaphysical assumptions, yet aim to vindicate a specific conception of practical reason. His arguments can be given, indeed they invite, an anti-metaphysical reading.

The central thought of Kant's account of public reason is simply that the standards of reason cannot be derivative. Any acceptance of other, 'external' authorities *of whatever sort* as sources of reason must fail. Just as a learner cyclist who clutches at passing objects and leans on them to balance thereby fails to balance at all, so a would-be reasoner who leans on some socially or civilly constituted power and authority that lacks reasoned vindication fails to reason.

This view is explicit in the quite distinctive way in which Kant characterises the difference between his conceptions of *public* and *private* uses of reason in various works of the 1780s and 1790s.[24] Here I shall refer only to two short essays of the 1780s, neglecting Kant's other extended discussions of

---

[22] *LP* 86–7; see also *TKMP* for further elaboration of ways in which Rawls sees his position on reason as different from Kant's.

[23] For discussion of some of Rawls's reasons for distancing himself from Kant, and some of the distinctive features of his conception of public reason, see Thomas McCarthy, 'A reasonable law of peoples' in Bohman and Lutz-Bachmann, *Perpetual Peace*, 201–17. For an anti-foundationalist reading of Kant's vindication of reason see Onora O'Neill, 'Vindicating reason' in Paul Guyer (ed.), *The Cambridge Companion to Kant* (Cambridge University Press, 1992), 280–308, and 'Kant's conception of public reason' in *Proceedings of the IXth Kant Kongress* (Berlin: de Gruyter, 2000). Both papers, and others on related themes, are included in O'Neill, *Constructing Authorities*.

[24] All references to Kant's works and all quotations are taken from the *Cambridge Edition of the Works of Immanuel Kant*, ed. Paul Guyer and Allen J. Wood (Cambridge University Press). The relevant volumes are *Practical Philosophy*, trans. Mary J. Gregor (1996), and *Religion and Rational Theology*, trans. Allen J. Wood and George Giovanni (1996). The volume and page references are to the Prussian Academy pagination, included in the margins of the Cambridge edition. The following

public and private reason and of related notions, including interpretation. In these essays Kant characterises uses of reason that appeal to rationally ungrounded assumptions, such as the civilly constituted authority of church or state, not as public but as private. In *What Is Enlightenment?* he speaks of the reasoning of military officers, of pastors of the established church and of civil servants in carrying out their roles as *private*: these functionaries derive their authority from their civil offices. Their official communications accept *and do not seek to justify* the authority of the civil power that establishes the relevant offices and their constitutive powers and rules. Kant states explicitly that 'the private use of reason is that which one may make of it in a certain *civil* post or office with which he is entrusted'.[25] It follows that the sorts of reasoning exhibited in democratic political debate and in communitarian thought, as well as in the civic reasoning Rawls commends, are all in Kant's view *private*, because each presupposes the authority of civilly and socially constituted roles, institutions and practices. Rawlsian peoples are not identifiable independently of their bounded territories and the constitutive institutional structures that secure these territories, distinguish citizen from noncitizen, and provide the contexts for their (democratic) government, including that part of (democratic) government that counts as foreign policy: hence Kant would see their reasoning as private.

Kant himself offers a quite different view of (fully) public reason as *intrinsically* non-derivative. He contrasts all 'private' uses of reason with 'the public use of one's own reason ... which someone makes of it *as a scholar* before the entire public of the *world of readers*',[26] a scholar 'who by his writings speaks to the public in the strict sense, that is, the world'.[27]

In these and other passages Kant sets out a dilemma. If we appeal to any civilly or socially constituted powers or authorities, let alone to mere brute force – if we try to view these contingencies as sources of reason – we lose the very justifications we seek. Discourse that defers to authorities that lack reasoned vindication achieves at best restricted scope and authority; those who buttress their conclusions by appealing to authorities they do not vindicate end up relying on the dubious merits of an argument from authority.

---

abbreviations are used: *What Is Enlightenment?*: WE (1784); *Groundwork of the Metaphysic of Morals*: G (1785); *What Does It Mean to Orient Oneself in Thinking?*: WO (1786); *The Metaphysic of Morals*: MM (1797); *Toward Perpetual Peace*: PP (1795); *On the Common Saying: That may be correct in theory, but is of no use in practice*: TP (1793); *Religion within the Boundaries of Mere Reason*: R (1793); *The Conflict of the Faculties*: CF (1798).
[25] WE 8:37.   [26] WE 8:37.   [27] WE 8:38.

Kant: public reason as freedom without lawlessness

Kant's criticism of *private* uses of reason is both convincing and problematic. It is convincing because it is clear enough what any appeal to contingently available authorities amounts to: the introduction of some arbitrary premise asserting the claims of that authority. And it is clear enough what it costs: the relativisation of conclusions to that arbitrary premise. It is easy to agree that reasoning is limited as soon as it takes for granted some civilly constituted authority, indeed any contingent 'authority' for which no justification is provided, and that independence from such assumptions would be needed to convince 'outsiders'. It is easy to see how this Kantian criticism of 'private' reason can be extended to undermine attempts to view *democratic, communitarian* and even *Rawlsian* (or other civic) conceptions of public reason as fundamental.

However, it is less easy to understand what we are going to be left with when all appeal to 'alien' authorities is set aside. Kant's favoured image of public reason is scholarly communication with the world at large. It has evident limitations. Perhaps Kant could find no better image of non-derivative reasoning than this; but we are more suspicious, and in my view rightly suspicious, about the relations between power and knowledge. Practices of scholarly communication include and exclude, highlight and suppress. Can we seriously expect to find or to live by communicative practices which do not introduce unargued assumptions – even if these assumptions change through history? (I personally doubt whether the much heralded emerging global communication regime, which some see as the basis for a deeper democratisation of political life, lives up to the Kantian ideal of public reason any better than the communication among scholars to which Kant points.)

Can we expect to say *anything* about the requirements of reasoned communication, other than making the negative point that it fails wherever it merely defers to the edicts and assumptions of civil or other powers or authorities? Reasoning surely cannot be merely a matter of discourse that does not defer – for if this were the case, every sort of gibberish and incoherence would count as reasoned, provided only that it did not draw on the authority or edicts of whatever powers there were.

Clearly Kant thinks that we can say more about the demands of public reason. He never maintains that reasoning has *merely* to be free and non-deferential. He sets out the other requirements of reasoning quite clearly in *What Does It Mean to Orient Oneself in Thinking?*, published soon after *What Is Enlightenment?* In the second essay he argues that nothing could deserve to be called reason if it was wholly without structure and discipline, because a minimal condition for any discourse to count as reasoned is that it be *communicable*, that it be *followable* by all whom it is to reach. And without a structure that can be followed there will be no communication, *a fortiori* no reasoning. Reasons are the sorts of things that we can give to others, receive or refuse to receive from others. Since Kant rejects the idea that reasons could be devised by the arbitrary fiat of individual reasoners, he rejects the thought that reasoning can be wholly unfollowable:

> how much and how correctly would we think if we did not *think* as it were in community with others to whom we *communicate* our thoughts, and who communicate theirs with us![28]

The standards of reason cannot be found in solitary thinking: on the contrary those who seek to reason *must* structure their thought, speech and communication in ways that others *can* follow. This double modal constraint is fundamental to the positive aspect of Kant's account of public reason, and a crucial part of his entire vindication of reason.

At times Kant uses a fiercely sarcastic rhetoric[29] to chastise those who try to purvey the illusion that reasoning could be without all structure or discipline and delude themselves that this 'lawless' freedom will be liberating, and that freedom is all there is to reasoning. He had clear targets in mind, including the fans of religious enthusiasm (*Schwärmerei*) and of exaggerated views of the powers of genius; today his targets might include a fair range of post-modernists, new-agers and deconstructionists. In each case he believes that the opponents of reason fail to see that *by itself* the unstructured liberation of thought and discourse that they crave will be a disaster, and an illusion:

> if reason will not subject itself to the laws it gives itself, it has to bow under the yoke of laws given by another; for without law, nothing – not even nonsense – can play its game for long. Thus the unavoidable consequence of *declared* lawlessness in thinking (of liberation from the limitations of reason) is that the freedom to think will ultimately be forfeited.[30]

The illusions of 'lawless' thinking end, Kant thinks, not merely in intellectual confusion, but in lack of defence against the very sorts of deference and subordination which enthusiasts for 'lawless' thinking wish to escape.

---

[28] *WO* 8:144.
[29] As those who seek to reason with post-modernists often discover, rhetoric is the only remaining way to engage with those who purport to dispense with reason and deny its authority.
[30] *WO* 8:145.

Because anarchic, 'lawless' thinking is no more than babble, it is defence-less in the face of the claims of superstition, of enthusiasm and of the ideas extolled by those who peddle religious and political dogmas.

Kant: public reason as lawlike

If 'lawless' thinking ends not in freedom of thought and communication, but in gibberish and isolation, even in superstition and cognitive disorientation, whose political consequences include vulnerability to tyrants and demagogues, then any activity in human life that can count as reasoned must be structured. This structure must enable us to distinguish better reasons from worse reasons, to distinguish claims we have reason to accept from those we ought to reject. Reasoning – whether theoretical or practical – will lack authority and normative force if it has no structure by which this distinction can be made. So if anything is to count as more than 'private' reason, in Kant's sense of the term, if there is to be anything that is to count as fully public reason, then its structure cannot be derived from the tenets of existing institutions and practices. What then can provide the internal, non-derivative discipline or structure of fully public reasoning? Kant's answer is straightforward:

> Freedom in thinking signifies the subjection of reason to no laws except *those, which it gives itself*; and its opposite is the maxim of a *lawless* use of reason.[31]

Public uses of reason must have *lawlike* rather than *lawless* structure, but since they are not to derive their lawlikeness from any external sources, it will have to be freely chosen: the discipline of reason is that of *self-legislation* or *autonomy*.

Kant's identification of reason with autonomy is initially startling, despite the fact that familiar passages in the *Groundwork of the Metaphysic of Morals* make it plain that he identifies *practical* reason with autonomy.[32] The reason that it is startling is, I believe, that contemporary conceptions of autonomy identify it with independence rather than with reason. But Kant distinguishes autonomy sharply from mere freedom or independence.[33] Unlike some recent 'Kantian' writers (and many of their critics), he

---

[31] *WO* 8:145.   [32] See especially *G* 4:440.
[33] Kant holds that various specific forms of independence (*Selbständigkeit, sibisufficientia*) are important, but are quite different from Kantian autonomy. A just, republican state is one where independence of action is safeguarded by the fact that nobody is either outside or above the law; active citizens need a degree of economic independence. *TP* 8:294–6; *MM* 6:314–15.

views autonomy or self-legislation as emphasising not some (rather amazing!) self that does the legislating, but rather 'legislation' that is not borrowed from unvindicated sources, that is not derivative, that is both freely chosen and has the form of law. Non-derivative 'legislation' cannot require us to adopt the actual laws or rules of some institution or authority; it can only require that any principle we use to structure thought or action be lawlike in form and have inclusive scope. Only those who freely choose principles that both have the 'form of law' and are in principle followable by all deploy a Kantian conception of public reason: indeed this is all that there is to his conception of practical reason, which explains why he can write: 'Now the power to judge autonomously – that is, freely (according to principles of thought in general) – is called reason.'[34] Another way of formulating the point is to note that Kant identifies public reason with meeting a double modal criterion: the *requirement* of structuring our thought, discourse and action in ways in which (we believe) all others *can* follow. A general statement of this criterion can be found at the end of *What Does It Mean to Orient Oneself in Thinking?*, where Kant identifies reasoning with the practice of adopting principles of thinking and acting that have the form of law, and could be adopted by all:

> To make use of one's own reason means no more than to ask oneself, whenever one is supposed to assume something, whether one could find it feasible to make the ground or the rule on which one assumes it into a universal principle for the use of reason.[35]

We are most of us more familiar with a restricted version of this principle, formulated specifically for the domain of action, which Kant rather pompously calls 'the supreme principle of practical reason' or 'the Categorical Imperative'.

Kant and domestic justice

Where does this account of the vindication of practical reason take Kant's account of justice, and specifically of justice beyond boundaries? I shall first comment briefly on Kant's account of domestic or 'internal' justice. His justification of political institutions appeals not simply to a version of social contract[36] or contractarian thought but to a more abstract Universal Principle of Justice. A particularly clear formulation of this principle is

---

[34] *CF* 7:27: the important phrase here is the one in parentheses!   [35] *WO* 8:146n.
[36] For Kant the term 'social contract' refers not to the fundamental principle of political justification, but to a specific step in the derivation of an account of just institutions from the Universal Principle

given early in the *Doctrine of Right* (the first part of the *Metaphysics of Morals*). It runs:

> Any action is *right* if it can coexist with everyone's freedom in accordance with a universal law, or if on its maxim the freedom of choice of each can coexist with everyone's freedom in accordance with a universal law.[37]

The Universal Principle of Justice makes no explicit reference to consent. Its justification lies rather in its relationship to the formulae of the Categorical Imperative, and so to Kant's vindication of practical reason as grounded in the necessary conditions for any possible fully public reasoning with universal scope. Kant's argument for justice begins simply from the requirement that reasoned thought and action adhere to principles that could be fully public, in the sense that they do not invoke arbitrary authority, but rather can be followed in thought or adopted in action by all, without presupposing any pre-established agreement, shared ideology or religion or other given (and unvindicated) source of coordination.

The most familiar generic statement of this requirement for the domain of practical reason is the Formula of Universal Law version of the Categorical Imperative '*act only in accordance with that maxim through which you can at the same time will that it become a universal law*'.[38] The generic principle covers maxims – practical principles – for all sorts of action, inward and outward, personal and public. By contrast the Universal Principle of Justice is restricted in two ways. First, it is concerned only with outward action, that is with the aspects of action that can be enforced (so not, for example, with inner virtue or with moral worth). Second, it is concerned only with the domain of *external freedom* that is the public domain (so not, for example, with outward aspects of personal conduct). The Universal Principle of Justice requires the rejection of basic principles for structuring the domain of the external use of freedom if they cannot be adopted by all.

Kant thinks that implementing this principle in the actual conditions in which we live is not straightforward. We find ourselves living on a

---

of Justice. Unlike that principle, the idea of the social contract takes cognisance of historically specific conditions, such as the fact that we live with moderate scarcity and limited altruism, yet in mutual proximity. Hence in our world the social contract has to accept state coercion, but only if state structures take a republican form. See Onora O'Neill, 'Kant and the social contract tradition' in *Constructing Authorities*, 170–85.

[37] *MM* 6:230.   [38] *G* 4:421.

spherical and finite globe that brings us into contact with others with whom we compete for scarce resources; and we are not reliably altruistic.[39] In our world external freedom will be perpetually insecure without at least limited forms of coercion, aimed at the 'hindering of a hindrance of freedom'.[40] In these conditions the Universal Principle of Justice can, as Kant sees it, best be implemented not by unlimited freedom – anarchy – but by establishing states with republican constitutions, which guarantee freedom within the law at least within bounded territories. Although such states will coerce, and although their boundaries create exclusions that would be unjust if they were not necessary, they provide a better realisation of justice than any universal state of nature: the first requirement of justice is therefore to leave the state of nature.[41] However, this requirement is not unconditional. Kant fiercely repudiates the Hobbesian view that any state whatever is to be preferred to the state of nature: tyranny can be worse than insecurity, and legitimate state power is always conditional rather than absolute.[42] On Kant's view, state power is not an intrinsic requirement of justice, but a compromise that we have to accept under actual conditions.

Kant's statement of the elements of this compromise is succinctly formulated in his statement of the requirements of a republican constitution in *Perpetual Peace*:

> A constitution established, first on principles of the *freedom* of the member of a society ... second on principles of the *dependence* of all upon a single common legislation ... third, on the law of their *equality* (*as citizens of a state*) – the sole constitution ... on which all rightful legislation of a people must be based – is a *republican* constitution.[43]

Republican justice is evidently not democratic justice, but I do not think it is trivial. Consider how much it rules out. Societies or states that do not secure the rule of law (e.g. anarchic or despotic societies), or that undermine or jeopardise external freedom for some, base their constitutions on principles that cannot be principles for all: they are unjust. Societies or states that leave some persons above or outside the law (monarchies,

---

[39] One might object that this shows that for Kant too boundaries are basic to justice; he differs from others only in considering what is enclosed within the bounded globe rather than within bounded societies. The analogy in fact fails. Kant views the boundedness of the earth as significant not because it excludes non-earthlings, but because the earth's finitude forces its numerous inhabitants into contact and rules out the possibility of solitary lives. If human life spread beyond the planet, the boundaries of Kantian justice would spread with it. Kant's recognition that the globe is bounded does not mean that his thinking on justice ceases to be cosmopolitan. See *MM* 6:352; *PP* 8:360–5.

[40] *MM* 6:231.   [41] *MM* 6:307; *TP* 8:302.   [42] *TP* 8:304.

[43] *PP* 8:350; cf. *MM* 6:340, *TP* 8:290ff.

dictatorships, states within states, slave states) undermine or jeopardise external freedom for some or for many, so base their constitutions on principles that cannot be principles for all: they are unjust. Societies or states that do not secure equality of status for all citizens under law (feudalism, caste societies) undermine or jeopardise external freedom for many or for all, so base their constitutions on principles that cannot be principles for all: they are unjust. It is plausible to think that Kant's account of domestic justice could be extended to show that patriarchal and undemocratic states, which also undermine or jeopardise external freedom for many, thereby base their constitutions on principles that cannot be principles for all, and will also be unjust.

Kant on justice beyond boundaries

I want now to indicate some advantages of approaching questions about justice across boundaries from a Kantian starting point. The most obvious advantage is that his conception of public reason is not premised on the status quo; it merely insists that all reasoned discourse, hence all justification, must be capable of being fully public. This seems to me a promising strategy: but how far can it take us? By contrast, claims that justification can appeal to the contingent fact that something is actually liked, or accepted, even reciprocally liked or accepted by lots of people, or even by lots of peoples, are in the end no more than (and no more convincing than) arguments from authority.

A second advantage is a corollary of the first. Because Kant's vindication of reason, hence of justice, does not presuppose any particular institutional structures, his basic arguments for principles of justice aim not to beg questions. In Kant's thought human rights, democracy, state power and other institutions, *including boundaries*, must all be shown to be just, rather than be accepted without justification.

For Kant a just world is one in which principles of justice that could be principles for all are *realistically institutionalised*. He argues that realistic institutions of justice will include not only states – and therefore boundaries – but further structures that secure international justice and cosmopolitan right, including a league of states.[44] Like Kant's arguments for just republican states, those for international justice and cosmopolitan right are grounded in the Universal Principle of Justice, which articulates the

---

[44] *PP* 8:357–60, 367, 385; *MM* 6:311, 352–7. See Flikschuh, *Kant and Modern Political Philosophy*; and Kleingeld, *Kant and Cosmopolitanism*.

requirements of public reason for the entire public domain and not only for bounded elements within that domain. In my view this may provide a better strategy for working towards an account of justice beyond boundaries than the one Rawls offers, not only because it aims deeper, but because it is *more realistic* and *more open*.

The greater *realism* lies in Kant's clear acknowledgement that republican states are not ideally just: they are a compromise that we have to make in order to build towards justice under real-world conditions. Unsurprisingly this compromise does not guarantee justice for all: the boundaries even of republican states are filters that institute and maintain patterns of inclusion and exclusion, of domination and of subordination, of vulnerability and power (Kant often points to the fatal effects on external freedom produced by wars between states and by colonisation). In itself, Kant takes it, a system of republican states will provide no more than a partial realisation of justice; often it will permit searing injustice. Yet although boundaries invariably create injustice, *bounded republican states coupled with institutions that contribute to international and cosmopolitan justice* achieve as good an approximation of justice as we can realistically hope for.

Kant's views on justice are also *more open* than those Rawls proposes, in that he recognises the need to reduce and limit the injustices that republican states too create and maintain. The picture of international and cosmopolitan order to which Kant points in *Perpetual Peace* is one in which justice is thought of not solely as internal to republican states, but as governing the relations between such states and their treatment of one another's citizens. It comprises the rejection of war, measures to make and maintain peace – including the formation of a 'pacific league' – as well as arrangements to provide security for individuals beyond the boundaries of their state of origin.[45] Many of Kant's specific institutional suggestions are inadequate to the twenty-first century: in particular we can no longer imagine that rights to hospitality deal adequately with justice to those who are beyond the boundaries of their own states. Nevertheless the scope of his thinking is wider and in some ways more generous than some contemporary discussion of international justice.

A reworking of this approach might be appropriate to the twenty-first century if it took realistic account of the many ways in which boundaries and their impact upon those whom they confine and exclude have changed since Kant wrote. In the world as we now know it, state boundaries are

---

[45] *PP* 8:357ff.

porous not in all but in many ways. They are for the most part highly porous to transfers of goods and capital, communications, and technologies; less so to movements of ideas, cultures and religions; still less so to flows of people and of public finance.[46] Ours is a world in which some activities that are open to the powerful are hardly impeded by state borders, allowing them to constrain the freedom of strangers far beyond boundaries, but in which the powerless are often disabled by distant powers that they cannot influence. In a more just world the structures that maintain such disparities of power and vulnerability, that form the matrix for countless injustices, would be reformed to prevent and limit injury to distant strangers as well as to those who are near and dear, and would seek to protect both their natural environments and their diverse cultures. First steps towards these changes might aim to reduce brutal poverty and brutal weapons; second steps to regulate and limit pollution of the natural and corruption of the human world.[47]

This vast agenda may seem mere hand-waving if we imagine that the only effective agents of change will be states themselves, but that states will be motivated to pursue only those changes that coincide with their self-interest. However, this supposedly realist picture of states and their motivation is obsolete, and in many respects evidently unrealistic. The world already teems with institutions that are not states, yet not powerless, and sometimes not powerless to achieve change or to work towards justice. A *genuinely realistic* approach to the tasks of justice should therefore begin by identifying, supporting and if necessary reforming and constructing *agents of justice*, with capacities to embrace and support an agenda of just reform.[48] Such an approach would reject the bogus realism that regards states, and states alone, as able to bring about change, and sees them as invariably dominated by a narrow conception of self-interest. It would

[46] By contrast, in Kant's day state boundaries may have been more pervious to people, but less so in other ways. For comments on ways in which boundaries have become more and less porous see Brian Barry and Robert E. Goodin (eds.), *Free Movement: Ethical Issues in the Transnational Migration of People and Money* (Philadelphia: Pennsylvania State University Press, 1992); and Warren F. Schwartz (ed.), *Justice in Immigration* (Cambridge University Press, 1995).

[47] For arguments for the obligations to seek these objectives see O'Neill, *Towards Justice and Virtue*, chs. 6 and 7.

[48] For some thoughts on the diversity of institutions that may contribute – positively or negatively – to justice beyond borders see Thomas Risse-Kappen (ed.), *Bringing Transnational Relations Back In: Non-State Actors, Domestic Structures and International Institutions* (Cambridge University Press, 1995); Robert O'Brien, Anne Marie Goetz, Jan Aart Scholte and Mare Williams, *Contesting Global Governance: Multilateral Economic Institutions and Global Social Movements* (Cambridge University Press, 2000); and Onora O'Neill, Chapter 11 'Agents of justice', below, 177–92.

recognise that varied agents of justice already exist, that new and perhaps more effective agents of justice can be constructed, and that the obstacles that prevent principles of justice from informing agendas of reform and development may be thought of as hindrances to justice rather than as guarantees that it is unattainable.

CHAPTER 7

Pluralism, positivism and the justification of human rights[1]
In memory of Michael Brock, 1920–2014

Empirical pluralism and value pluralism

A great many discussions of pluralism in many disciplines focus not on 'value pluralism' as Isaiah Berlin understood it, but on empirical claims that there are a lot, or at any rate a number, of things of various sorts. This is obviously true, and any approach to ethics and political philosophy must take account of empirical pluralities. Accounts of justice have, for example, to assume that a plurality of people will be subject to its demands: solipsists don't have to worry about justice. Early modern writers often link the fact that there are many subjects of justice to competition for scarce resources: Locke, Hume and Kant all saw the fact that many share a finite earth as among the basic circumstances of justice.

A second range of empirical claims about pluralities focuses not on the plurality of subjects of justice, but on their varying conceptions of the world and their varying ethical and political views. Empirical evidence that people hold many different moral and political views was of great importance in early modern discussions of toleration and free speech. However, they acquired wider importance in political philosophy in the twentieth century, both through Isaiah Berlin's writings, and because John Rawls and others later persistently emphasised that pluralism of beliefs and outlooks is ineradicable. Rawls held that 'the fact of reasonable pluralism' is a 'permanent feature of democratic societies', whose 'citizens affirm irreconcilable and incommensurable conceptions of the good'.[2] He concluded that while people whose conceptions of the good differ can reach agreement on a conception of justice, normative justification cannot reach beyond matters of justice.

---

[1] The Isaiah Berlin Lecture for 2014, given at Wolfson College Oxford.
[2] John Rawls, *Justice as Fairness: A Restatement*, ed. Erin Kelly (Boston, MA: Harvard University Press, 2001), 84.

Isaiah Berlin was mainly concerned not with the *fact* that people hold a plurality of beliefs and values, but with the bearing that this has on attempts to justify substantive moral and political claims, including liberal claims, and thereby also claims about human rights. However, unlike Rawls, Berlin does not think that reasonable agreement among fellow citizens can justify principles of justice.

Towards the end of his life he noted that:

> I have for many years thought the problem of the incommensurability, and still more the incompatibility, of some values to be central to all ethical, social, political and aesthetic issues.[3]

The distinction between 'value pluralism' and 'value monism' was a lasting feature of Berlin's thought,[4] and while the phrase 'value monism' is not now much used, it is easy to grasp his concern. He is worried not by the empirical fact that there are a number of world views or ethical outlooks, or by run-of-the-mill ethical and political disagreements, but by the lack of any robust way of resolving fundamental ethical disagreement.

Many philosophical discussions of the plurality of values people actually hold claim – or at least hope – that this is not an insurmountable problem. Writers who locate justification in agreement accept that we can't have the deep justification that 'value monism' would (supposedly) provide, but claim that the right solution is to take a less demanding view of justification. If deep justification is not available, we should settle either for barefaced relativism, or for one or another version of the thought that justifications themselves can be plural, each of them anchored in whatever agreement can be reached in particular societies or communities at particular times, or within particular sorts of discourse. For example, John Rawls (particularly in his later work) sees normative justification as internal to bounded, liberal, democratic societies, within which citizens can reason and come to agreement on a conception of justice, even if they cannot agree on any wider conception of the good. Habermas too subordinates the project of justification to reasoning that allows for free exchange of views, such as can be secured in democratic deliberation, and so sees

---

[3] Quoted in Henry Hardy, 'Berlin's big idea', *Philosophers' Magazine* 11 (2000), 15–16.
[4] See Isaiah Berlin, *The Hedgehog and the Fox: An Essay on Tolstoy's View of History* (London: Weidenfeld & Nicolson, 1953), 1–2: 'There exists a great chasm between those, on one side, who relate everything to a single central vision ... and, on the other side, those who pursue many ends, often unrelated and even contradictory ... The first kind of intellectual and artistic personality belongs to the hedgehogs, the second to the foxes.'

justification as civic. Communitarians have appealed to culturally narrower forms of agreement as sources of justification.

Value monists, as Berlin characterises them, aim higher. Their ambition would be satisfied only if objective ethical values could be justified by appeal to a single set of premises, for example by deriving them from a single metric of value such as Utilitarians invoke, or appealing to a single authority such as the Divine Will. But without 'value monist' foundations, Berlin concluded, some values that matter may turn out to be incommensurable or incompatible with others, and deep justification of values, or specifically of claims about justice or about rights, may simply elude us.[5]

Human rights: 'political' and 'positive' justifications

Does it matter if we cannot offer any deep justification for human rights? Human rights have never been more widely endorsed than they are today, although respect for and realisation of them remains very patchy across the world. But this acceptance does not reflect any wider or deeper agreement that human rights can be justified. Rather, justification has come to seem less urgent (even a waste of time) to many, in part because human rights have been beneficiaries of their own worldly success.

There is a degree of convergence. Many political philosophers follow Rawls in arguing that, despite the plurality of views people hold, *political* justifications of principles of justice are feasible. Many human rights lawyers and activists, and others, reach rather similar positions by appealing to 'positive' legal enactments. Human rights are now incorporated into 'the international architecture' and transposed into treaties and legislation, so now constitute 'positive' requirements. Rights that were once merely declared or disputed have now been incorporated into international Covenants and Conventions; very often they have been ratified by states, and in consequence states are committed to respecting and realising human rights – even if many of them make rather little effort to do so. Both philosophical pluralists and legal positivists conclude that deeper justification is unnecessary: political or legal facts can trump, or perhaps merely short-circuit, hankerings for deeper justification.

But can we really set aside the aim of justifying human rights claims, and substitute appeals to public agreement or state action? Are human

---

[5] Many other philosophers have shared Berlin's view, including Judith Jarvis Thomson, Bernard Williams, Charles Taylor, Charles Larmore, John Kekes, Michael Stocker, David Wiggins and Christine Swanton.

rights adequately seen just as matters of agreement, treaty and law? What are the costs of relying on 'justifications' that are no more than *political* (in the Rawlsian sense of that term) or no more than *positive* (in the legal sense of the term)? Has the project of trying to justify the human rights proclaimed in the *Universal Declaration of Human Rights* (UDHR) of 1948 or in the *European Convention on Human Rights* (ECHR) of 1950, or in other human rights documents, really been made redundant by a happy convergence between moral and political pluralism and legal positivism?

Many others remain sceptical about both *political* and *positivist* substitutes for deeper justifications.[6] Some reject these substitutes for justification because they reject the human rights proclaimed in UDHR and ECHR, and elsewhere, seeing them as attempts to impose 'Western' standards, or even as a mask for imperialism. They deny that the mere facts of declaration or ratification provide *any* justification, and sometimes argue that there should be different rights for different societies, and that the Declaration rights should *not* have universal scope. Others do not argue that human rights are a 'Western' imposition, but are well aware that UDHR and ECHR reflect recent history and its preoccupations, so take a guarded rather than a reverential view of the rights declared, and do not think agreement or enactment provides an adequate substitute for justification.

The historical points adduced by sceptics about justification are largely accurate. Those who framed the leading human rights documents indeed drew on earlier 'Western' claims about natural rights and of the rights of man, and what they produced reflected a specific historical situation in which 'Western' values were riding high.[7] The Declaration is a central part of the post-WWII settlement and the institutional structures it established. The rights declared were to be acknowledged by the accession of states to the United Nations, and later by their ratification of the more specific versions of human rights subsequently set out in international Covenants and Conventions.

So while some answers to the question 'Why are human rights binding?' will indeed be either *political* or *positive*, these answers have weight only in

---

[6] Philosophers who do *not* think the project of justifying rights obsolete include John Finnis, James Griffin, John Tasioulas, Amartya Sen, John Simmons, Jeremy Waldron and Nicholas Wolterstorff. Most are not value monists.

[7] Mary Ann Glendon, *A World Made New: Eleanor Roosevelt and the Universal Declaration of Human Rights* (New York: Random House, 2001); Samuel Moyn, *The Last Utopia: Human Rights in History* (Cambridge, MA: Harvard University Press, 2010).

contexts in which appeals to positive law or enactments, or to political agreements, are appropriate. These approaches duck rather than address fundamental questions of justification. They take either prior exercises of state authority or prior agreement as the basis of human rights. By bracketing questions about any deeper justification of human rights standards they lose any basis for criticising political cultures or states that do not endorse human rights. *Positive* or *political* 'justifications' are limited, and time limited, and may lose their appeal as the legitimacy, powers and enactments of states change, as indeed they have been and are being changed by processes of globalisation and conflict. One would, I think, expect those who purport to take these standards seriously to be concerned about the limits of pluralist and positivist support for human rights standards, and to be worried that human rights might at some point come to lack status in the jurisdictions and cultures in which they are currently (if tenuously) anchored.

Indeed, many strong supporters of UDHR rights see the dangers of this approach, and maintain that positivist and pluralist approaches to justification are inadequate, and that human rights are *more than* the agreements or enactments of a particular historical moment, to which states have committed themselves, at least for the time being. For better or for worse, human rights are still very widely seen as fundamental moral claims that human beings can make on one another, and in particular on states and their institutions and officials, even (or *especially*) when existing institutional structures fail to recognise, protect or secure those claims. When the citizens of rogue states are arbitrarily tortured, or imprisoned without trial, or deprived of their livelihoods, nobody says 'that's OK: those states have not signed up to the relevant human rights instruments', or regards it as acceptable if they have signed up, but have taken no effective steps to meet or to secure the standards to which they signed up (unfortunately not uncommon).

Most supporters of human rights hold that they have deeper and more substantial justification than could be provided by the mere facts of political agreement, or of state ratification and institutionalisation. Rogue states are not seen as escaping, but as flouting human rights claims. Criticism is directed not only at blatant flouting, but also at persisting failure to create the basic institutions for respecting and protecting human rights (the rule of law; a competent and non-corrupt judiciary). In short, human rights are still typically seen *neither* as *positive* rights nor as matters of contingent *political* consensus, but as fundamental rights held by all human beings. Indeed, unless proponents of human rights take it that there are deeper justifications that are neither merely *positive* nor merely *political*, they will be unable to offer reasons for respecting human rights to those who are disinclined to take them seriously. That is where *pluralist* and *positivist* attempts to domesticate questions of justification strand us.

Monism and justification: Berlin's conclusions

Isaiah Berlin did not argue that standards of justification should be weakened, but only that we are not in a position to meet their demands. He takes it that values are objective, and would have seen both *positivist* and *political* substitutes for justification as inadequate. But he also thought that value monism was not available, since it requires strong metaphysical or theological underpinnings, which we cannot supply. The real cost of value pluralism is therefore high, indeed tragically high, because it leaves us without deep justifications:

> The notion of the perfect whole, the ultimate solution in which all good things coexist, seems to me not merely unobtainable – that is a truism – but conceptually incoherent ... Some among the Great Goods cannot live together. That is a conceptual truth. We are doomed to choose, and every choice may entail an irreparable loss.[8]

Do these strong but tragic conclusions follow from our lack of a monistic vindication of all values? May there not be other routes to justifying *at least some* fundamental principles, including those most relevant for the public sphere, such as (some) human rights standards? Might a metaphysically less demanding view of justification be possible, that does not reduce justification to contingent matters of *positive* law or *political* agreement? I shall explore parts of these questions by considering a further type of

---

[8] Isaiah Berlin, 'The pursuit of the ideal' in his *The Crooked Timber of Humanity* (London: Fontana Press, 1991), 13. See also his bleak but clear-eyed insistence that lack of justification must be endured, and that it is immature to ask for more: 'It may be that the ideal of freedom to choose ends without claiming eternal validity for them, and the pluralism of values connected with this, is only the late fruit of our declining capitalist civilisation: an ideal which remote ages and primitive societies have not recognised, and one which posterity will regard with curiosity, even sympathy, but little comprehension. This may be so; but no sceptical conclusions seem to me to follow. Principles are not less sacred because their duration cannot be guaranteed. Indeed, the very desire for guarantees that our values are eternal and secure in some objective heaven is perhaps only a craving for the certainties of childhood or the absolute values of our primitive past. "To realise the relative validity of one's convictions", said an admirable writer of our time, "and yet stand for them unflinchingly is what distinguishes a civilised man from a barbarian." To demand more than this is perhaps a deep and incurable metaphysical need; but to allow such a need to determine one's practice is a symptom of an equally deep, and more dangerous, moral and political immaturity': 'Two concepts of liberty' in his *Four Essays on Liberty* (Oxford University Press, 1969), 172.

approach to the justification of human rights claims. I do not assume that human rights claims are the only normative claims that raise questions of justification, but I take them to be an important case, and also (as I hope to show) a relatively tractable set of standards for justifications that are neither positivist nor pluralist and that are available even if we cannot establish any form of value monism. This, I shall argue, is because any system of universal rights has to meet at least three rather demanding formal conditions.

Interpreting rights, implementing rights

The most fundamental feature of human rights standards is their scope: whatever else they are, human rights are standards *for everyone*. This is not to say that questions of scope need no justification, and Berlin often pointed in horror at positions such as slavery or Nazism that deny recognition or moral standing to some human beings. I think – but will not argue the matter here – that it is possible to justify the thought that at least some principles must be taken to have universal scope by reflecting on the assumptions about others to which we unavoidably commit ourselves in action. Once we think of others as agents who can affect us by their action and of ourselves as agents who can affect them by ours, however indirectly or remotely, we must see others too as agents, and must align at least some judgements that we make about their case to the judgements we make about our own case.

Yet even if we accept that at least some normative principles must have universal scope, why should we think that the specific principles set out in the human rights documents such as the *Universal Declaration of Human Rights* (UDHR) or the *European Convention on Human Rights* (ECHR) are the right places to start? Might not these lists be incomplete, or defective, or in need of revision? Why is so much discussion of the justification of human rights so accepting, even relaxed, about the *actual* lists of rights declared in 1948, or 1950? Are there reasons (other than inconclusive *positivist* and *political* reasons) to accept these specific lists of rights?

I have come to think that the fact that so many are prepared to accept the standard list of human rights is not because they are confident that these are *the right lists*, let alone *demonstrably the right lists*, but rather because the rights listed are highly indeterminate, so that some interpretation of virtually all of them would be included in any plausible list of universal rights. The magic that secures such widespread agreement to human rights is largely that the list in UDHR allows people to bracket much that is contentious or about which they disagree.

So it is not after all very surprising that so many who think that human rights standards require deeper justification are nevertheless quite accepting of the UDHR list. It does not follow that there is wide agreement about which of many possible *interpretations* of the rights it lists is to be preferred. There are persistent disputes about the adequacy or inadequacy of interpretations of, for example, *freedom of expression* and *rights to privacy*, or of *rights to life* and *rights to security*, which illustrate the point. So do earlier disputes about the *right to work* (a *free labour market* or the *right to be assigned a job*? – a major dispute between market and centrally planned societies before 1990) and current disputes about the *right to marry* (*opposite sex partners* only, or *same or opposite sex partners?*). The UDHR list of rights poses rather than resolves difficult questions of justification. Those questions can only be addressed by selecting (or rejecting) more specific interpretations of each indeterminate right.

The indeterminacy of the UDHR rights reinforces the point that justification cannot be derived from the mere fact that some (or many) states have signed up to and ratified the relevant international instruments, or that some (but fewer) have legislated to realise their commitments, or that some (but still fewer) try to enforce the legislation they have enacted. The situation is rather that relatively indeterminate standards provide *starting points* for reaching a justifiable interpretation of rights, although rather different sets of starting points might also have proved adequate. For the hard issues arise further ahead, and must be addressed in moving from indeterminacy towards one or another coherent and more specific interpretation of the range of rights. However, here there can be rigorous standards for justification.

The issues and concerns that have to be addressed in selecting or rejecting various possible interpretations of rights are not technical questions about *implementation* (which also matter). They are more fundamental questions on which legislators, commentators and (in democracies) citizens need to form and to justify their views. While implementations can be ranked by relatively uncontentious criteria (such as efficacy, efficiency, expense), there are no similarly technical standards for ranking interpretations. However, the necessary constraints on any adequate interpretation of the declaration or convention rights turn out to be rather powerful. They rule out many alternatives, so make it possible to go a long way towards justifying human rights.

Human rights are for everyone

Even if we lack the metaphysical or theological foundations that could satisfy the standards that Berlin sets for a monistic justification of all values, a robust justification of demanding constraints on any adequate interpretation of human rights standards is feasible. This is because any coherent interpretation of the UDHR rights has to satisfy at least *three* formal constraints. It must secure consistency between interpretations of the various rights held by each person; consistency between the interpretations of the rights of each person and others' like rights; and consistency between interpretations of the rights of each person and the action needed to secure respect for those rights.

An immediate corollary of requiring that any interpretation of rights for all be consistent in these three respects is that few rights can be seen as unconditional. *At most* a few important liberty rights might be interpreted as absolute. The right not be tortured and the right not to be enslaved are often said to be *absolute*, meaning that no other consideration, and no other right, provides an acceptable reason for restricting them. But most human rights have to be constrained in numerous ways if the rights of each person are to be compatible with one another, compatible with others enjoying the same rights, and compatible with the action needed to respect or realise those rights.[9]

The task of interpreting human rights, other than the few that may be absolute, is sometimes described as a matter of *balancing* one right against others. This metaphor misleads. Its proper context is in characterising judicial decision-making about *particular* cases, where balancing considerations is a matter of taking multiple facts into account. In considering the justification of human rights we are dealing not with particular cases, but with principles, and since there is no particular case, there are no facts of the case to be balanced. There is no *metric* for rights, analogous to the metrics used for physical balances. What is actually required is in the first place *an interpretation of each right that adjusts* it to others held by the same individual, takes account of the fact that each right is to be enjoyed by all, and does not obstruct or prevent the action that respect for each right requires – i.e. allows for the performance of the counterpart duties needed

---

[9] It is common to speak of some non-absolute rights as *limited* and others as *qualified*. Some human rights may be *limited* by statute, as the right to liberty is *limited* by legislation that specifies when a prison sentence or detention for reasons of mental health is permitted. Other human rights may be *qualified* for wider reasons than those set out in statute, such as the need to protect the rights of others or wider society.

to make a reality of rights. Difficult questions must be decided. For example, what line should be drawn between rights to freedom of expression and rights to privacy? In which ways can rights to life, liberty and security for all be made compatible with rights to fair trials for those accused of endangering others' life, liberty and security? How are rights to food to be met compatibly with respecting food producers' rights to freedom, to work and to property?

Constraints and justification

In solving problems it is sometimes helpful to have more rather than fewer constraints, since this narrows down the range of possibilities. We are all familiar with equations that can be solved only if one knows enough constraints, or for that matter with crossword puzzles where solving each clue constrains possibilities and is helpful for completing the puzzle. Justifications of specific interpretations of human rights can also, I suggest, make headway by focusing on the necessary constraints on any set of rights that can be rights for all.

The power of consistency constraints is easily missed if one tries to think about rights or their interpretation one-right-at-a-time. Even the *first* of these consistency requirements – that the several rights of a given individual be mutually consistent – cannot be resolved by thinking about an individual's rights one-by-one. For example, if we consider rights one-at-a-time it is all too easy to imagine that the best interpretation of a given right must be a *maximal* interpretation. However, this will be at the cost of overlooking what is needed for individuals to enjoy other rights. If *A* had a *maximal* right to liberty, she could not also have a right to security, since some measures required to protect her security would restrict her liberty. Unfortunately some enthusiasts for particular rights overlook this elementary consistency requirement, and waste time searching for maximal interpretations of their favourite right, without attending to the ways in which a maximal interpretation of a given right is likely to distort or obstruct the interpretation of other rights of the same individual (let alone those of other individuals).

The *second* consistency requirement sets even more powerful constraints on any adequate interpretation of rights. Human rights are *rights for everyone* – for all human beings, not merely for some privileged ones. So no interpretation of rights is acceptable if it implies that the right could be held only by some, but not by all. There cannot, for example, be universal rights to positional goods: there can be no universal right to win, to be the richest or the best, or to enjoy upward social mobility.[10] (None of us lives in the magical world of Lake Woebegon, where *all* the children are above average.) If rights are universal we must reject as spurious any interpretation of a right under which it *could not* be held by all. Nor can any adequate interpretation of rights endorse supposed rights whose successful exercise would prevent others from enjoying like rights: so there can therefore be no rights to coerce, to destroy or to control others, since they would all evidently undermine others' like rights. Nor can anybody's freedom of movement be interpreted as an unrestricted right to occupy any chosen location on the surface of the earth – since this would be incompatible with others enjoying a like right. These reasons against considering rights one-right-at-time filter out many unsatisfactory possibilities: *A*'s right to privacy must be construed in ways that are compatible with *B*'s right to a fair trial; *C*'s right to liberty must be construed in ways that are consistent with *D*'s right to security; *E*'s right to food must be construed in ways that are consistent with *F*'s rights to grow and sell food, and so on and on.

A *third* powerful consistency constraint on any adequate interpretation of rights arises from the fact that rights cannot be respected or realised unless there are others – individuals or institutions, depending on the case – who are required to discharge the counterpart duties that can realise the right. No way of adjusting rights to one another can guide action unless it also leaves room for the action and forbearance required if they are to be respected or realised. So any adequate interpretation of human rights for a given society at a given time has to take a clear view about whose action is required to respect those rights. In thinking about these questions we have to ask not only which rights can consistently be held by all, but also which counterpart duties on others (themselves right holders) are compatible with everyone's rights. It is not enough merely to accept or assume that everyone has each listed right: rights shorn of counterpart duties are no more than rhetoric and gesture, and the fundamental task of justifying rights is to find an interpretation under which each person can coherently have all of a range of rights, and these rights are not mere rhetoric because they can be matched to and secured by a pattern of duties that can respect and realise those rights. Following through the ways in which these constraints interact is analogous to solving a moderately complicated simultaneous equation.

---

[10] Unless, as Thomas Pogge suggests, social status could be perfectly coordinated with age.

These three consistency constraints have partially differing implications for the interpretation of liberty rights and of rights to goods and services. Consider first the simpler case of classical liberty rights. Each person's liberty rights will be incomplete unless *everyone* else has a duty to respect them. Your right to freedom of expression will be vulnerable if *anybody* has a right to censor, silence or gag you, but may have to be shaped in specific ways to make it compatible with your other rights and with others' like rights. Your right to freedom of movement will be vulnerable if *anybody* has a right to prevent or restrain your movement, but may have to be limited to secure like rights for others (for example by limiting the freedom of movement of those convicted of serious crimes). A system of liberty rights makes demands *on everyone*. Moreover liberty rights will not be secure if they are construed merely as demands not to interfere with each right holder. Liberty rights are likely to be fragile without institutional backing to ensure that people actually respect rather than violate them. So, while the primary duties that correspond to liberty rights must be held by *all* individuals and institutions, securing respect for them typically requires secondary action by specified state and other institutions that back up performance of these duties and sanction breaches and failures.

Things are more complex in the case of rights to goods or services – rights to food or to health care, for example. Here the required counterpart duties must be carried by specified persons or institutions rather than by all others: it is literally impossible for *everyone* to feed each hungry person or to look after each person's health. Unless the primary duties to provide food or health care are *allocated*, moreover allocated effectively to specific individuals and institutions with competence and capacity to discharge them, at least some people's rights to food or health care will be ignored or violated – or both. Allocating duties to provide goods and services (let alone enforcing them) is a hugely demanding task. Typically states that try to realise some adequate interpretation of these rights build on existing cultural and institutional patterns of requirement, seeking to adjust them where they risk violating or failing to secure rights, or to buttress them where compliance is weak. The international human rights architecture makes this explicit by assigning second-order duties to introduce an effective allocation of duties, if an existing or customary assignment of duties is inadequate; and this task too is constrained by the three types of consistency requirement described here.[11]

---

[11] See Chapter 12 'The dark side of human rights', below, 193–207.

The complexity of these interlocking consistency requirements means that any coherent interpretation of a plurality of rights has to meet exacting criteria. The full set of rights must be given an interpretation under which *any given individual* can have the *range of rights*; under which *all* individuals can have that range of rights; and under which the duties that must be met in order to respect and realise those rights can be met. This is quite a tall order. It may not show that there is a single optimal interpretation of human rights, but it is likely to provide a robust way of identifying inadequate interpretations that should be rejected. The justification of human rights seen in this way is a task to be achieved, rather than something supplied by a value monist algorithm or intuition. An interpretation of rights that meets all three consistency tests will not demonstrate that there is one and only one justifiable configuration of human rights, but will offer a robust justification that rules out many possibilities, and allows only for limited variation.

Justification without value monism

The approach to justifying human rights that I have sketched does not reinstate, or indeed refer to, any version of value monism. Nor does it establish anything about values that lie beyond the framework of rights. This is not because rights are the only important ethical or political values, but rather because this is a domain of reasoning about action in which consistency constraints can do some heavy lifting. In thinking about human rights we must consider interlocking universal entitlements to others' action and requirements to act. In my view there are also arguments that can justify at least some values that lack corresponding rights, although I shall not discuss them here.

However, I hope I have shown that we need not settle either for *political* or for *positivist* 'justifications' of human rights and their counterpart duties. There are reasons for taking human rights seriously that we can offer to those who are not inclined to do so. The temptation of the fashionable 'justification lite' approaches to rights that pluralists and positivists have proposed are immense, and the ways in which they have been argued in the last half century are often impressive. Yet I do not think they are adequate. Precisely because they are predicated on appeals to the *facts* of agreement, the *facts* of ratification, the *facts* of enactment – where there are such facts – *pluralist* and *positivist* substitutes for justification have nothing to say to others who do not agree, or who are not fellow citizens, or whose states ignore human rights. Isaiah Berlin was, I think, right to think that 'value pluralism' fails as justification, but not in fearing that we can therefore offer no reasons for taking rights seriously that should weigh with others who do not agree with us, or who are not fellow-citizens. There are powerful strategies for justifying rights, that can lead us a long way.

PART III

Action across boundaries

CHAPTER 8

From Edmund Burke to twenty-first-century human rights: abstraction, circumstances and globalisation[1]

Edmund Burke on revolutions and rights

Critical comments on appeals to the rights of man played a central and memorable part in Edmund Burke's thought. What might he have thought about the human rights proclaimed in the *Universal Declaration of Human Rights* and other international documents, such as the *European Convention of Human Rights*, that have achieved global resonance in our times? Would he have reiterated his criticisms of the 'abstract' character of the supposed rights of man, and dismissed twentieth-century human rights and aspirations for their global reach as one more form of abstract and defective liberalism that fails to take account of the circumstances of particular times and situations? Or would he have concluded that contemporary commitments to 'realise' human rights save them from mere abstraction, and that it is feasible to embed them in our times and our communities?

Edmund Burke took a complex, sometimes surprising, view of the revolutionary movements of his day, and of their claims about rights. In many writings he celebrates natural rights and those constitutions that respect and further them; in others he excoriates what he calls 'abstract' rights, such as the rights of man of the French Revolution, and those who claim and pursue them. In the decades before he published *Reflections on the Revolution in France*[2] he argued for conciliation with the American revolutionaries, wrote scathingly about the oppression of Catholics in Ireland and attacked the abuses of the East India Company. In each case he commented on the injustice of what was being done and on the need to protect the rights of the oppressed, and argued for reform. But in the 1790s

---

[1] Given as the first Edmund Burke Lecture at Trinity College Dublin, 22 April 2014. References to Burke's work are to *Writings and Speeches of Edmund Burke*, ed. Paul Langford et al. (Oxford: Clarendon Press, 1988), followed by volume and page numbers.

[2] Edmund Burke, *Reflections on the Revolution in France* (1790), in *Writings and Speeches*, vol. VIII.

he castigated the revolutionaries of France and their commitment to the Declaration of the Rights of Man and the Citizen of 1789. Across more than two centuries Burke's admirers and critics have repeatedly discussed this tension – some of them at considerable length. But they have reached no consensus.

Opinions were highly divided among Burke's contemporaries and near contemporaries. Coleridge claimed that nobody could doubt Mr Burke's consistency, and that any contrary impression arose because Burke argued from the same principles in differing circumstances, legitimately reaching differing conclusions.[3] Hazlitt quotes this passage, but promptly charges Burke with inconsistency in an essay with the pointed title *On the Character of Mr. Burke*:

> It is not without reluctance that we speak of the vices and infirmities of such a mind as Burke's: but the poison of high example has by far the widest range of destruction: and, for the sake of public honour and individual integrity, we think it right to say, that however it may be defended upon other grounds, the political career of that eminent individual has no title to the praise of consistency. Mr. Burke, the opponent of the American war, and Mr. Burke, the opponent of the French Revolution, are not the same person, but opposite persons – not opposite persons only, but deadly enemies. In the latter period, he abandoned not only all his practical conclusions, but all the principles on which they were founded. He proscribed all his former sentiments, denounced all his former friends, rejected and reviled all the maxims to which he had formerly appealed as incontestable ... The burthen of all his speeches on the American war was conciliation, concession, timely reform, as the only practicable or desirable alternative of rebellion: the object of all his writings on the French Revolution was, to deprecate and explode all concession and all reform, as encouraging rebellion, and as an irretrievable step to revolution and anarchy.[4]

Wordsworth concluded that Burke had simply changed his mind: and did the same.[5]

[3] Samuel Taylor Coleridge, *Collected Works* (London: Routledge & Kegan Paul, 1983), vol. VII.i, *Biographia Literaria*, 'Opinions in religion and philosophy', 191: 'He will find the principles exactly the same, and the deductions the same but the practical inferences almost opposite, in the one case, from those drawn in the other; yet in both equally legitimate and confirmed by the results.'

[4] William Hazlitt, 'On the character of Mr Burke', *Edinburgh Review* 28 (1817), 513.

[5] William Wordsworth had at first greeted the French Revolution with total enthusiasm ('Bliss was it in that dawn to be alive / But to be young was very heaven'), but in a late version of *The Prelude* wrote admiringly of Burke: 'While he forewarns, denounces, launches forth / Against all systems built on abstract rights, / Keen ridicule; the majesty proclaims / Of Institutes and Laws, hallowed by time; / Declares the vital power of social ties / Endeared by Custom; and with high disdain / Exploding upstart

These disagreements about Burke's claims and positions persist.[6] Was he inconsistent? Did he simply change his mind? Should we count Burke a friend or an enemy of rights? What is the evidence? Although it is hard to demonstrate consistency between all of Burke's many comments on rights, it seems to me that he is committed *both* to natural rights *and* to their institutionalisation. This is clearly his position in many of his writings, at many stages of his life.

In his 1780 speech on *Mr Fox's East India Bill* he asserts that:

> The rights of men, that is to say, the natural rights of mankind, are indeed sacred things; and if any public measure is proved mischievously to affect them, it ought to be fatal to that measure, even if no charter at all could be set up against it.[7]

He then adds that to have institutions that realise these sacred rights is still better:

> If these natural rights are further affirmed and declared by express covenants, if they are clearly defined and secured against chicane, against power, and authority, by written instruments and positive engagements, they are in a still better condition: they partake not only of the sanctity of the object so secured, but of that solemn public faith itself, which secures an object of such importance ... The things secured by these instruments may, without any deceitful ambiguity, be very fitly called *the chartered rights of men*.[8]

These claims suggest that Burke might have endorsed many of the human rights that now command wide assent, including many of those listed in the *Universal Declaration of Human Rights* (1948) and the *European Convention on Human Rights* (1950), but that he would also have argued for these rights to be institutionalised or 'chartered' and thereby 'secured against chicane, against power, and authority, by written instruments and positive engagements'. Although he might have had misgivings about

---

Theory, insists / upon the allegiance to which men are born'. See William Wordsworth, *The Prelude 1799, 1805, 1850*, ed. Jonathan Wordsworth, M. H. Abrams and Stephen Gill (New York: W. W. Norton, 1979), 255.

[6] E.g. Charles Parkin, *The Moral Basis of Burke's Political Thought: An Essay* (Cambridge University Press, 1956), reissued 2011; Conor Cruise O'Brien, *The Great Melody: A Thematic Biography of Edmund Burke* (University of Chicago Press, 1992); Jesse Norman, *Edmund Burke: Philosopher, Politician, Prophet* (London: William Collins, 2013).

[7] Edmund Burke, 1 December 1783, *Speech on Fox's India Bill*, in *Writings and Speeches*, vol. VI, 383.

[8] *Ibid.* 383–4, and see also see also the distinction between real and false rights in *Reflections on the Revolution in France*, vol. VIII, 109: 'Far am I from denying in theory, full as Far from withholding in practice (if I were of power to give or to withhold) the *real* rights of men. In denying their false claims of right, I do not mean to injure those which are real, and are such as their pretended rights would totally destroy.'

one or another specific right now taken to be important, the core of contemporary views of human rights would have met with his approval.

If this is plausible, Burke's position is not wholly remote from that set out in the two great International Covenants of 1966, which take the tasks of securing respect for and realisation of human rights seriously. These Covenants offered a partial answer to those who feared that the Universal Declaration had merely proclaimed 'manifesto rights' or aspirations – in effect, abstract rights – while saying too little about securing respect for or realising those rights. The *International Covenant on Civil and Political Rights*[9] demands that each state party to the Covenant 'respect and ensure to all individuals within its territory and subject to its jurisdiction the rights recognized' and that it 'promote universal respect for, and observance of, human rights and freedoms'. The *International Covenant on Economic, Social and Cultural Rights* demands that each state party 'undertakes to take steps, individually and through international assistance and cooperation, especially economic and technical, to the maximum of its available resources, with a view to achieving progressively the full realization of the rights recognized in the present Covenant'.[10] Since then the duties of states party to the Covenants have been repeatedly emphasised, sometimes extended and frequently ignored.

The Covenants, however, say remarkably little about the duties either of individuals or of non-state institutions: their focus is entirely on the second-order duties on states to respect and realise rights by legislating, constructing institutions and enforcing law. The two Covenants do not assume that rights can be realised regardless of circumstances, but they do assume a specific, *statist* view of the circumstances that are to make it possible to secure respect for and realisation of rights.

1776 and 1789: abstraction and circumstances

Burke's account of the realisation of rights is in large measure developed in the course of criticising what he characterises as 'abstract rights', and contrasting them with views of rights that pay due attention to 'circumstances'. He had articulated this view as early as the 1760s and 70s when he described the American revolutionaries as entitled to and maintaining the historical and acknowledged rights of Englishmen, rather than as making claim to any 'abstract rights'. In 1775 he wrote:

[9] *International Covenant on Civil and Political Rights*, Part II, Art. 2.
[10] *Ibid.* (1): For more detail see Chapter 12 'The dark side of human rights', below, 193–207.

> First, the people of the Colonies are descendants of Englishmen ... They are therefore not only devoted to Liberty, but to Liberty according to English ideas, and on English principles. Abstract liberty, like other mere abstractions, is not to be found.[11]

Here he contrasts so-called 'abstract' liberty with the liberties of particular societies or communities. Although his comments are about *liberties*, rather than (more broadly) about *rights*, this is hardly surprising. The Constitution of the United States did not initially speak explicitly of individual rights, which became explicit when the first ten amendments, known as the 'Bill of Rights', were added to the Constitution (with other amendments).[12]

These amendments seemingly promulgate abstract rights of the very type that Burke later criticised in his comments on the French revolutionaries. And that is how these rights have often been seen: as rights that have, as it were, been inserted on top of, rather than derived from, a living constitutional tradition. This is also how the US Bill of Rights is often seen today. For example, President George W. Bush claimed 'The true [American] revolution was not to defy one earthly power, but to declare principles that stand above every earthly power – the equality of each person before God, and the responsibility of government to secure the rights of all.'[13] Did Burke ever have second thoughts about the American revolutionaries with whom he had sympathised in 1776? Might he have come to think that in agreeing to a Bill of Rights their successors had fallen under the spell of 'abstract' rights? If not, what was the difference? Or would Burke have continued to hold that, since the circumstances in which American rights and liberties had been promulgated included the rule of law, the common law, and a shared political tradition, this meant that these were no mere abstract rights?

By contrast, Burke's criticisms of 'abstract' rights throughout *Reflections on the Revolution in France* (and in other writings) are fierce and sustained. He criticises the revolutionaries of France for their reckless assertion of the 'abstract' rights to be found in the Declaration of the Rights of Man and of

---

[11] Burke, *Conciliation with America* in *Writings and Speeches, 1775*, vol. III, 120; cf. Burke, *Reflections on the Revolution in France*, vol. VIII, 110: 'their abstract perfection is their practical defect'.

[12] They were adopted by the House of Representatives on 21 August 1789, formally proposed by joint resolution of Congress on 25 September 1789 and came into effect as Constitutional Amendments on 15 December 1791, after ratification by three-fourths of the states. While twelve amendments were proposed by Congress, only ten were originally ratified.

[13] Speech at the 2003 rededication of 'Rotunda for the Charters of Freedom' at the US National Archives in Washington, DC.

the Citizen, and for their failure to respect and develop the ancient
constitutional traditions and laws of France:

> I flatter myself that I love a manly, moral, regulated liberty as well as any
> gentleman of that society, be he who he will; and perhaps I have given as
> good proofs of my attachment to that cause, in the whole course of my
> public conduct. I think I envy liberty as little as they do, to any other
> nation. But I cannot stand forward, and give praise or blame to anything
> which relates to human actions, and human concerns, on a simple view of
> the object, as it stands stripped of every relation, in all the nakedness and
> solitude of metaphysical abstraction. Circumstances (which with some
> gentlemen pass for nothing) give in reality to every political principle its
> distinguishing colour and discriminating effect. The circumstances are what
> render every civil and political scheme beneficial or noxious to mankind.[14]

In arguing that circumstances may render specific ways of institutionalising
rights either beneficial or noxious, Burke may have something useful to
tell us.

We can see *parts* of what Burke had in mind in asserting that the
circumstances of the American and French revolutions differed. But it is
less clear why he identifies the problem with French claims about the
Rights of Man as due to their *abstraction*. To *abstract* is simply to omit, or
leave out, or bracket explicit reference to some of the features of the matter
under discussion. It is unavoidable in all uses of language, since we cannot
make every feature or aspect of matters we discuss explicit. What then is
wrong about an account of liberties or of rights 'stripped of every relation,
in all the nakedness and solitude of metaphysical abstraction'? Speech may
be more or less abstract; it may abstract from some features of a situation
but not from others: but all speech is abstract in countless ways. Burke –
like many later writers[15] who criticise claims about rights or about liberalism for being *abstract* – must have some more specific defect in mind.
There are several possibilities.

In some cases what is labelled 'abstraction' appears not to leave some
things out, but to smuggle in *idealised*, hence *false*, assumptions. For
example, many economic and social theories assume *idealised* models of
man or of rationality, which are not to be found in real life. Idealisations
make fictitious, indeed false, rather than merely abstract assumptions,

---

[14] Burke, *Reflections on the Revolution in France*, vol. VIII, 57–8.
[15] Criticisms of 'abstraction' have been made repeatedly, for example by Hegel (mainly of Kant), by
contemporary communitarians (of liberals) and by many feminists (generally of liberals). Cf.
Chapter 5 'Ethical reasoning and ideological pluralism', above, 79–98.

which is a good reason for being cautious about them. But this is not the failing of which Burke accuses the defenders of abstract rights.

Other critics of abstraction suggest that the problem is not that false or misleading idealisations are covertly introduced, but that a misleading impression is given by omitting important or material aspects of the matter at hand. This, I think, is closer to Burke's concerns. The danger in focusing exclusively on an abstract account of rights is that we may omit circumstances that matter, which Burke thinks include the existing constitutions, conventions, traditions, habits, duties, virtues and sentiments of actual human societies and cultures. However, not every actual circumstance is relevant to realising rights, and not every circumstance should be preserved. If circumstances may be either 'noxious or beneficial', those that are noxious should surely be challenged and if possible abolished or changed, rather than left intact.

So if we are to consider how rights are to be realised it is not enough to criticise abstraction. We need to work out *which* circumstances we face at a given time or place, *which* to preserve or protect, *which* to ignore, and *which* to (seek to) change. Without understanding clearly why some circumstances must or may be left intact, and others changed, Burke's insistence on the importance of circumstances combined with his hostility to 'abstract' rights tells us little. It may be true that we do not aim 'to give praise or blame . . . on a simple view of the object in all the nakedness and solitude of metaphysical abstraction',[16] but we need to attend to the circumstances we face in actual situations. Taking realistic account of circumstances does not damage rights: ignoring them is likely to undermine attempts to respect or to realise rights.

Circumstances, institutions and cultures

In his early 1766 essay opposing the penal laws in Ireland, Burke had argued passionately that

> Everybody is satisfied, that a conservation and secure enjoyment of our natural rights is the great and ultimate purpose of civil society; and that therefore all forms whatsoever of government are only good as they are subservient to that purpose to which they are entirely subordinate.[17]

---

[16] Burke, *Reflections on the Revolution in France*, vol. VIII, 58.
[17] Edmund Burke, *Tracts on the Popery Laws*, vol. IX, 413 434–82, 464.

But he repeatedly tempered this view with the claim that we can only tell what is needed to pursue this 'great and ultimate purpose' in specific circumstances. If so we need to know which circumstances are relevant, and which irrelevant now, in the circumstances in which we are to act. The mere fact that Burke mentions a wide range of institutional and cultural circumstances – our ancient constitution and liberties, accepted views and traditions, the happiness or misery of the people[18] – does not show which are still relevant, let alone essential, to realising the rights he thinks important, or which new circumstances are relevant. Our circumstances are not Burke's circumstances, and we cannot simply adopt his claims about what is needed if rights are to be respected and realised. Some of the circumstances he thought essential for securing rights are no longer there to be maintained. Others remain, but may no longer be important, or may even be damaging to human rights. Yet others may be essential for realising rights in our circumstances.

The practical point is surely then not to 'avoid abstraction', but to identify and to maintain circumstances that make it *possible* to reach a determinate and coherent interpretation of rights, and *feasible* to respect and realise those rights. This is not best done by preserving the circumstances that Burke singles out as important. Circumstances, such as the fact that some of our rights have an ancient pedigree, indeed were inherited from our forefathers, seem to me unlikely to be useful, let alone necessary, either for interpreting or for realising rights. What we have inherited may be inadequate, or inadequate in our present circumstances; it may be in part noxious, in part decayed, or in part now irrelevant to or destructive of respect for and realisation of rights. Realism about actual circumstances is indispensable if rights are to be realised.

Burke's realism: interpretations and implementations

Burke is realistic and not anachronistic in some of his claims about the fundamental circumstances in which rights can be respected and realised. His realism is clearest when he insists that realisable rights require counterpart duties:

> What is the use of discussing a man's abstract right to food or medicine? The question is upon the method of procuring and administering them.

---

[18] See *ibid.* 320: 'The happiness or misery of multitudes can never be a thing indifferent. A law against the majority of the people is in substance a law against the people itself; its extent determines its invalidity.'

In that deliberation I shall always advise to call in the aid of the farmer and the physician rather than the professor of metaphysics.[19]

Rights without counterpart duties are illusory. No right can be respected or realised without competent duty bearers, who are to do what is required. Some rights, such as those to food or medicine (or to other goods and services), demand strenuous action by *specified* others. Others, such as liberty rights, may require less strenuous duties, but demand them of *all* others. Unless duties are allocated to individuals and institutions that can discharge them, there can be no effective rights. The striking silence about duties in many contemporary discussions of rights no doubt reflects immense cultural shifts from a world centred on social and ethical duties, to one in which legal requirements and their enforcement by states are seen as fundamental, and in which individuals are commonly seen as having rights – but little is said about their duties. But rights cannot be secured merely by assigning second-order duties to enforce them. Somebody has to shoulder the primary duties, and enforcement is not likely to work unless it is clear who ought to do what for whom.

The most fundamental circumstance that is needed for rights to be respected or realised is an adequate *interpretation of rights*. Since rights are typically declared or listed or asserted in relatively abstract language, it may seem that it should not be hard to reach a shared understanding of what they require. But as soon as we consider any specific right closely, it becomes evident that each has to be interpreted so as to be consistent with an interpretation of all other rights. How are rights to freedom of expression to be adjusted to rights to privacy? How are rights to liberty to be shaped so that they do not undermine others' rights to security? How are 'rights to food' to be secured without undermining the rights to work and to property of farmers and of others who store, distribute, prepare and sell food? How are 'rights to medicine' (to health care) to be secured without undermining many of the rights of physicians and other health care providers? Adequate answers to these questions depend on complex cultural and institutional arrangements, without which these rights indeed remain abstract, and may be useless. Here, perhaps, Burke may have something to tell us today: but it is not something simple.

I doubt whether it is possible to identify a unique or optimal way of interpreting and configuring the full *range* of rights that we meet in the contemporary Declarations and Covenants, or to arrive at a unique

---

[19] Burke, *Reflections on the Revolution in France*, vol. VIII, III.

interpretation of the counterpart duties.[20] Even if we are convinced of the importance and merits of human rights standards, we cannot assume that the interpretations of human rights proposed at a given time are beyond question and need no revision.

Currently favoured ways of adjusting rights to one another may not be optimal, or may be optimal for some circumstances and suboptimal or even impossible in others. For example, current interpretations of rights to privacy may not prove adequate, or even feasible, in the face of revolutions in communications, encryption and data mining technologies. Current interpretations of rights to family life may not prove adequate, or even feasible, in the face of transformations in family structures. Current interpretations of rights to citizenship, which are often tightly tied to conceptions of family structure, may not prove adequate as those structures change. The abstract human rights standards listed in the Declarations and Conventions may remain widely accepted, but their interpretation is not likely to remain either constant or undisputed.

Secondly, changes in circumstances may require changes in the ways we think of enforcement. Enforcement fails unless it is based on a realistic view of the actual capacities both of those who enforce and of those who are to comply. Current assumptions about enforcement load the task onto states. But states can only discharge the second-order duties to ensure that rights are respected and realised if they have the necessary capacities to enforce the performance of duties and thereby respect for and realisation of rights. Yet many states that have ratified the Covenants of 1966 lack or refuse to exercise these capacities. Some are failed states, some are rogue states, some are merely weak states, and cannot – however enthusiastically they ratified the relevant instruments – enforce duties or ensure that rights are respected and realised.

And in some respects even well-governed states that secure both order and the rule of law internally now face challenges to enforcement that were hard to imagine fifty years ago. The Covenants of 1966 were drafted at a distinctive time at which decolonisation was seemingly moving forward, but globalisation was only beginning. It was a *Westphalian* moment, at which it was possible to imagine a future world consisting of sovereign states with well-defined and effectively controlled borders, and adequate powers to enforce duties to respect and to realise human rights within their borders. So it made sense to assign states the task of enforcing respect for

---

[20] See Chapter 7 'Pluralism, positivism and the justification on human rights', above, 120–33, for further discussion of constraints on adequate interpretations of rights.

and realisation of rights. But circumstances have changed in at least two ways that do not fit this picture. First, it has become clearer that a large number of states have not developed the power or the will to enforce the relevant duties, not only for a transitional but for a longer period. Secondly, the powers of states that are taken to have the will and capacity to secure respect for and realisation of rights have been reshaped, sometimes reduced, as state borders have become more porous and as the powers of many non-state actors have grown at their expense. The emergence of powerful transnational corporations and of 'offshore' havens that allow the rich or powerful to escape tax (or regulation, or standards of corporate governance, or all of these) all now limit the capacities of states.[21]

The Westphalian moment has passed, and even states with robust laws and a strong commitment to human rights can find it hard to secure all rights for all persons who are (wholly or partly, continuously or episodically) within their borders. More porous borders have produced increasing migration; increasing tax evasion; competitive tax reductions that reduce revenues; financial cross border crime on a large scale; increasing 'offshoring' of corporate governance and economic power; and many other changes that can be used by a wide range of non-state actors, many of them intent on gaining power and wealth by locating aspects of their activities advantageously. All these changes can reduce and reshape state powers and revenues and make it harder for states to respect or to realise all rights. These trends have been recognised by academic commentators, and are now seen as fundamental at the heart of the United Nations discussions of human rights. Both the UN global compact initiative (begun under Kofi Annan)[22] and John Ruggie's report[23] to the UN on the 'Protect, Respect and Remedy Framework' take it that some duties to respect and realise rights may have to be assigned to non-state actors; but the implications of these changes remain unclear.

---

[21] Some of the ways in which states have retreated or become less effective are discussed in Susan Strange, *The Retreat of the State: The Diffusion of Power in the World Economy* (Cambridge University Press, 1996); Nicholas Shaxson, *Treasure Islands: Tax Havens and the Men who Stole the World* (London: Vintage, 2011); and Tim Büthe and Walter Mattli, *The New Global Rulers: The Privatization of Regulation in the World Economy* (Princeton University Press, 2011).

[22] 'The Global Compact asks companies to embrace universal principles and to partner with the United Nations. It has grown to become a critical platform for the UN to engage effectively with enlightened global business.' UN Secretary-General Ban Ki-moon, www.unglobalcompact.org.

[23] 'Guiding Principles on Business and Human Rights: Implementing the United Nations "Protect, Respect and Remedy" Framework' proposed by UN Special Representative John Ruggie and adopted by UNHRC in 2008, www.business-humanrights.org/SpecialRepPortal/Home/Protect-Respect-Remedy-Framework/GuidingPrinciples.

Circumstances indeed matter, and changes in circumstances can create reasons for rethinking human rights and their counterpart duties. While effective rights require a clear interpretation that is systematically linked to a clear interpretation of the counterpart duties there is no reason to assume that this must always be exactly what finds favour at a given moment either with the states party or among human rights lawyers or activists, or with other political or economic actors. Nor is it to be expected that current ways of implementing rights (or current aspirations for doing so) will, or even can, remain unchanged in changing circumstances.

When we speak of the 'progressive realisation' of human rights, it is easy to be led into imagining that there is a single path forward towards full compliance with all human rights standards in all jurisdictions. But we should be cautious about suggestions that there is a unique path of progress that all must follow to a single destination. Burke would have been mistaken if he had assumed that the circumstances that shaped the realisation of rights in his day – in particular an inherited tradition and constitution – provided the only route forward. We would repeat this mistake if we imagined that the approaches to respecting and realising rights that seemed obvious in the heyday of state power will remain adequate, or even feasible, in a globalising world. If we seek to realise rights, we must be realistic about the circumstances in which we seek to do so, and about ways in which circumstances have changed, are changing and may change further.

Practicalities and judgement

Human rights are explicitly *universal* – they are for everybody – but they do not prescribe *uniformity*. Because human rights standards are inevitably to some degree abstract and indeterminate, their interpretation *may* and *must* vary with circumstances. It is therefore highly likely that the established view of human rights laws and procedures of a given time and place could be improved; and even if they do not currently need changing, will come to need revision as circumstances change.

I have suggested that the first task in respecting and realising rights is to interpret their varying demands in ways that are mutually consistent. This task is often characterised in the abstract (!), as a matter of 'balancing' rights, or of finding a proportionate or appropriate way of doing so. I believe that the ubiquitous use of these abstract phrases does not do justice to the real task or its difficulty. There is no metric for this balance, and the task cannot be compared to that of a judge considering a large range of evidence about a particular case, who may indeed be able to balance the various features *of that particular case*. In working out how to adjust different rights to one another, we are not considering particular cases, and there are no 'facts of the case' to balance. Rather the task of adjusting rights to one another is a matter of selecting among possible policies. It therefore rightly, indeed necessarily, involves bringing a multiplicity of considerations together, and reaches conclusions that are always less than perfect and less than permanent.

In judging how to secure effective respect for or realisation of human rights, policy-makers have to take account not only of the full range of rights, but of many other specific circumstances. How secure is the rule of law? Which matters are best secured by legislating and which by 'softer' means? Which sanctions are likely to be effective in actual circumstances, and which are not? How much complexity and how much detailed regulation are useful for realising specific rights? Which sorts of provision are unnecessary, or likely to prove counterproductive? What do smarter regulation and more intelligent accountability require?[24] Is the proposed assignment of duties clear? Is it feasible for those to whom they are assigned? Is their performance of these duties compatible with respecting or realising the other duties they also hold? Are the public funds required to realise a given right, using the proposed procedures, available? Are the methods for checking that rights are not violated adequate, and are they likely to work?

Working towards schemes for respecting and realising human rights is a political and practical task, and no evaluation of such schemes can be convincing unless it considers the *full* task, and the ways in which rights and duties have been adjusted to one another, to the available financial and human resources, and to actual cultural and social capacities – and readjusted to changes in these circumstances.

A question that in my view remains open is whether there are (sometimes or always) further considerations that ought to play a part in the practical task of implementing human rights standards. It has become a standard trope of liberal political philosophy during recent decades that we live in a morally pluralistic world, that we should be agnostic about the good for man, and that we should not introduce wider, perhaps contentious, ethical considerations (such as appeals to values other than rights) in

---

[24] Cass R. Sunstein, *Simpler: The Future of Government* (New York: Simon & Schuster, 2013); Onora O'Neill, 'Trust, trustworthiness and accountability' in Nick Morris and David Vines (eds.), *Capital Failure: Rebuilding Trust in Financial Services* (Oxford University Press, 2014), 172–89.

specific circumstances that go beyond human rights standards are needed in working out how we are to move from a *coherent interpretation* of the entire range of rights towards a *feasible implementation* of those rights for a given time and place. For example, a range of moderately abstract ethical standards such as decency, civility and moderation may be essential for identifying feasible ways of implementing human rights in specific circumstances. A merely 'political' liberalism, which takes no wider view about what matters, may not then offer an adequate basis for realising rights in various circumstances.

CHAPTER 9

From statist to global conceptions of justice[1]

Overt and covert statism in conceptions of justice

Many theories of justice of the modern period have been either openly or discreetly theories of just states. From Hobbes to Rawls[2] we find an agreement that the context of justice is the state, although disagreement whether justice should be sought only in political or also in economic and social arrangements. What is misleadingly called *international* justice, and would more accurately be called *interstatal* justice, is then treated as a supplementary topic, which presupposes the existence of states – and not necessarily of just states, as the doctrine of non-intervention reminds us.

Evidence that this is the common order of construction of theories of justice may be found not only in the classical texts of modern political philosophy, but in their curious evasions of certain topics. For example, until late in the twentieth century, discussions of justice often treated state boundaries as presuppositions rather than as problems for an account of justice. Although there have been many discussions of the justice of boundaries, they have usually been discussions about the just placing of this or that boundary, and have presumed that boundaries are not in themselves unjust. Yet unless we have presupposed that states provide the proper context for justice, we can hardly take for granted that state boundaries (wherever they are drawn) can be just. On the face of it, the boundaries of states limit many rights and duties to a certain territory, and this fundamental institutional structure requires justification rather than bland acceptance.

---

[1] 'From statist to global conceptions of justice', in Christoph von Hubig (ed.), *XVII Deutscher Kungress für Philosophie* (Berlin: Akademie Verlag, 1997), 368–79.

[2] Rawls insisted that his is a theory not of just states, but of just bounded societies: 'I shall be satisfied if it is possible to formulate a reasonable conception of justice for the basic structure of society conceived for the time being as a closed system isolated from other societies': Rawls, *A Theory of Justice*, 8. For discussion of this position, and the extent to which bounded societies differ from states, see Caney, *Justice beyond Borders*, and Chapter 6 'Bounded and cosmopolitan justice', above, 99–119.

More surprisingly, a careful consideration of the *Universal Declaration of Human Rights* also reveals how prevalent statism remained in its approach to justice. The universality of the rights proclaimed in the Declaration is constantly linked to the point that for any individual these rights may legitimately be differentiated by state boundaries. This is why the Declaration is so careful to insist that everyone has the right to a nationality[3] (in the sense of membership of a state) in Article 15, and to differentiate the freedom of movement that each is to enjoy in his or her *own* state (Article 13) from the right of asylum which he or she may have in *other* states (Article 14). A basic feature of a just international order – interstatal order – as outlined in the Declaration is that any given individual's rights to travel, take up abode, work, own property and vote, as well as their corresponding duties, may justly be circumscribed by the boundaries of the state where he or she is a citizen, or more broadly a member.[4]

Of course, there is a rosy view of the world in which the segmentation of justice by the boundaries of states does no harm. On this rosy view each of us may have the full range of rights guaranteed by his or her state, states are effective deliverers of those rights, and nobody finds their rights infringed or lessened by being a member of one rather than another state. In fact, as we well know, the present world order is a grotesque parody of this rosy story. Many states fail to guarantee various rights, including basic rights of the person, for some or many of their citizens; many others cannot guarantee various rights (in particular economic, social and cultural rights) for many of their citizens. And there are many stateless persons.

It seems that current institutions and much current thinking about human rights does not go very far towards securing rights for those whose states do not secure them, or for those who have no state. The situation of refugees and migrants is often harsh and uncertain, and rarely ends up with the full or secure enjoyment of rights. Intervention in other states has taken place only for grossest violations of human rights, and then only occasionally, and then often for mixed motives, and then often

---

[3] Article 15 of the Declaration has two parts: '1. Everyone has a right to a nationality; 2. No one shall be arbitrarily deprived of his nationality nor denied the right to change it.' The text suggests that the sense in which *nationality* is intended has to do not with descent and ethnicity, which cannot be changed, but with membership and citizenship in a state which can be removed.

[4] The term 'citizen' is too narrow to define those who enjoy rights in a given state. The term 'member' can be used to cover resident aliens (who have many but not all rights, and in particular no political rights), *Gastarbeiter* (who may have many rights, but not that of permanent residence) and also children of citizens (who have many rights, but not yet those of full citizens). The topic was extensively discussed in Walzer, *Spheres of Justice*.

unsuccessfully. The institutions for successful intervention do not exist at present: the agenda of UN reform is much discussed, but makes little progress.[5] Where then, if anywhere, can consideration of global justice gain a foothold? Where should one begin?

Moral cosmopolitanism

A favourite starting point for global justice, paradoxical as it may seem, has been to insist that the only subjects of moral concern are individual agents. If all individuals, wherever they may be, are equally owed justice, then it might seem that we have the appropriate starting point for a genuinely cosmopolitan account of justice, in which rights and duties are not differentiated by membership of states. And of course we can find a great deal of abstract cosmopolitanism or moral cosmopolitanism in contemporary moral and political philosophy.[6] Yet these more abstract approaches also often present us with surprising difficulties in offering an account of global justice. Some of these difficulties can I think be attributed to a tendency in cosmopolitan thinking, even when it does not take up the more evidently statist assumptions of the UN Declaration and subsequent International Covenants, to think about justice in terms of human rights.[7]

The lofty rhetoric of human rights, even when not specifically tied to the claims of the Universal Declaration, insists that all human beings (I leave the animals aside for the moment) have the same rights. Although this resonant claim sounds as if it should provide a promising way of thinking about global justice, it leads straight into difficulties. In particular, the assumption that the category of rights is fundamental for thought about justice creates difficulties. Roughly speaking, I believe, much abstract cosmopolitan thinking has difficulty in moving on from abstraction to a discussion of institutions *because* it treats the category of rights as fundamental. The difficulty begins to show as soon as we ask who bears obligations to meet these rights and whether all human beings have the same obligations.

If all human rights were liberty rights the matter would be, if not simple, still not in principle difficult. A liberty right (e.g. to freedom of movement, to freedom of speech) is incomplete if there are *any* others who have no

---

[5] Not much was changed by enthusiastic promotion of an additional international norm known as the *Responsibility to Protect* ('R2P') at the 2005 World Summit.

[6] Cf. Thomas Pogge, 'Cosmopolitanism and sovereignty' in Brown, *Political Restructuring in Europe*, 89–122; he has developed these themes in many later publications. Caney, *Justice beyond Borders*.

[7] See Chapter 12 'The dark side of human rights', below, 193–207.

obligation to respect that right. A right to freedom of speech is damaged if even one other – particularly one powerful other, for example, Frederick the Great![8] – has the right to breach or override it. This fact makes it possible to move from an abstractly cosmopolitan account of liberty rights to an abstractly cosmopolitan account of the corresponding obligations. On a libertarian conception of justice, there are both universal liberty rights and counterpart universal obligations to respect liberties: the duties of man match the rights of man.

However, this simple correspondence fails for liberty rights as soon as we seek to move from abstract to more institutional thinking about justice. Any institutional embodiment of liberty rights will have to differentiate the obligations assigned to different individuals, office holders and institutions. Even a basic liberty right, such as a right not to be tortured, cannot be established and enforced without quite complex institutions that assign obligations to the police, to courts, to tax payers and to other institutions, perhaps including independent monitoring and publicising bodies (e.g. Amnesty International; Human Rights Watch; national human rights institutions).[9] In thinking our way from rights to obligations we have to acknowledge that a cosmopolitanism of rights leaves institutional questions wide open.[10] It leads us only to the thought that rights, including liberty rights, are to be secured by some just scheme or other.

The difficulties become even more acute when we consider rights of other sorts – and much cosmopolitan thinking claims that there are other sorts of rights. In particular, the economic, social and cultural rights which form so large a part of the discourse of human rights are all of them rights to action by others that cannot be delivered by everybody acting in concert. Here universal rights cannot plausibly be matched by universal obligations. A right to food cannot be a matter of all others having an obligation to contribute an aliquot amount of food. A right to development cannot be a matter of all others having the obligation to make an equal contribution to development. It is not plausible to assert that all universal rights are matched by universal obligations. It seems that we do

---

[8] Cf. Immanuel Kant, *An Answer to the Question: What Is Enlightenment?* (1784) in *Practical Philosophy*, 8:35–42.

[9] Again, this has long been recognised, as in Henry Shue, *Basic Rights: Subsistence, Affluence and US Foreign Policy* (Princeton University Press, 1980, 2nd edn 1996).

[10] Evidence of this indeterminacy can be found not only in the variety of legal formulations for securing rights within a state, but in the suggestions by certain libertarians that unregulated markets, including markets in dispute resolution and enforcement, would do the job better and perhaps secure justice better than state regulation can.

little more than gesture in talking in abstraction from institutions about universal rights to goods or services, since we cannot identify which sets of obligations held by specific individuals or institutions would correspond to universal economic, social or cultural rights. Merely abstract thinking tells us remarkably little about rights to goods and services, since the counterpart obligations cannot be universal – yet if nothing is said about the counterpart obligations, the rights that are proclaimed will not have been taken seriously. If we are to take rights seriously, we have to say something about the way in which the obligations that support them should be allocated to individuals, office holders and institutions.[11]

For these and other reasons I believe that thinking about global justice has at a very early stage to go beyond the claims of abstract cosmopolitanism. Yet it cannot, I believe, rely mainly on claims about rights, or specifically on the claims made in UDHR. Even if all rights were liberty rights, we would need to think about obligations and about institutions.

However, it does not follow from the need to think institutionally that an account of global justice will be best supported either be assuming that fundamental obligations should be held by anti-cosmopolitan institutions such as states, or by constructing unflinchingly cosmopolitan institutions, such as a world state. If our thinking begins from this familiar starting point we shall have to repeat the long and difficult intellectual trek from accounts of justice in one state to accounts of international (interstatal) justice to an account of global justice. Not only is this not the only route by which to try to think about global justice: it may be an unpromising route.

Institutions and territoriality: land or people?

One feature that distinguishes modern states from other institutions is that they are intrinsically territorial. Each of them has, or claims, a certain territory as exclusively its own, and sees the limits of this territory as the limits of the state. It is no wonder that in thinking about states we now generally follow the Weberian definition and take ourselves to be focusing not merely on entities that claim the monopoly of legitimate use of

---

[11] Libertarians have a solution, up to a point. If all rights are liberty rights, all humans have both the same rights and the same obligations. However, all but the most anarchist of libertarians find it hard to give up on the claim that states, at least minimal states, are needed because enforcement is needed. And once a plurality of states comes into the picture there must be some retreat from abstract or moral cosmopolitanism in the direction of statist and institutional thinking.

violence, but specifically on entities that claim the monopoly of legitimate use of violence *within a given territory*. For us, states are invariably associated with land, and the boundaries of a state can be represented by lines on the map.[12] Yet we know the linkage of the monopoly of (legitimate) use of force with territory that we find in the Weberian conception of the state is by no means inevitable. Many earlier conceptions of states represent them as exercising a monopoly of (legitimate) power over one or many peoples, and make no immediate reference to exclusive control of territory. If we are to think about the ways by which we might work towards a global conception of justice I believe we may do well not to insist that we should start with this exclusive focus on a set of mutually exclusive (and more or less jointly exhaustive) territorial units, each claiming monopoly of the legitimate use of force.[13]

We might in fact do well to consider a much wider range of institutions that exercise substantial power, but which are not intrinsically territorial. Non-territorial institutions are, of course, locatable. But their influence is not identified with a bounded territory. Many of them might be thought of as networking institutions that link dispersed persons, officials and institutions. Among familiar examples of networking institutions we might include the international banking system; transnational corporations; communications networks including transnational communications organisations; transnational NGOs such as Amnesty, Caritas, Oxfam and Médecins sans Frontières; research and educational networks.

The powers exercised by networking organisations may, of course, differ greatly from those exercised by territorial organisations. Territorial organisations are (sometimes!) good at enforcing requirements on those within their territory, but often less good at achieving certain other sorts of changes. Other sorts of institutions, and in particular networking institutions, may have limited capacities to enforce requirements, but can be good at exercising productive power.

This is not a novel point. It is often formulated from a statist point of view as a complaint that certain institutions, particularly networking institutions, *evade* the exercise of state power. For example, transnational corporations can (and often do) locate dirty production processes where

---

[12] The territory is not always connected or unitary (former Pakistan; island states), but it is taken to be exclusive – and sometimes disputed.

[13] Cf. Thomas Baldwin, 'The territorial state' in Hyman Gross and Ross Harrison (eds.), *Jurisprudence: Cambridge Essays* (Oxford University Press, 1992).

environmental legislation is weakest, or their profits where taxation is lowest.[14] Global communications organisations can and often do locate their hardware, their editorial policies and their profits wherever may be advantageous – where advantage is often a matter of escaping certain state requirements. An alternative, non-statist or less statist view of these institutions and others like them is that they are evidently not readily subordinated to states, and that any approach that assumes that they can or should be is doomed. Yet if networking institutions escape the control of states, how is an account of justice to deal with them more directly?

All this is really by way of refocusing aspects of political philosophy, and so far my conclusions are largely negative: it is not obvious that the state is the sole port of call in thinking about the institutions of justice; it is not likely that an account of international (interstatal) justice by itself can offer an adequate account of just networking institutions.

Just networks and sovereignty

Networking institutions do not of course wholly escape the regulation of states. Their officials and offices and laboratories are located in state territories, or rather in the territories of many states. The problem is rather that they are not located in any one state, and that they escape many sorts of regulation and control in this way. One strategy of trying to squeeze them into accounts of justice that begin with states is to construct international (interstatal) and intergovernmental bodies to regulate the networking institutions, and ensure that they meet certain standards of justice. The much noted difficulty of this strategy is that interstatal and intergovernmental institutions have to work by laborious procedures of negotiation, in many cases by procedures that demand unanimity. The regulatory regimes produced may be slow and inefficient or leave central issues unregulated. To choose an obvious example of escape from regulation, consider the Internet? While cyber romantics insist that its escape from state control must be preserved, others fear the emergence of unaccountable power.

Laborious approaches can seem unavoidable if we are in thrall to the Weberian conception of the state. For if legitimate monopolies on the use of power are all held by intrinsically territorial institutions, then surely the regulation of other institutions must ultimately be in their hands.

---

[14] Shaxson, *Treasure Islands.*

Sovereignty on this account *must* ultimately be located in intrinsically territorially institutions.

This thought can be sustained only if sovereignty is intrinsically indivisible. Hobbes offered a classic formulation of the indivisibility of sovereignty: the Leviathan is a mortal God. Already in the eighteenth century the thought that sovereignty must be indivisible was challenged for the case of internal sovereignty. The doctrine of the division of powers is tantamount to insistence that internal sovereignty had better be divisible. The arguments for so doing have many of them been arguments against the concentration of power, and in particular against concentration of institutional power, which tends to absolute power. The indivisibility of internal sovereignty was challenged in the name of demands of justice, and in particular of the demands of liberty and democracy. Moreover the challenge has proved institutionally sustainable. Those states which institutionalise a division of powers in their constitutions are not intrinsically weakened or unable to function. On many accounts they function rather better – and go to war less often – than monolithic states.

Has the time now come for reconsidering the form which external sovereignty should take? Could external sovereignty be divided? Would this threaten justice? Or might it help secure justice? Much realist thought on international relations has insisted that undivided external sovereignty for each state is essential, the guarantor if not of justice then at least of security. Only states unite powers to tax, to fight and to enforce law. Since states alone have sufficient internal sovereignty, they alone should have external sovereignty.

This picture blurs as soon as we remember that not all states enjoy the sort of external sovereignty imagined. States are typically multiply interconnected with one another, with a range of interstatal and intergovernmental institutions, and with major non-state actors, including networking institutions. A government that has to float a bond issue may find that the international banking system controls what it can do, every bit as much as a bank might find itself limited by government action. A state may find that the culture and orientation of its citizens is formed by broadcasting networks and the Internet, which are both in some ways extraterritorial. Of course, states can try to reassert the territorially limited and defined sovereignty that they used to enjoy, for example by keeping the networking institutions out of their territories. Quite apart from questions of the rights of citizens that might then be infringed, the development of technology is hostile to this old-fashioned way of asserting sovereignty.

If networking institutions are not readily regulable by states, acting either individually or in concert, it may be that we should view them too as primary institutions for achieving justice. The immediate objection may be that there is no obvious way of bringing networking institutions to account, and that they escape political, including democratic control. Yet it may be possible to aim for accountability. One route to accountability is through state regulation, but others are imaginable and constructible, and some have emerged: there are already many non-state regulators that work across many jurisdictions.[15] Networking institutions can provide effective and trusted forms of accountability, even if they lack aspects of the sorts of sovereignty that territorial states can indeed monopolise. However, some of the ways in which they are accountable do not conform to statist – or democratic – models of accountability: forms of commercial or cultural accountability often suit networking institutions better. We have yet to understand what this means for ensuring that these institutions do not act unjustly.

---

[15] They are particularly significant in financial and product standards regulation. See Büthe and Mattli, *The New Global Rulers*.

CHAPTER 10

Global justice: whose obligations?[1]

Cosmopolitan rights and state obligations

Many respected and prominent accounts of justice have cosmopolitan aspirations, yet provide a poor basis for thinking about the demands of justice in a globalising world and especially for thinking about economic justice. Typically they endorse some account of cosmopolitan principles of justice, then assume without argument, or without sufficient argument, that the *primary agents of justice* must be states. Other agents and agencies are seen as *secondary agents of justice*, whose contribution to justice is regulated, defined and allocated by states. These approaches to justice are cosmopolitan in assuming that justice is owed to all human beings, wherever they live and whatever their citizenship, yet anti-cosmopolitan in assuming that many significant obligations stop or vary at state or other boundaries.

There are tensions, and perhaps incoherencies, in thinking that anti-cosmopolitan institutions such as bounded states and their subordinate institutions can shoulder primary obligations of cosmopolitan justice. On the surface, states are fundamentally ill-suited and ill-placed to secure or strengthen justice beyond their own borders. Their primary responsibilities are to their own maintenance and to their inhabitants. Historically the states that have secured a measure of justice beyond their borders – *pax Romana, pax Britannica, pax Americana* – have generally been imperial states that exercised power beyond their borders, or obliterated certain borders, or made them more porous in certain respects. These facts are so obvious that it is remarkable that anyone should see the pursuit of justice for those beyond their borders as a primary task of states. And, of course, many have made no such assumptions. Unlike cosmopolitans, would-be

---

[1] 'Global justice: whose obligations?' in Deen K. Chatterjee (ed.), *The Ethics of Assistance: Morality and the Distant Needy* (Cambridge University Press, 2004), 242–59.

realists about international relations have always argued that states should do nothing about injustice beyond their borders, except where it is important to their own survival and interests.

The lamentable but strong evidence that states have failed to secure justice, and in particular economic justice, beyond their borders should not surprise us. Although 'humanitarian interventions' to curb major violations of human rights have become more numerous since the ending of the Cold War, even massive violations do not always lead to intervention (and there can be good prudential reasons for refraining: non-intervention in Chechnya or in China would be wholly realistic).[2] Even when there has been intervention it has often been late or ineffective, or both (consider former Yugoslavia or Somalia). And the supposed attempts of richer states and of international agencies to reduce poverty in less developed countries have also often been ineffective. In the 1990s the gap between rich and poor often grew rather than shrinking.[3] Assigning obligations to secure justice beyond their borders to states may be no more sensible than assigning obligations to supervise hen houses to foxes.

It is not only practitioners who combine cosmopolitan and anti-cosmopolitan rhetoric. Many prominent political and philosophical approaches to justice also combine cosmopolitan aspirations with statist assumptions. One example is the *Universal Declaration of Rights* of 1948, which demands 'the promotion of universal respect for and observance of human rights',[4] then assumes that this noble goal can be pursued by assigning to states the counterpart obligations to respect these rights. The poor drafting of the Declaration obscures this hiatus: the text refers promiscuously to 'countries', 'member-states' and 'nations'. However, a careful reading makes it quite plain that obligations to secure universal rights are assigned to states, almost always to the state of which an individual is a citizen or member.[5] Rights against states of which an individual is not a citizen or member, if any, are far less extensive. For example, the Declaration distinguishes the rights to freedom of movement and association that states should guarantee their citizens or members from those they should guarantee non-members (contrast: 'the right to freedom of movement and residence within the borders of each state', Art. 13;

---

[2] Michael Doyle, 'The new interventionism', *Metaphilosophy* 32 (2001), 212–35.
[3] See Thomas Pogge, 'Priorities of global justice', *Metaphilosophy* 32 (2001), 6–24.
[4] *Universal Declaration of Human Rights*, 1948, reprinted in Ian Brownlie (ed.), *Basic Human Rights Documents* (Oxford: Clarendon Press, 1981), 21–7, Preamble.
[5] For more detailed comments see Onora O'Neill, *Bounds of Justice* and 'Agents of justice', Metaphilosophy 32 (2001), 180–95 'Bounded and cosmopolitan justice', and Chapter 6; above, 99–119.

'the right to leave any country, including his own, and to return to his country', Art. 13; and 'the right to seek and enjoy in other countries asylum from persecution', Art. 14).

John Rawls's theory of justice offers a more philosophical account of principles of justice of universal scope that links them to a substantially statist view of agents of justice. Rawls gives priority to an account of 'domestic' justice: he aims initially to 'formulate a reasonable conception of justice for the basic structure of society conceived for the time being as a closed system isolated from other societies'.[6] This initial assumption recurs constantly in his writings; it is not discarded even in his late writings on justice beyond borders. Consequently a latent statism marks even Rawls's most explicit attempts to arrive at a wider account of justice. His account of global justice remains an account of 'international' justice, in which the supposed legitimacy of assigning control of bounded territories to 'peoples' is presupposed, and limits and perhaps undermines his arguments for justice beyond borders.[7]

Could abstract cosmopolitanism be enough?

Looked at with hindsight, the gigantic costs of assuming that states (or even Rawlsian 'peoples') are the primary agents of justice may seem obvious. Yet what are the alternatives? One possibility would be to offer an account of international justice that says *nothing* about the allocation of obligations, assuming only that all agents and agencies are bound by the same basic principles of justice. Cannot an abstract account of universal rights of cosmopolitan scope be matched by an equally abstract account of universal obligations of cosmopolitan scope? Indeed, could we not adopt an abstract account of universal obligations and then forget about any account of universal rights? The latter approach was adopted by Peter Singer in his still much discussed 1972 article on famine, affluence and morality, which argues that anybody with more than he or she needs ought to give the surplus to the relief of poverty.[8] Utilitarian

---

[6] Rawls, *A Theory of Justice*, 8.

[7] See Rawls, *The Law of Peoples*. Rawls maintains that his account of justice is designed for *peoples* not *states*. However, his conception of a people is not cultural but political. It builds on notions of territoriality, boundaries and a monopoly of coercive power: most political philosophers would deem anything with these properties a state. See Kuper, 'Rawlsian global justice; and Onora O'Neill, 'Political liberalism and public reason: a critical notice of John Rawls, *Political Liberalism*', *Philosophical Review* 106 (1998), 411–28.

[8] Singer, 'Famine, affluence and morality'.

and similar consequentialist positions subsume justice in generalised beneficence, obliging each to do whatever is likely to contribute most to aggregate happiness or welfare. Judgements about what is likely to contribute most to happiness or welfare will, of course, always be made against complex background assumptions and evidence about others' action, about institutions and about resources, about the effects of possible action, and about the value of those effects. Such judgements will not, however, be derived from or presuppose any independent views about rights: they may or may not support the rights promulgated in the Universal Declaration, or in other manifestos and charters; they will regard distance and borders, hence states, as lacking intrinsic moral significance.

Utilitarian and other consequentialist approaches to global justice have considerable weaknesses. In placing all conclusions at the beck and call of claims about the value of outcomes and about the vastly complex causal connections that determine outcomes, they gain a spurious precision. Such reasoning may seem to anchor moral requirements in empirical calculation, but when evidence, data and calculations (not to mention units of account) are all hazy, those requirements will be elastic, if not indeterminate. They may foster a rhetoric of cosmopolitan justice, yet fail to determine *who* ought to do *what* for *whom*. Of course, utilitarian reasoning can also be deployed more circumspectly – or possibly more ambitiously – to work out which institutions should be constructed and how obligations should be allocated among them, leaving the resolution of particular cases to the normal functioning of these institutions. But here too, very demanding calculations are needed to see just *who* should do *what* to help 'rear the fabric of felicity by the hands of reason and of law'.[9]

So if we think that ethical requirements are universally important, we have reason to look for accounts of rights and obligations that have firmer anchoring than utilitarian thinking or alternative forms of abstract cosmopolitanism can provide. Moreover, we will have strong reasons to think that it will not be possible to anchor an account of rights without offering an account of obligations. The abstract cosmopolitanism that Declarations of Rights favour has practical import only when we can determine *who* ought to do or provide *what* for *whom*.

This may look unproblematic: surely universal rights are secured by universal performance of obligations. If all agents and agencies have the

---

[9] Bentham, *An Introduction to the Principles of Morals and of Legislation*, ch. 1, para. 1, 125.

same obligations why should any further allocation of obligations be needed? However, this neat parallel is illusory. Although all agents and agencies can be bound by the same *underlying* obligations of justice, many of the more specific forms of action required to implement the rights promulgated in the Declaration and subsequent documents have to be discharged by specific agents and agencies. This may not be the case for the core obligations corresponding to liberty rights, but is generally true of obligations to provide goods and services, of obligations to construct institutions that may be relevant for poverty reduction, and also of obligations to enforce the obligations corresponding to liberty rights.

Up to a point, statist approaches to anchoring the obligations of justice may, it seems, be on the right track. They do not leave rights claims floating free, or rely on a merely abstract claim that obligations are universal, leaving it entirely open *who* is obliged to meet or secure *which* rights for *which* others. In viewing states as primary *agents of justice* realists recognise that rights are mere rhetoric unless there are counterpart obligations, and take seriously the need to assign specific tasks to institutions and individuals.

Despite these merits, statist approaches to cosmopolitan justice are now implausible. The initial assumption that states alone are *primary agents of justice* views states, and states alone, as having the will and the capabilities to discharge, delegate or assign all obligations of justice. The problem with statist approaches is not that they seek to allocate the obligations that are the counterparts to human rights, but that they allocate them in ways that may not work. Despite the supposed realism of those who assign obligations to states, their approach to international justice – and above all to development issues – is often quite unrealistic.

There are at least three quite different reasons for thinking that it is not enough to view states as primary agents of justice, which allocate and determine the obligations of other, secondary agents of justice. One reason that has been much discussed – it was all too evident in 1948 – is that many states are unjust: they lack the will to shoulder the obligations proclaimed in the Declaration and other documents. Although such states may have the competence and capacity to be primary agents of justice, they abuse that role and inflict and institutionalise forms of injustice. Tyrannies and rogue states constantly violate the rights of their inhabitants (it is often misleading to speak of them as *citizens*). They quite often violate the rights of outsiders. Even when the United Nations and 'the international community' seek to impress on such states the importance of respecting human rights, the sanctions that can be brought to bear are always limited, and often risk provoking or causing further harm to the very inhabitants whose rights are being violated. If rogue states could be reformed they would deliver justice, and only their reform can deliver full political justice. But as things are they deliver not only political but other forms of injustice.

A second reason for thinking that states are not always appropriate primary agents of justice is that many states are incapable of securing justice for their citizens or members: even if they have the will, they lack the capabilities to shoulder the obligations assigned them by the Declaration and other international documents, so cannot effectively assign obligations to secondary agents of justice or secure their compliance. Like rogue states and tyrannies, weak states and failing states (sometimes labelled 'quasi states') fail to secure the supposed rights of their inhabitants. But they typically do so in quite different ways. They may fail to enforce the law rather than enforce unjust laws or policies; they may leave individuals without redress in the face of corruption and banditry; they may fail to challenge unjust and criminal activities; they may fail to provide elementary infrastructure or health or educational services; they may fail to provide the basic conditions for economic activity, let alone prosperity or economic justice. Sometimes they cannot even exercise effective control of central state institutions, such as the police, the customs or the armed services.

A third reason for thinking that states cannot be the sole agents of justice is that even states with some capacities to secure rights, and in particular the rights of their own citizens, often find that processes of globalisation require them to make their borders more porous, thereby weakening state power and allowing powerful agents and agencies of other sorts to become more active within their borders. For example, weak states often cannot do much to control the activities of transnational corporations or of international crime within their borders, and may not succeed in regulating legitimate business either.

Given that there are many bad states, many weak states and many states too weak to prevent or regulate the activities of supposedly external bodies within their borders, the thought that justice must always begin by assigning primary obligations to states is implausible. Yet we have seen that the thought that we might say *nothing* about who holds these obligations, hence *nothing* about the allocation of specific tasks needed for justice, is also implausible. This should, I think, leave both political philosophers and thoughtful citizens with a strong feeling of unease: yet often it does not. It is not obvious why there is so little unease, but I shall offer a suggestion on that point before going on to consider briefly which agents and agencies other than states might carry obligations of justice beyond borders.

Practical questions and retrospective questions

Discussions of the moral agency of states, as of other institutions, have sometimes been viewed as implausible on the grounds that neither states nor other institutions can be held responsible or blamed for moral failures. Moral blame and fault, it is said, can be ascribed to individuals but not to institutions and collectivities. For example, individuals can feel guilt and remorse; states or groups cannot. Taken neat, this 'realist' view queries not only specific claims about the appropriate allocation of obligations, but the underlying view of agency needed for accounts of justice.

There are indeed large differences in the ways that individuals and institutions can respond to their own past failings. But a retrospective focus on past failings is not the same as a prospective focus on present and future obligations. It conflates questions about past and about future responsibility. *Practical questions* about what a given agent or agency should do are quite different from *retrospective questions* about failure and the proper response to failure.

Forward- and backward-looking ethical questions may seem inseparable if one takes a rather specific, complex and hostile view of obligations, such as the one Bernard Williams criticises in *Ethics and the Limits of Philosophy*, in a chapter where he discusses a construct that he calls 'the morality system'.[10] 'The morality system' is a way of looking at ethical requirements that links them closely to issues about blame and other retrospective attitudes. This way of looking at ethics deliberately lumps together *forward-looking practical questions* – 'What ought I, or we, or this institution to do?' – and judgemental, *retrospective questions* – 'What view should we take of those who fail to do what they ought?' The conflation is often made by those who (unlike Williams) speak mostly of *responsibilities* rather than *obligations*, who often implicitly privilege a retrospective stance.

It seems to me unfortunate to conflate these two types of questions. There may be a lot to be said about moral requirements that does not entail anything much about retrospective attitudes or action. In particular, claims about the requirements of justice may be quite distinct from claims about what should be done when these are flouted. Blaming and shaming, punishing and rewarding and other retrospective attitudes and action may

[10] Williams, *Ethics and the Limits of Philosophy*, ch. 10.

be out of place, or need to take distinctive forms, when institutional agents are concerned. We evidently take quite different views of punishing states and punishing individuals, and do not generally ascribe the full range of retrospective attitudes to past moral failure of states or of other institutions. We do not expect them to feel guilt, or regret or remorse, although we may sometimes think that they should compensate, or even apologise. Of course, it may be that these retrospective issues have also loomed too large in personal ethics. Williams may be right in holding that questions about blame and other reactive attitudes should have a more limited place in personal ethics than some suppose.

Even if retrospective questions have very little part in an account of justice, practical questions are not out of place in thinking about institutional agents: like individuals, institutions can have obligations. Most political philosophers would hold that states have obligations of justice ranging from obligations not to conduct aggressive wars to obligations to honour treaties, from obligations not to commit crimes against humanity to obligations to protect their citizens. Yet we are curiously diffident in speaking about the obligations, including the obligations of justice, of institutions other than states and those bodies that represent or derive from them (governments, international agencies). In thinking of states as the primary *agents of justice*, many would-be advocates of cosmopolitan justice maintain positions that are less distant from the realist positions they reject than one might imagine. They view non-state institutions as having only *secondary obligations of justice*, defined by their required compliance with state requirements. It is as if they viewed states alone as active global citizens and all other institutions as passive global citizens.

Agents and agencies

There is nothing very unusual or surprising about ascribing obligations to institutions, including states. Institutional agents and agencies, like individual agents, bring cognitive and decision-making capacities and capabilities to bear on choices that initiate action and affect what happens. The fact that institutional capabilities exist only with the support and participation of individuals does not show that institutions have no moral obligations. For it is equally true that many individual capabilities arise only through the action of others and through participation in institutions and practices (there is a sense in which *natural persons* have *artificial capabilities*). Both individual and institutional capabilities are determined not only by the intrinsic abilities of the agent or agency, but also by the capabilities that are constituted when intrinsic abilities are deployed using determinate resources and institutional powers. Individual and institutional capabilities can be exercised in many specific areas of life, although little is gained by trying to classify them into types of agency such as 'moral agency', 'legal agency', 'political agency' and the like. It is probably more useful to replace these ways of talking with less reifying modes of speech, and to distinguish types of constraint and capability, rather than types of agency.

We can, I suggest, ask of any agent or agency – an individual, an institution, or a collectivity – whether he or she, or we, it or they, can be bound by specific constraints or principles, such as economic constraints, or moral constraints, or prudential constraints, or professional constraints. In particular we can ask whether an agent or agency of a specified type could be bound by certain sorts of normative requirements, such as those that correspond to securing or respecting aspects of a conception of justice. The answers we can plausibly give will depend on the relationship between the propositional content of principles of justice and the actual capabilities of the putative agent or agency. Agents and agencies can only be obliged to act in ways for which they have an adequate set of capabilities. Where there is an effective primary agent of justice, the allocation of specific obligations to other agents and agencies with coherent and effective capabilities to discharge them is feasible.

So, for example, we may think that a child of fifteen could be required to study a second language, but hardly that a financial services company could be so required; that a corporation could be required to demonstrate compliance with health and safety legislation, but hardly that a five year old could be so required; that a university could be required to comply with a complex financial memorandum, but hardly that a market stall holder could be so required. And so on with banal specificity. Only if we conclude that an agent – individual, institution or collectivity – *can* carry a certain obligation does the further question arise whether it *ought* to carry that obligation. Of course, where we can establish that a specific obligation – say, an obligation not to obstruct free speech – is held by every competent agent, no *further* argument is needed to show that it falls on all agents and agencies with the capability to avoid obstructing free speech. But, as we have noted, some specific obligations that are important for justice can be discharged only by specific agents and institutions, with the competence to carry (at least parts of) the relevant task. Assuming falsely that the primary obligation of allocating other obligations of justice can always be assigned to states, even if they are weak and incompetent, indeed incapable of making and enforcing an effective allocation of the tasks of justice, is an inadequate approach to justice.

It is not enough merely to *assume* that there will always be an effective and decent state to assign obligations of justice to other institutions. Any adequate assignment must allocate specific obligations to those with the necessary powers, skills and resources (other considerations may also be relevant). Police forces with adequate resources and ordinary degrees of freedom from intimidation can be required to keep order and prevent torture: they cannot be required to provide health care. Hospitals and medical practitioners can be required not to deceive patients: they cannot be required to maintain national security. States and the governments that represent them at a given time can be required to live up to undertakings made in treaties: they cannot be required to farm the land. Individuals can be required not to assault or defraud others: they cannot be required to secure world peace. In these and other cases, obligations cannot be coherently ascribed to agents or agencies that are incapable of carrying them.

Ought and can

I have argued so far that both institutions and individuals can have obligations *if, but only if,* they have adequate capabilities to fulfil or discharge those obligations. This is a more guarded thought than some interpretations of the adage '*ought* implies *can*', which can be misinterpreted as suggesting that having used money for frivolous purposes I now am released from a debt I could otherwise have repaid. The thought that obligations presuppose capabilities for their discharge, so lapse when agents and agencies do not have and cannot acquire them, needs a lot of further explication. Nevertheless, I think there are robust links between obligations and capabilities for action: in particular, lack of capability always counts against an ascription of obligations, except where the lack is chosen. Individuals cannot be obliged to resolve the problems of world hunger, or to grow wings and fly; institutions cannot have obligations to perform tasks for which they lack capabilities.

If this is convincing, then weak states cannot coherently be required to carry tasks for which they are not competent. Nor can weak international institutions. Yet we are constantly tempted to assume that weak states and weak international bodies can carry obligations that exceed their capabilities. We often hear claims that states and the governments that represent them should solve a wide range of social problems, or that the United Nations or 'the international community' should deal with an even wider range of requirements of justice. And yet we know that weak states and the UN, and all their respective subordinate institutions, often have inadequate resources and capabilities for these tasks. The UN has not been designed or resourced to have effective powers to deal with large ranges of problems, which commentators commonly suggest it should solve. The traditional conception of states as sovereign is wholly at odds with the multiple and real limitations on the powers of many states, including the multiple ways in which (like other agents) they are dependent on other, more powerful institutions that may oppose, prevent or demand certain uses of state power. Weak states are always ill equipped to enforce or secure respect for central human rights, even for their own citizens.

Conventional responses to these points often stress the need to build up weak states and to reform international institutions. Both strategies are important. However, such reform is evidently taking a long time, and in the meantime many lives are lived and lost. Supplementary strategies may be needed. States are not the only institutional agents that can make a difference to respect for human rights. Some powerful non-state actors have capabilities that can make a difference to some aspects of justice. For example, some religious groups and institutions, some professions, some transnational corporations and some non-governmental organisations may *in certain circumstances* be able to help secure respect for certain aspects of justice, even within failing states. This is significant because some non-state actors are powerful. For present purposes I shall set religious institutions and professions aside, and consider very briefly some tasks that certain other non-state actors, in particular TNCs and NGOs, might take on.

I select these examples because TNCs and NGOs are numerous and sometimes influential in weak states, and because their activities may be important for global justice or injustice. In 2000 the United Nations Conference on Trade and Development estimated that there were over 60,000 transnational corporations compared with 37,000 in 1990. These transnational corporations had around 800,000 foreign affiliates, compared with some 170,000 foreign affiliates in 1990, and millions of suppliers and distributors.[11] A census of non-governmental organisations would also run into many tens and probably hundreds of thousands.[12]

---

[11] See Mary Robinson, UN High Commissioner for Human Rights, BP Lecture (29 November 2001), www.bp.com/centres/press/s_detail.asp?id=142.
[12] For some thoughts on the diversity of institutions that may contribute – positively or negatively – see Risse-Kappen, *Bringing Transnational Relations Back In*; O'Brien et al., *Contesting Global*

Although many NGOs have limited powers and objectives, and many are single issue organisations, and although many are highly dependent on funders and founders, some have considerable power and resources, and a few have structures of governance that allow them to act on a wide range of issues.

But here is the rub. Where states are weak, who is to allocate obligations to particular non-state actors? Where there are no (adequate) primary agents of justice, how can there be any (adequate) secondary agents of justice? An alternative view would be that, if they have the relevant capabilities, non-state actors *need not, indeed ought not, hold back on meeting their basic obligations.* In exploring this thought I am not suggesting that either TNCs or NGOs can wholly supplant states. In particular, they are unlikely to be able to assign obligations of justice across a society (any that can do this have become states within a (weak) state). They are, however, quite likely to be able to find specific ways of carrying *some* of the underlying obligations of justice that fall on all agents and agencies; and they may even sometimes find ways of taking up some tasks that are usually carried by primary agents of justice. There is no reason for thinking that the underlying obligations of justice should be neglected by non-state actors simply because no effective state enforces legal requirements or allocates specific tasks.

In powerful states with effective legislation and institutions, non-state actors may reasonably view obligations of justice as a matter of conforming to laws and requirements established and enforced by those states. They can rightly see themselves merely as *secondary agents of justice.* Not so in weak states. Where states are too weak to allocate obligations, relatively powerful non-state actors may be particularly well placed to contribute to – or to damage – aspects of justice. Attention is often given to the ways in which non-state actors may take advantage of a lack of state power to inflict injustice: those who accuse some TNCs of lack of respect for human rights clearly take it that they are potential agents of justice, and actual agents of injustice. But there are other possibilities. For example, TNCs can contribute to justice by instituting economic and social policies that bear on human rights, on environmental standards or on labour practices, and even on wider areas of life. For example, they may introduce local accounting and tendering practices that move a business culture away from corruption and towards accountability.

Governance; and Onora O'Neill, 'Agents of justice', and 'Bounded and cosmopolitan justice', respectively Chapters 11, below, 177–92, and 6, above, 99–119.

They may bear down on a culture of bribery by making it known that any 'facilitation fees' will be made public in their accounts. They may institute environmental and safety standards that go beyond local legal requirements. They may publicly refuse to take part in customary forms of nepotism and cronyism. They may strive for labour relations that meet high standards. They may make demands in these areas on their suppliers and employees. Because TNCs are often major powers in weak economies, with which many local businesses want connections, these standards can ripple beyond the contexts in which they are introduced. Some TNCs might argue that setting standards and influencing local practice has little to do with the bottom line and shareholder value; others, in particular those whose business is long term, may judge matters differently. In any case, these are not unrealistic ideas: in the last few years they have been affirmed in a growing dialogue between international business and the UN, and in the policies of certain TNCs.[13]

NGOs are often less powerful than major TNCs, although the largest have considerable powers, and some administer programmes funded by (richer) states and international organisations. It is conventional to assume that NGOs can contribute to justice more readily than TNCs, because TNCs have shareholders. Realities may be more differentiated. Some NGOs have ideological commitments, or specific agendas that can hamper their contributions to justice. As noted, some TNCs have found ranges of action where they can contribute. Where either sort of institution is capable of acting to improve justice, obligations of justice come into play.

Like TNCs, some NGOs can deploy good employment and environmental policies. More importantly, in a weak state an NGO whose funding is not local may be able to pursue employment and purchasing policies that implement standards that the government does not, indeed cannot, institute or achieve. Some NGOs may take responsibility for aspects of welfare and educational provision, even for constructing infrastructure and providing health care. Even when they acquire a major role in these and similar areas, they will not become primary agents of justice: they are unlikely to take on the task of allocating obligations to other institutions, or of enforcing compliance with that allocation. Equally they

---

[13] This is accepted UN policy: see the 1999 Global Compact initiative, which asks corporations to sign up to nine principles covering support for human rights, good labour relations and care for the environment, www.un.org/partners/business/fs1.htm. For a corporate response to the initiative see British Petroleum's policies as set out at www.bp.com/key_issues/social/human_rights.asp.

will not simply be secondary agents of justice, pursuing policies set by government and working under the authority of the relevant ministries. Rather they can use the area of discretion that lack of state power opens up to support changes that may lead towards more just and effective policies.

Where power is dispersed and in part privatised, in the sense that it is in large part non-statal, the distinction between primary and secondary agents of justice falters. Non-state actors, who in other contexts would be secondary agents of justice, may find themselves able to carry more aspects of those obligations of justice that hold for all agents and agencies, which well-functioning states orchestrate. Their contribution to justice can and ought then to take advantage of opportunities before them. They can choose to support and promote justice, to wash their hands, or to take advantage of the situation by acting unjustly. We need only think that they are obliged not to act unjustly to see that only the first of these options is acceptable.

When no available state agency can carry significant obligations of justice it can be destructive, even deluded, to assume that they will do so. It does not follow that those who think justice important should or can wait for the construction of more effective state institutions, and of a more just polity. Lives, indeed generations, may pass before that transformation is achieved. A more realistic view may be to accept that in the meanwhile some tasks *may be and should be* taken on by institutions that statist views of justice would regard merely as secondary agents of justice, lacking clear obligations in the absence of an adequate primary agent of justice. In some circumstances certain obligations of justice, and in particular of economic justice, may be carried by TNCs and NGOs. Although TNCs and NGOs cannot take on *all* the tasks that states, international agencies or political institutions might carry if they had the capabilities, they may be adequately placed to deliver *some* of them.

Is it risky for institutions like TNCs and NGOs to step beyond the roles that they would have in relatively effective states, in which they would be only secondary agents of justice? One danger might arise because many obligations of justice require exemptions from certain standard ethical requirements. We traditionally accord states and other institutions a partial exemption from certain other obligations, when they need this for discharging their obligations. A police force may be exempt *to a limited degree* from a prohibition on coercion, or a peacekeeping force exempt *to a limited degree* from a prohibition on seizure of property, but only because these exemptions are needed if their broader obligations are to be met. A government may be exempt *to a limited degree* from a general prohibition on hoarding in a food emergency, but only because it has to look to the equity and feasibility of maintaining food distribution. Could we accept that a TNC or an NGO should have any exemption from such requirements where they shoulder obligations of justice?

It may be helpful to consider why we allow exemptions from certain moral constraints. In general we do so *if, but only if,* those exemptions are needed for carrying obligations. For example, we allow parents certain powers over their children *because* they are required to care for them (absentee parents lose these powers). We allow the state certain exemptions from obligations not to coerce *because* it is responsible for enforcing law. Entitlement to exemptions is related to task, not to status. Where non-state actors take on certain obligations of justice the same standards are relevant. An NGO that is organising food distribution need be no less exempt from restrictions on hoarding than a government that is handling food delivery itself.

Non-state actors, including TNCs and NGOs, are in practice likely to rely more on negotiation and persuasion, backed by the real threat of withdrawing business or benefits, rather than on replication of the ordinary structure of state powers. Both sorts of non-state actor often adapt work in tandem with weak states. Although there will always be some aspects of justice, including political justice, to which they can contribute rather little, there will be others, including economic justice, to which they often can and ought to contribute a lot.

Reconfiguring realism

Political philosophers and others who assign extensive obligations to states have often done so in the name of *realism*. Their thought is often that states enjoy sovereignty, hence states and states alone have the power and the obligation to deliver justice, at least within their own boundaries, and to ensure that others respect rights within those boundaries. In international affairs, the thought has often been parallel. States and states alone have the power to establish and maintain a social and political order that lives up the demands of the Universal Declaration, or an economic system that secures adequate food, water, shelter and basic health care for all: non-state actors are powerless. This is a most unrealistic form of realism, and increasingly unrealistic as globalisation reconfigures power.

If we are to be seriously realistic, we need to think about the full range of agents and agencies that can carry obligations, and can *if they choose* contribute to securing wider respect for certain rights. The obligations that institutions and individuals carry can never exceed their capabilities. Those capabilities are seldom adequate to secure the full range of rights proclaimed in the Universal Declaration. If states alone could initiate an increase in justice, then the situation of those in weak states would often be profoundly depressing: where institutions and individuals are weak there will be few competent obligation-bearers, few obligations will be secure, and few rights will be respected. In a weak state whose revenue raising institutions are inadequate there will be no effective rights to tax-supported welfare systems; in a failing state where the rule of law is fragile there will be no effective obligations to bring criminals to justice – and so on.

But we need not take this passive view of state capability failure as making entitlement failure for others inevitable. It is often beside the point – a reversion to retrospective thinking about blame rather than practical thinking about obligations – to respond to such cases simply by reasserting that rights have been violated. In these cases neither individuals nor institutions had the requisite ranges of capabilities to carry these obligations. There may be a future time at which institutions with more extensive and reliable capabilities are established, when more extensive obligations can be discharged, and when wider ranges of rights can be respected and even secured. Persistent ascription of obligations to meet rights to an institutional structure that lacks the capabilities to discharge them replaces forward-looking practical reasoning with blame: it is wholly unrealistic.

A more realistic approach might be to raise questions about obligations to construct, improve and strengthen the capabilities of institutions and of individuals, and in particular about the need to think about the allocation of obligations among individuals and institutions. Many distinguished approaches to this topic have been exclusively statist or quasi-statist, often because they have looked mainly at questions of political justice. It may, I believe, be more convincing – and more realistic – to look at matters more opportunistically. If we allow that whatever capabilities there are, including those held by non-state actors including TNCs and NGOs, may be and should be deployed not only to avoid injustice, but to contribute where possible to a more just social order, then there may be much to be done even where states are weak and failing and cannot (in the short run) achieve either definitive allocations of the obligations of justice or any adequate form of political justice.

The realism about international justice – realism with a rather small 'r' – that I am commending does not mean that those whose lives are led in weak states that cannot secure their rights have fewer rights *in the abstract* than those in strong states. They have exactly and only those rights for which sound arguments can be given, as do those in strong states. (There is little reason for expecting sound arguments to support all and only those rights that have been promulgated in the Universal Declaration or any other document.)[14] What those in strong states have, and those in weak states lack, is *justiciable rights*, where obligations to respect and enforce are allocated to agents with the necessary capabilities. What those in weak states need is a process of institution building by which justiciable rights are increasingly secured. Much of this process may indeed aim to strengthen state institutions, and to secure a greater degree of political justice, which in turn may deliver economic justice. But the task does not have to await the emergence of competent and politically just states. There may be additional routes towards greater justice if obligations of justice can be discharged without waiting for a definitive allocation or enforcement of tasks. Where non-state actors can contribute to justice, fundamental obligations that in other circumstances are secured by compliance with state requirements demand that they do so. If we take the universalism of obligations as seriously as we have often taken the universalism of rights, we need to look realistically at actual agents and agencies, with their actual powers and vulnerabilities. We do not need to assume that non-state actors will be paralysed in weak states, or that all progress to justice must be endlessly postponed until more competent and just states emerge.

---

[14] James Griffin, 'Discrepancies between the best philosophical account of human rights and the International Law of Human Rights', Presidential Address, *Proceedings of the Aristotelian Society* (2001), 1–28. See Chapter 7 'Pluralism, positivism and the justification of human rights', above, 120–33.

CHAPTER II

Agents of justice[1]

Cosmopolitan principles and state institutions

Many of the best-known conceptions of justice are avowedly cosmopolitan – when considered in the abstract.[2] They propose basic principles of justice that are to hold without restriction. Whether we look back to Stoic cosmopolitanism, to medieval natural law theory, to Kantian world citizenship or to twentieth-century theory and practice – John Rawls and the UN *Universal Declaration of Human Rights* of 1948, for example – the scope of *principles* of justice is said to be universal or cosmopolitan, encompassing all humans. As is well known, such principles have been compromised in various ways, for example by the exclusion or partial exclusion of slaves, women, labourers or the heathen from the scope of justice; these exclusions have been a focus of much debate, and recent cosmopolitan conceptions of justice have condemned them.

However, there are other less evident exclusions created by the commonplace assumption that cosmopolitan principles are to be instituted in and through a system of states. Many recent challenges have argued that the exclusions that borders create are further injustices, and that they should be addressed by abolishing borders, or at least by reducing the obstacles they present to movements of people, goods or capital. Some conclude that justice requires the construction of a world state;[3] others that

---

[1] 'Agents of justice', *Metaphilosophy* 32 (2001), 180–95; and in Thomas Pogge, *Global Justice* (Oxford: Blackwell, 2001), 188–203.

[2] Some relativists, communitarians and nationalists are avowedly anti-cosmopolitan, but often with less startling conclusions than the conceptual resources of their starting points might permit.

[3] There are many versions of the thought that suprastatal or global governance should replace states, often if somewhat inaccurately seen as a Kantian position. See, for example, Habermas, 'Kant's idea of perpetual peace' Thomas Mertens, 'Cosmopolitanism and citizenship: Kant against Habermas', *European Journal of Philosophy* 4 (1996), 328–47; and Onora O'Neill, 'Cosmopolitanism then and now' in Stefano Bacin, Alfredo Ferrarin, Claudio La Rocca and Margit Ruffing (eds.), *Kant und die Philosophie in weltbürgerlicher Absicht: Akten des XI. Kant-Kongresses* (Berlin: Walter de Gruyter, 2013), 357–68.

borders should be (more) open to the movement of peoples;[4] others that powerful regional and global institutions can mitigate or redress inequalities that states and borders create.[5] I am at least partly sceptical about those attempts to realise cosmopolitan principles by means of global institutions without showing what is to prevent global governance from degenerating into global tyranny and global injustice. Big may not always be beautiful, and institutional cosmopolitanism may not always be the best route to universal justice. It is worth exploring a more realistic, and also (I hope) a more robust view of the plurality of agents of justice that might play some part in institutionalising cosmopolitan principles of justice.

A plausible initial view of agents of justice might distinguish primary *agents of justice* with capacities to determine how principles of justice are to be institutionalised within a certain domain from *other, secondary agents of justice*. Primary agents of justice may construct other agents or agencies with specific competencies: they may assign powers to and build capacities in individual agents, or they may build institutions – agencies – with certain powers and capacities to act. Sometimes they may, so to speak, build from scratch; more often they reassign or adjust tasks and responsibilities among existing agents and agencies, and control and limit the ways in which they may act without incurring sanctions. Primary agents of justice typically have some means of coercion, by which they at least partially control the action of other agents and agencies, which can therefore at most be secondary agents of justice. Typically, secondary agents of justice are thought to contribute to justice mainly by meeting the demands of primary agents, most evidently by conforming to any legal requirements they establish.

There is no fundamental reason why a primary agent of justice should not be an individual, for example a prince or leader; and in some traditional societies that has been the case. Equally there is no fundamental reason why a primary agent of justice should not be a group with little formal structure, for example a group of elders or chieftains, or even a constitutional convention; and in other instances this has been the case. However, in modern societies institutions with a considerable measure of formal structure, and pre-eminently among them states, have been seen as the primary agents of justice. All too often they have also been agents of injustice.

[4] E.g. Joseph Carens, 'Aliens and citizens: the case for open borders', *Review of Politics* 49 (1987), 251–73.
[5] Thomas Pogge, 'An egalitarian law of peoples', *Philosophy and Public Affairs* 23 (1994), 195–224.

A low-key view of the matter might be simply this: it is hard to institutionalise principles of justice, and although states quite often do not do very well as primary agents of justice, they are the best primary agents available, and so indispensable for justice. Institutions with a monopoly of the legitimate use of coercion within a given, bounded territory often behave unjustly, both to those who inhabit the territory and to outsiders, but we have not found a better way of institutionalising justice. On such views the remedy for state injustice is not the dismantling of states and of the exclusions their borders create, but a degree of reform and democratisation coupled with international (that is interstatal) agreements.

This very general response seems to me to take no account of the fact that states may fail as primary agents of justice for a number of different reasons. Sometimes they have the power to act as primary agents of justice, but use that power not to achieve justice, but for other ends. When these ends include a great deal of injustice we often speak of *rogue states*; and these are common enough. But on other occasions states fail because they are too weak to act as primary agents of justice: although they are spoken of as states, even as sovereign states, this is no more than a courtesy title for structures that are often no more than *dependent states* or *quasi-states*.

These two types of failure pose quite different problems for other agents of justice. Powerful rogue states confront all other agents and agencies with terrible problems. Compliance with their requirements contributes to injustice rather than to justice; non-compliance leads to danger and destruction. These problems and conflicts formed a staple of twentieth-century political philosophy, in which discussions of the circumstances that justify or require revolution and resistance against established states, or non-compliance with state requirements, or at least conscientious objection, have been major themes. But when failure of supposed primary agents of justice arises not from abuse but from lack of state power, the problems faced by other agents and agencies are quite different. In such cases it is often left indeterminate what the law requires, and the costs of complying with such laws as exist are increased, if only because others do not even aim to comply. Unsurprisingly, many of the stratagems to which agents and agencies turn when states are weak are themselves unjust. Where agents and agencies cannot rely on an impartially enforced legal code they may find that in order to go about their daily business they are drawn into bribery and nepotism, into buying protection and making corrupt deals, and so become complicit in riding roughshod over requirements of justice. If the agents and agencies that could in better circumstances be secondary agents of justice are reduced to these sorts of action in weak states, why should we continue to think of them as agents of justice?

Cosmopolitan rhetoric and state action in the Universal Declaration

These issues are often obscured because much of the cosmopolitan rhetoric of contemporary discussions of justice is unclear about the agents and agencies on which the burdens of justice are to fall. Nowhere is this more evident than in the text of the *Universal Declaration of Human Rights* of 1948. In this brief and celebrated text, nations, peoples, states, societies, countries are variously gestured to as agents against whom individuals may have rights. Little is said about any differences between these varying types of agent, or about their capacities and vulnerabilities, and there is no systematic allocation of obligations of different sorts to agents and agencies of specific types. If we inhabited a world in which all states were strictly nation-states, and in which no nation spread across more than one state, or formed more than one society, the failure to distinguish these terms and the entities to which these terms refer might matter rather less. But that is not our world. Few states are nation-states; many nations spread across a number of states; the individuation of societies, peoples and countries is notoriously complex. It may seem a scandal that the Universal Declaration is so cavalier about identifying agents of justice.[6]

Even if it is cavalier, I think that it is fairly easy to understand why the framers of the Universal Declaration felt no need for precision. The Declaration approaches justice by proclaiming rights. It proclaims what is to be received, what entitlements everyone is to have; but it says very little about which agents and agencies must do what if these rights are to be secured. Like other charters and declarations of rights, the Universal Declaration looks at justice from a recipient's perspective: its focus is on recipience and rights rather than on action and obligations. Hence it is about rights and right-holders that the Declaration is forthrightly cosmopolitan. It identifies the relevant recipients clearly: rights are ascribed to 'all human beings' (Art. 1), and more explicitly to 'everyone ... without distinction of any kind, such as race, colour, sex, language, religion, political or other opinion, national or social origin, property, birth or other

---

[6] I suspect that in the middle of the twentieth century it was common to speak of *states* as *nation-states*, and then to refer to them simply as *nations*. See Hans J. Morgenthau, *Politics among Nations: The Struggle for Power and Peace* (New York: Knopf, 1948, rev. 1978). For the influence of this book see John A. Vasquez, *The Power of Power Politics: From Classical Realism to Neo-Traditionalism* (Cambridge University Press, 1988).

status ... [and] no distinction shall be made on the basis of the political, jurisdictional or international status of the country or territory to which a person belongs, whether it be independent, trust, non-self-governing, or under any other limitation of sovereignty' (Art. 2). Human rights are to reach into all jurisdictions, however diverse.

So far, so cosmopolitan: the universalist aspirations are unequivocal. However, since nothing is said about the allocation of obligations to meet these aspirations, it is unclear whether these universal rights are matched and secured by universal obligations, or by obligations held by some but not by all agents and agencies. This is a more complex matter than may appear. Whereas traditional liberty rights for all have to be matched by universal obligations to respect those rights (if any agent or agency is exempt from that obligation, the right is compromised), other universal rights cannot be secured by assigning identical obligations universally to all agents and agencies. Universal rights to goods and services, to status and participation, cannot be delivered by universal action. For these rights the allocation of obligations matters, and some means of designing and enforcing effective allocations is required if any ascription of rights is to have practical import.

The Universal Declaration in fact resolves this problem by taking a non-universalist view of the allocation of obligations. For example, Articles 13–15 reveal clearly that the primary agents of justice are to be states (referred to in several different ways).[7] In these articles the Declaration obliquely acknowledges that different agents are to be responsible for securing a given right for different persons, depending on the state of which they are members. The import of these articles is probably clearest if they are taken in reverse order.

The two clauses of Article 15 read

1 Everyone has a right to a nationality.
2 No one shall be arbitrarily deprived of his nationality nor denied the right to change his nationality.

Evidently the term 'nationality' is not here being used in the sense that is more common today, to indicate a specific ethnic or cultural sense of identity. If the Declaration used 'having a nationality' to mean 'having an ethnic or cultural identity' it would not need to prohibit deprivation of nationality, or to assert rights to change of one's nationality: it would need rather to speak of rights to express, foster or maintain one's nationality. 'Having a nationality' as it is understood in the Declaration is a matter of

---

[7] On this see also Chapter 12 'The dark side of human rights', below, 193–207.

being a member of one or another state:[8] such membership is indeed something of which people may be deprived, and which they can change, and which some people – stateless people – lack.

A right to a nationality, in the sense of being a member of some state, is pivotal to the Declaration's implicit conception of the agents of justice. It is by this move that a plurality of bounded states – explicitly anti-cosmopolitan institutions – is transformed into the primary agents of justice, who are to deliver universal rights. This becomes explicit in Articles 13 and 14, which make the following contrasting claims:

Art. 13

1 Everyone has the right to freedom of movement and residence within the borders of each state.
2 Everyone has the right to leave any country, including his own, and to return to his country.

Art. 14

1 Everyone has the right to seek and enjoy in other countries asylum from persecution.
2 This right may not be invoked in the case of prosecutions genuinely arising from non-political crimes or from acts contrary to the purposes and principles of the United Nations.

The rights proclaimed in Articles 13 and 14 make it clear that the Declaration assumes a plurality of bounded states and exclusive citizenship. It is only in a world with this structure that it makes sense to distinguish the rights of freedom of movement, of exit and of re-entry that an individual is to enjoy in whichever state recognises him or her as a member, from the quite different right to asylum which a persecuted individual may have in states of which he or she is not a member. Rights, it appears, may legitimately be differentiated at boundaries: my rights in my own state will not and need not be the same as my rights in another state. In a world without bounded states these distinctions would make no sense. Here it becomes quite explicit that the Declaration views states as the primary

---

[8] Evidently the framers of the Declaration could not speak of *citizenship*, since they were working in a world in which there were numerous colonies, trust territories and dependent territories whose inhabitants were not (full) citizens. Even today, when there are fewer such territories, the term *citizenship* would be inappropriate, since there are many members of states who do not enjoy full citizenship status, including minors and resident aliens, whose rights are nevertheless important.

agents of justice: a cosmopolitan view of rights is to be spliced with a statist view of obligations.

The statism of the Declaration should not surprise us. Its preamble addresses Member States who 'have pledged themselves to achieve, in co-operation with the United Nations, the promotion of universal respect for and observance of human rights and fundamental freedoms'. Yet since states cannot implement justice, let alone global justice, without constructing and coordinating many other agents and agencies, it is a matter for deep regret that the Declaration is so opaque about allocating the obligations of justice. The reason for regret is that in the end obligations rather than rights are the active aspects of justice: a proclamation of rights will be indeterminate and ineffective unless obligations to respect and secure those rights are assigned to specific, identifiable agents and agencies which are able to discharge those obligations.

If the significant obligations that secure rights and justice are to be assigned primarily to states, much would have been gained by making this wholly explicit. In particular it would have exposed the problems created by rogue states and weak states, and the predicaments created for other agents and agencies when states fail to support justice. Such explicitness might also have forestalled the emergence of the free-floating rhetoric of rights that now dominates much public discussion of justice, focuses on recipience and blandly overlooks the need for a robust and realistic account of agents of justice who are to carry the counterpart obligations. This rhetoric has (in my view) become a prominent and often damaging feature of contemporary discussions of justice.

Cosmopolitan rhetoric and state action: Rawls's conception of justice

It is not only in the *Universal Declaration of Human Rights* and the attendant culture of the Human Rights Movement that we find cosmopolitan thinking about justice linked to statist accounts of the primary agents of justice. This combination is also standard in more theoretical and philosophical writing that assigns priority to universal rights: as in declarations of rights, so in theories of rights, giving priority to the perspective of recipience distracts attention from the need to determine which agents of justice are assigned which tasks. More surprisingly, statist views of the primary agents of justice can also be found in theoretical and philosophical writing on justice that does *not* prioritise rights.

A notable example of hidden statism, but without an exclusive focus on rights, is John Rawls's political philosophy. This is the more surprising

because Rawls hardly ever refers to states, and then often with some
hostility. He claims throughout his writings that the context of justice is
a 'bounded society', a perpetually continuing scheme of cooperation which
persons enter only by birth and leave only by death, and which is self-
sufficient.⁹ In his later writing he increasingly relies on a *political*
conception of bounded societies, seeing them as domains within which
citizens engage in public reason, which he defines as 'citizens' reasoning in
the public forum about constitutional essentials and basic questions of
justice'. He consequently views *peoples* rather than states as the primary
agents of justice. Yet his account of peoples is surprisingly state-like:

> Liberal peoples do, however, have their fundamental interests as permitted
> by their conceptions of right and justice. They seek to protect their
> territory, to ensure the security and safety of their citizens, and to preserve
> their free political institutions and the liberties and free culture of their civil
> society.¹⁰

However, Rawls maintains that in speaking of a bounded society and its
citizens he is *not* speaking of a territorial state. This is surely puzzling: if
nobody is to enter except by birth or leave except by death, the boundaries
of the polity must be policed; the use of force must be coordinated, indeed
monopolised in the territory in question. If there is a monopoly of the use
of legitimate force for a bounded territory we are surely talking of entities
that fit the classical Weberian definition of a state.

The reason why Rawls so emphatically denies that states are the
primary agents of justice appears to me to be that he has in mind one
specific and highly contentious conception of the state. In *Law of Peoples*
he explicitly rejects the realist conception of state that has been of great
influence in international relations. He sees states as 'anxiously concerned with their power – their capacity (military, economic, diplomatic)
to influence other states – and always guided by their basic interests'.¹¹
He points out that

---

⁹ This formulation is found from the first pages of Rawls's *A Theory of Justice*, and remains constant in
Political Liberalism and *The Law of Peoples*. In the latter two works he emphasises not only bounded
societies but liberal democracy and universal citizenship, which together form the basis for his
conception of 'political' justification.

¹⁰ Rawls, *The Law of Peoples*, 29. Note also the following passage: 'The point of the institution of
property is that, unless a definite agent is given responsibility for maintaining an asset . . . that asset
tends to deteriorate. In this case the asset is the people's territory and its capacity to support them *in
perpetuity*; and the agent is the people themselves as politically organized', *ibid*. 39.

¹¹ *Ibid*. 28.

What distinguishes peoples from states – and this is crucial – is that just peoples are fully prepared to grant the very same proper respect and recognition to other peoples as equal.[12]

In Rawls's view states cannot be adequate agents of justice because they necessarily act out of self-interest: they are rational but cannot be reasonable.

However, this supposedly realist conception of the state is only one among various possibilities. Rawls's choice of *peoples* rather than *states* as the agents whose deliberations are basic to justice beyond boundaries is, I think, motivated in large part by an inaccurate assumption that states *must* fit a certain 'realist' paradigm, hence are unfit to be primary (or other) agents of justice. Yet states, *as we have actually known them* do not fit that paradigm particularly well.[13] The conception of states and governments as having limited powers, and as bound by numerous fundamental principles in addition to rational self-interest, is part and parcel of the liberal tradition of political philosophy, and central to contemporary international politics. States *as they have really existed and still exist* never had and never have unlimited sovereignty, internal or external, and have never been exclusively motivated by self-interest.[14] States *as they actually exist today* are committed by numerous treaty obligations to a limited conception of sovereignty, to restrictions on the ways in which they may treat other states, and by demands that they respect human rights. Peoples, *as they once lived* before the emergence of state structures probably did not have bounded territories; those peoples who developed the means to negotiate with other peoples, to keep outsiders out and to make agreements, did so by forming states and governments by which to secure bounded territories.

The motive of self-interest ascribed to states or other agencies in would-be realist thinking is so open to multiple interpretations that I do not believe that we are likely to get far in trying to determine whether agents or agencies – whether states or companies or individuals – are or are not

---

[12] *Ibid.* 35.

[13] Theorists of international relations acknowledge that many of the states we see around us fall far short of the realist paradigm of statehood: they speak of quasi-states and dependent states. Rawls acknowledges that realism provides a poor account of state action – yet leaves realists in possession of the concept of the state. *Ibid.* 46.

[14] A recent comment runs: 'From the days of E. H. Carr . . . on, realists have claimed that their theories are empirically accurate, robust and fruitful, empirically sound guides to practice, and explanatorily powerful . . . But what has been found is that the realist paradigm has not done well on any of these criteria' (Vasquez, *The Power of Power Politics*, 372). Although a 'revealed' (ascriptive, interpretive) view of self-interest may seemingly rescue the claim that states act only out of self-interest from this and other empirical defects, this is a Pyrrhic victory. As with analogous moves in discussions of individual motivation, a 'realist' insistence that state action *must* be self-interested survives only by offering a trivialising and unfalsifiable interpretation of self-interested motivation.

always motivated by self-interest, or *necessarily* motivated by self-interest, however interpreted. I suspect that ascriptions of self-interest often have a plausible ring only because they are open both to a tautologous and to an empirical interpretation. If the empirical interpretation of self-interested motivation fails for agents and agencies of any sort, the tautologous interpretation lingers in the background sustaining an unfalsifiable version of 'realism' by which the action of states (or companies, or individuals) is taken to define and reveal their motivation and their interests.

Once we have shed the assumption that all states (or other agents and agencies) must conform to this 'realist' model, we can turn in a more open-minded way to consider the capacities for action that agents and agencies of various sorts, including states, actually have. In particular, we may then be in a position to say something about predicaments that arise when some states are too weak to act as primary agents of justice.

States as agents of justice: capabilities and motivation

Once we set aside the 'realist' paradigm of state agency, many questions open up. Perhaps states are agents of a more versatile sort than 'realists' assert, and capable of a wider range of motivation than self-interest (as has been argued by various 'idealist' theorists of international relations). Perhaps states are not the only agents of significance in building justice: various non-state actors may also contribute significantly to the construction of justice. Perhaps a system of states can develop capacities for action that individual states lack.

These are very large questions, and the literature on international relations has dealt in part with many of them. However, for the present I want to take a quite restricted focus, with the thought that it may be useful to work towards an account of agents of justice *by attending specifically to their powers rather than to their supposed motives.*

A focus on the powers of states may *seem* to return us to classical discussions of sovereignty. That is not my intention. An analysis of *state power* is not an account of *state powers*; nor is an analysis of the *power* of other agents and agencies an account of their *powers*. The powers of all agents and agencies, including states, are multiple, varied and often highly specific. These specificities are worth attending to, since it is these capacities that are constitutive of agency, and without agency any account of obligations (and hence any account of rights or of justice) will be no more than a gesture.

Amartya Sen has introduced the useful notion of a *capability* into development economics; it can also be helpful in discussing the powers of states, and of other agents and agencies.[15] Agents' capabilities are not to be identified with their individual capacities, or with their aggregate power. An agent or agency, considered in the abstract, may have various capacities or abilities to act. For example, a person may have the capacity to work as an agricultural labourer, or an ability to organise family resources to last from harvest to harvest; a development agency may have the capacity to distribute resources to the needy in a given area. However, faced with a social and economic structure that provides no work for agricultural labourers or no resources for a given family to subsist on or for an agency to distribute, these capacities lie barren. From the point of view of achieving justice – however we conceptualise it – agents and agencies must dispose not only of capacities which they could deploy if circumstances were favourable, but of *capabilities*, that is to say of *specific, effectively resourced capacities which they can deploy in actual circumstances*. Capabilities are to capacities or abilities as effective demand is to demand: it is the specific capabilities of agents and agencies in specific situations, rather than their abstract capacities or their aggregate power, that are relevant to determining which obligations of justice they can hold and discharge – and which they will be unable to discharge. The value of focusing on capabilities is that this foregrounds an explicit concern with the action and with the results that agents or agencies can achieve in actual circumstances, so provides a *seriously realistic reference point for normative reasoning*, including normative claims about rights.

A focus on capabilities quickly reveals how defective weak states may be as agents of justice, and makes vivid why it is important also to think about other possible agents of justice, particularly but not only in weak states. Weak states may simply lack the human, material and organisational resources to do very much to secure or improve justice within their boundaries. They may lack capabilities to regulate or influence the action of certain other agents or agencies, or to affect what goes on in certain regions of the state, or to achieve greater justice. They may fail to

---

[15] For present purposes I do not intend to discuss the links which Sen draws between capabilities and their actualisation in an agent's functionings, or his arguments to identify which functionings, hence which capabilities, are valuable. See Amartya Sen, *Development as Freedom* (Oxford University Press, 1999), and 'Capability and well being' in Martha C. Nussbaum and Amartya Sen, *The Quality of Life* (Oxford: Clarendon Press, 1993), 30–53. The usefulness of a focus on capabilities does not depend on basing it on one rather than another theory of value, or one rather than another account of justice, rights or obligations.

represent the interests of their citizens adequately in international fora, and agree to damaging or unsupportable treaties or loans. They may lack the capabilities to end or prevent rebellions and forms of feudalism, insurgency and secession, banditry and lawlessness, or to levy taxes or enforce such law as they enact in the face of powerful clans or corrupt factions. Often when we speak of such entities as 'states' the term is used in a merely formal sense, as a largely honorific appellation, and it is widely acknowledged that they lack capabilities that would be indispensable in any primary agent of justice.

Sometimes the lack of capabilities of states arises because other agents and agencies within or beyond the state have usurped those capabilities. The weakness of the Colombian state across many years reflected the military and enforcement capabilities acquired by Colombian drug cartels; the weakness of a number of African states reflects the military capabilities achieved by secessionist and insurgent groups and movements within those states. However, even in cases where non-state agents have acquired selected state-like capabilities, which they use to wreak injustice, they do not enjoy the range of capabilities held by states that succeed in being primary agents of justice. When weak states lack capabilities to be primary agents of justice, there is usually no other agent or agency that has acquired these missing capabilities. The fact that a state is incapable of securing the rule of law, or the collection of taxes, or the provision of welfare within its terrain is no guarantee that any other agent or agency has gathered together these missing capabilities. An unpropitious bundling or dispersal of capabilities may simply leave both a weak state and the agencies that are active within and around it incapable of securing (a greater measure of) justice.

When states fail as agents of justice the problem is therefore not always a general lack of power. It is rather a lack of the specific ranges of capabilities needed for the delivery of justice, and specifically for the coordination and enforcement of action and obligations by other agents and agencies. Unfortunately, weak states often retain considerable capabilities for injustice even when wholly unable to advance justice. In these circumstances other agents and agencies may become important agents of justice.

Non-state actors as agents of justice

The odd phrase 'non-state actor' as currently used in international relations is revealing. It identifies certain types of agent and agency *by reference to what they are not*. In an area of inquiry in which states have classically been thought of as the primary agents (not only of justice), the phrase 'non-state actor' has been invented to refer to a range of agencies that are neither states nor the creations of states. Etymology might suggest that all agents and agencies other than states – from individual human agents to international bodies, to companies and non-governmental institutions – should count as non-state actors. In fact the term is usually used more selectively, to refer to institutions that are neither states, nor international in the sense of being interstatal or intergovernmental, nor directly subordinate to individual states or governments, *but which interact across borders of states or state institutions.* Some non-state actors may acquire capabilities that make them significant agents of justice – or of injustice.

Examples of non-state actors in this relatively restricted sense include (at least) those *international non-governmental organisations that operate across borders* (INGOs), *transnational or multinational companies or corporations* (TNCs/MNCs), and *numerous transnational social, political and epistemic movements that operate across borders* (sometimes known as 'global social movements' or GSMs).[16] Here I shall refer to a few features of certain INGOs, TNCs and GMSs, but say nothing about other types of non-state actors.

Nobody would doubt that some non-state actors aspire to be and sometimes become agents of justice; others become or may become agents of injustice. However, their mode of operation in weak states is quite different from the standard activities of secondary agents of justice. Non-state actors do not generally contribute to justice by complying with state requirements: in weak states those requirements maybe ill-defined; and where adequately defined, compliance may contribute to injustice. Sometimes INGOs seek to contribute to justice in weak states by helping or badgering them into instituting aspects of justice which a state with more capabilities might have instituted without such assistance or goading. INGOs may do this by mobilising external powers (other states, international bodies, public opinion, GSMs), by advocacy work that assists weak states in negotiations with others, by mobilising First World consumer power, or by campaigning for and funding specific reforms that contribute to justice in a weak or unjust state. The typical mission and raison d'être of INGOs is to contribute to specific transformations of states, governments and polities; quite often to a single issue or objective.

---

[16] For discussion of some ways in which global social movements may act transnationally see O'Brien et al., *Contesting Global Governance.*

Although INGOs cannot themselves become primary agents of justice, they can contribute to justice in specific ways in specific domains. Even when they cannot do much to make states more just, they may be able to help prevent weak states from becoming wholly dysfunctional or more radically unjust. Their difficulties and successes in doing so are not different in kind from the long and distinguished tradition of reform movements and lobbies within states, whose ambitions for justice do not extend beyond improvements within (certain aspects of) that particular polity or state.

Some non-state actors, in particular INGOs, may contribute to justice precisely *because* the states in which they operate are relatively weak, *because* they can act opportunistically and secure an unusual degree of access to some key players, *because* they are not restricted by some of the constraints that might face non-state actors in states with greater and better coordinated capabilities. Their successes and failures as agents of justice are therefore analogous *neither* to the achievements and failure of stronger states with the capabilities to be primary agents of justice, *nor* to those of secondary agents of justice within stronger states.

Other non-state actors are not defined by their reforming aims, and it may seem that they are less likely to be able to contribute to justice in weak states. For example, TNCs are often thought of as having constitutive aims that prevent them from being agents of justice at all, except insofar as they are secondary agents of justice in states that have enacted reasonably just laws. If this were correct, TNCs could not contribute to justice in weak states where laws are ill defined or ill enforced, and the very notion of compliance with law may be indeterminate in many respects. Companies, we are often reminded, have shareholders; their constitutive aim is (controversially) said to be only to improve their bottom line. How then could they be concerned about justice, except insofar as justice requires conformity to law?

This view of TNCs seems to me sociologically simplistic. Major TNCs are economically and socially complex institutions of considerable power; their specific capabilities and constitutive aims are typically diverse and multiple. To be sure they have to worry about their shareholders (even institutions that lack shareholders still need to balance their books and worry about the bottom line). Yet a supposition that companies must be concerned *only* about maximising profits seems to me on a par with the 'realist' supposition that states can *only* act out of self-interest. The notion of the *responsible company* or *responsible corporation* is no more incoherent than the notion of the liberal state; equally the notion of the *rogue company* or *rogue corporation* is no more incoherent than that of the rogue state. If these notions *seem* incoherent it may be because claims that some company pursues only economic self-interest (understood as shareholder interest) are shielded from empirical refutation by inferring interests from whatever is done: *whatever* corporate behaviour actually takes place is defined as pursuit of perceived shareholder interest.[17]

Much popular and professional literature on TNCs wholly disavows this trivialising conception of the pursuit of self-interest, and accepts that TNC action can be judged for its contribution to justice – or to injustice. For example, TNCs have often been criticised for using their considerable ranges of capabilities to get away with injustice: for dumping hazardous wastes in states too weak to achieve effective environmental protection; for avoiding taxation by placing headquarters in tax havens; for avoiding safety legislation by registering vessels under 'flags of convenience'; or by placing dangerous production processes in areas without effective worker protection legislation. If the critics who point to these failings *really* believed that TNCs cannot but profit maximise, these objections would be pointless: in fact they assume (more accurately) that major TNCs can choose among a range of policies and actions. Yet surprisingly little is said – outside corporate promotional literature – about the action of companies that insist on decent environmental standards although no law requires them to do so, or on decent standards of employment practice or of safety at work even where they could get away with less. In some cases TNCs operating in weak states with endemic corruption may go further to advance justice, for example by refusing complicity with certain sorts of corruption or by insisting on widening the benefits of investment and production in ways that local legislation does not require and that local elites resist.

These commonplace facts suggest that it is more important to consider the capabilities rather than the (supposed) motivation of TNCs. Many TNCs are evidently *capable* of throwing their considerable weight in the direction either of greater justice, or of the status quo, or of greater injustice. In many cases it may be a moot point whether their motivation in supporting greater justice is a concern for justice, a concern to avoid the reputational disadvantages of condoning or inflicting injustice, or a

---

[17] The UN evidently does not see business in this way, as is shown both by Kofi Annan's *Global Compact* initiative and by the UN's adoption of the 'Ruggie Principles' for business. See John Ruggie, *Just Business: Multinational Corporations and Human Rights* (New York: W. W. Norton, 2013).

concern for the bottom line *simpliciter*. However, unclarity about the motivation of TNCs does not much matter, given that we have few practical reasons for trying to assess the quality of TNC motivation. What does matter is what TNCs can and cannot do, the capabilities that they can and cannot develop.

If these thoughts are plausible, it is plain that TNCs can have and can develop ranges of capabilities to contribute both to greater justice and to greater injustice. Shareholder interests are of course important to all TNCs, but they underdetermine both what a given TNC can and what it will do. Fostering justice in specific ways is an entirely possible corporate aim; so unfortunately is contributing to injustice. Although TNCs may be ill-constructed to substitute for the full range of contributions that states can (but often fail to) make to justice, there are many contributions that they can make, especially when states are weak. Corporate power can be great enough to provide the constellation of individuals and groups with influence in weaker states with powerful, even compelling, reasons to show greater respect for human rights, to improve environmental and employment standards, to accept more open patterns of public discourse or to reduce forms of social and religious discrimination. Corporate power can be used to support and strengthen reasonably just states. Equally TNCs can accept the status quo, fall in with local elites and with patterns of injustice, and use their powers to keep things as they are – or indeed to make them more unjust.

In the end, it seems to me, any firm distinction between primary and secondary agents has a place only where there are powerful and relatively just states, which successfully discipline and regulate other agents and agencies within their boundaries. But once we look at the realities of life where states are weak, any simple division between primary and secondary agents of justice blurs. Justice has to be built by a diversity of agents and agencies that possess and lack varying ranges of capabilities, and can contribute to justice – or to injustice – in more diverse ways than is generally acknowledged in those approaches that have built on supposedly realist, but in fact highly ideologised, views of the supposed motivation of potential agents of justice.

CHAPTER 12

The dark side of human rights[1]

In his *Reflections on the Revolution in France* Edmund Burke asks

> What is the use of discussing a man's abstract right to food or medicine? The question is upon the method of procuring and administering them. In that deliberation I shall always advise to call in the aid of the farmer and the physician rather than the professor of metaphysics.[2]

Burke's question is sharp. What is the point of having a right? More specifically what is the point of having an abstract right, unless you also have a way of securing whatever it is that you have a right to? Why should we prize natural or abstract rights if there is no way of ensuring their delivery? And if we need to secure their delivery, are not 'the farmer and the physician' not merely of greater use than abstract or natural rights, but also of greater use than positive rights to claim food or medicine? For a hungry person, positive and justiciable rights to food are to be sure better than abstract rights that are not justiciable: but those who know how to grow, harvest, store and cook food are more useful, and having the food is better still. When we are ill, positive and justiciable rights to health care are to be sure better than abstract rights that are not justiciable: but skilled doctors and nurses are more useful, and receiving their care better still.

In a way it is surprising to find Burke discussing abstract rights to food or health care, for these presumed rights came to full prominence only in the late twentieth century. They are commonly called welfare or social rights, and contrasted with liberty rights. This, I think, is a misnomer. The salient feature of these rights is not that they contribute to the welfare of the recipient (although they are likely to do so), but that they are rights to goods or services. If there are to be rights to goods or services, those goods

---

[1] 'The dark side of human rights', *International Affairs* 81 (2005), 427–39.
[2] Edmund Burke, *Reflections on the Revolution in France*, ed. Conor Cruise O'Brien (London: Penguin Books, 1984), 151–2.

and services must be provided, and more specifically provided *by someone* – for example, by the farmer and the physician.

Most of the abstract rights against which Burke campaigned were the rights proclaimed in the *Declaration of the Rights of Man and of the Citizen* of 1789 (*Declaration of 1789*). They are what we now call liberty rights. The short list in Article 2 of the *Declaration* states succinctly 'the natural rights of man, which must not be prevented ... are freedom, property, security and resistance to oppression'.[3] Needless to say, the right to property is to be understood not as a right to some amount of property, but as a right to security of tenure of property: it too is a liberty right, not a right to any goods or services.[4] Much of the *Declaration of 1789* is concerned with the rights to process needed to make liberty rights justiciable: rights to the rule of law, to habeas corpus, to what we would now call accountable public administration. The rights of the *Declaration of 1789* are rights against *all* others and *all* institutions. Liberty rights are universal – and so are the corresponding obligations. They are compromised if *any* others are exempt from those counterpart obligations. If anyone may infringe my rights to freedom, property and security, or to resist oppression, I have only incomplete and blemished rights of these sorts.

On closer consideration, matters have turned out to be rather more complicated. The institutions for securing and enforcing liberty rights require an allocation of certain obligations to specified others rather than to all others. First-order obligations to respect liberty rights must be universal, but second-order obligations to ensure that everyone respects liberty rights must be allocated. There is no effective rule of law without law enforcement, and law enforcement needs law enforcers who are assigned specific tasks; there is no effective accountability of public administration without institutions that allocate the tasks and responsibilities and hold specified office-holders to account. Nevertheless, the asymmetry between abstract liberty rights and abstract rights to goods and services is convincing: we can know who violates a liberty right without any allocation of obligations, but we cannot tell who violates a right to goods or services unless obligations have been allocated.

---

[3] *Declaration of the Rights of Man and of the Citizen*, 1789, www.magnacartaplus.org/french-rights/ 1789.htm.

[4] Note also Article 17 of the *Declaration of 1789*: 'Property, being an inviolable and sacred right, no one may be deprived of it; unless public necessity, legally investigated, clearly requires it, and just and prior compensation has been paid.'

This well-known point has not impeded the rise and rise of an international human rights culture that is replete with claims about abstract rights to goods and services, now seen as universal human rights, but often muddled or vague, or both, about the allocation of the obligations without which these rights not merely cannot be met, but remain undefined. The cornucopia of universal human rights includes both liberty rights[5] and rights to goods and services, and specifically rights to food and rights to health care. The right to food is proclaimed in Article 11 of the 1966 *International Covenant on Economic, Social and Cultural Rights* (CESCR), which asserts 'the right of everyone to an adequate standard of living for himself and his family, including adequate food, clothing and housing, and to the continuous improvement of living conditions'[6] (the *continuous improvement* is a nice touch!). Article 11 of CESCR has been adopted as a guiding principle of the Food and Agriculture Organisation (FAO), which has made its mission 'food security for all'.[7] The right to health (to *health*, not just to *health care*: another nice touch!) is proclaimed in Article 12 of the CESCR, which recognizes 'the right of everyone to the enjoyment of the highest attainable standard of physical and mental health'.[8] Article 12 has been adopted as the guiding principle of the World Health Organization (WHO).[9]

There is an interesting difference between Articles 11 and 12 of CESCR. The right to food is viewed as a right to *adequate food*, not to the *best attainable food*; the right to health is viewed as a right to the *highest attainable standard ... of health*, and not as a *right to adequate health*. One can see why the drafters of the Covenant may have shrunk from proclaiming a *right to adequate health*, but in qualifying this right as a *right to the highest attainable standard of health* many questions were begged. Is this right only a right to the standard of health that a person can attain with

---

[5] Set out in the UN *International Covenant on Civil and Political Rights*, 1966 (CCPR). This Covenant also 'recognises' various rights that are not liberty rights. See www.magnacartaplus.org/uno-docs/covenant.htm.

[6] CESCR, Art 11. See www.unhchr.ch/html/menu3/b/a_cescr.htm.

[7] See the FAO website at www.fao.org/UNFAO/about/index_en.html.

[8] CESCR, Art 12. The two Articles expand on rights proclaimed in Article 25 of the *Universal Declaration of Human Rights* of 1948 (UDHR), which runs: 'Everyone has the right to a standard of living adequate for the health and well-being of himself and of his family, including food, clothing, housing and medical care and necessary social services, and the right to security in the event of unemployment, sickness, disability, widowhood, old age or other lack of livelihood in circumstances beyond his control.' For the text of the UDHR see www.bee-leaf.com/universaldeclarationhumanrights.html.

[9] The WHO's objective, as set out in its Constitution, is 'the attainment by all peoples of the highest possible level of health', defined expansively as 'a state of complete physical, mental and social well-being and not merely the absence of disease or infirmity': www.who.int/about/en.

locally available and affordable treatment – however meagre that may be? Or is it a right to the highest standard available globally – however expensive that may be? The first is disappointingly minimal, and the latter barely coherent (how can everyone have a right to the best?). And what is required of the farmer, the physician and others who actually have to provide food and health care? Uncertainties of this sort are unavoidable unless the obligations that correspond to rights to goods and services are well specified.

Norms, aspirations and cynicism

Does any of this matter? Perhaps we should view the Declarations and Covenants that promulgate human rights as setting out noble aspirations, which it is helpful to articulate and bear in mind when establishing institutions, programmes, policies and activities that allocate obligations. In effect, we would concede that the rhetoric of universal human rights to goods or services was deceptive, but defend it as a noble lie that helps to mobilise support for establishing justiciable rights of great importance. There is something to be said for this view of human rights Declarations and Covenants as ideological documents that can help mobilize energy for action that makes a difference, but many would see this as cynical.

In any case, this interpretation of human rights claims would be wholly at odds with ordinary understandings of rights. Both liberty rights and rights to goods and services are standardly seen as *claim rights* or *entitlements* that are valid against those with the counterpart obligations. Rights are seen as one side of a normative relationship between right-holders and obligation-bearers. We normally regard supposed claims or entitlements that nobody is obliged to respect or honour as null and void, indeed undefined. An understanding of the normative arguments that link rights to obligations underlies daily and professional discussion both of supposedly *universal* human rights, and of the *special* rights created by specific voluntary actions and transactions (treaty, contract, promise, marriage, etc.). There cannot be a claim to rights that are rights against nobody, or nobody in particular: universal rights will be rights against all comers; special rights will be rights against specifiable others.

Only if we jettison the entire normative understanding of rights in favour of a merely aspirational view, can we break the normative link between rights and their counterpart obligations. If we take rights seriously and see them as normative rather than aspirational, we must take obligations seriously. If on the other hand we opt for a merely aspirational view, the costs are high.

For then we would also have to accept that where human rights are unmet there is no breach of obligation, nobody at fault, nobody who can be held to account, nobody to blame and nobody who owes redress. We would in effect have to accept that human rights claims are not real claims.

Most advocates of human rights would be reluctant to jettison the thought that they are *prescriptive* or *normative* in favour of seeing them as merely *aspirational*.[10] We generally view human rights claims as setting out requirements from the standpoint of recipients, who are *entitled to* or *have a claim to* action or forbearance by others with corresponding obligations. From a normative or prescriptive view, the point of human rights claims would be eroded if nobody were required to act or forbear to meet these claims. A normative view of rights claims has to take obligations seriously, since they are the counterparts to rights; it must view them as articulating the normative requirements that fall either on all or on specified obligation-bearers. Few proponents of human rights would countenance the thought that there are human rights that nobody is obliged to respect. (The converse thought is unproblematic: there can be obligations even where no claimants are defined; such 'imperfect' obligations are generally seen as moral obligations, but not as obligations of justice with counterpart rights.)

The claim that rights must have well-specified counterpart obligations is not equivalent to the commonplace piety that rights and responsibilities go together, which asserts only that right-holders are also obligation-bearers. This is often, but not always, true. Many agents – citizens, workers, students, teachers, employees – are both right-holders and obligation-bearers. But some right-holders – infants, the severely disabled, the senile – cannot carry obligations, so have no responsibilities. By contrast, the claim that rights must have counterpart obligations asserts the exceptionless logical point that where anyone is to have a right there must be identifiable others (either all others or specified others) with accurately corresponding obligations. From a normative view of rights, obligations and claimable rights are two perspectives on a single normative pattern: without the obligations there are no rights. So while obligations will drop out of sight if we read human rights 'claims' merely as aspirations rather than require-ments, so too will rights, as they are usually understood. Unsurprisingly, aspirational readings of human rights documents are not popular. How-ever, such readings at least offer an exit strategy if we conclude that claiming rights without specifying counterpart obligations is an

---

[10] See Griffin, 'Discrepancies between the best philosophical account'.

unacceptable deception, and find that we can't develop an adequate normative account of obligations and rights.

Clearly it would be preferable to offer a serious account of the allocation of obligations that correspond to all human rights. But do Declarations and Covenants provide an account – or even a clue – to the allocation of the obligations that are the counterparts to rights to goods and services? This point was complicated at the birth of human rights by the unfortunately obscure drafting of the 1948 UDHR,[11] which gestures to the thought that certain obligations lie with states, then confusingly assigns them indifferently to nations, countries and peoples as well as states. Not all of these have the integrated capacities for action and decision-making needed for agency, and so for carrying obligations. For present purposes I shall leave problems arising from this unfortunate drafting aside, and rely on the fact that in later documents, including CESCR, these ambiguities are apparently resolved in favour of assigning obligations to the states party, that is to the signatory states.

This approach has apparent advantages – and stings in its tail. The first sting is that states that do not ratify a Covenant will not incur the obligations it specifies: not a welcome conclusion to advocates of universal human rights, since these states thereby escape obligations to respect, let alone enforce, the rights promulgated. The second sting is sharper. The obligations created by signing and ratifying Covenants are *special*, not *universal* obligations. So the rights which are their corollaries will also be *special* or *institutional rights*, not *universal human rights*. Once we take a normative view of rights and obligations, they must be properly matched. If human rights are independent of institutional structures, if they are not created by special transactions, so too are the corresponding obligations; conversely if obligations are the creatures of convention, so too are the rights.

These unwelcome implications of taking the human rights documents at face value might be avoided in several ways. One well-known thought is that so long as we confine ourselves to liberty rights there is no allocation problem, since these rights are only complete if *all* others are obliged to respect them. We can coherently see universal liberty rights as independent of institutions or transactions, and read the parts of instruments that deal with liberty rights as affirming rather than creating those rights (justifying such claims would be a further task). But the fact that liberty rights do not face an allocation problem (although enforcing them raises just that

---

[11] The text can be found at www.imcl/biz/docs/humanrights.pdf. For further comments on some confusions about obligations and agency in UDHR, see Chapter 11 'Agents of justice', above, 177–92.

problem) offers small comfort to those who hope to show that rights to goods or services, for example to food or medicine, are universal human rights rather than the creatures of convention. A normative view of human rights cannot view rights to food and medicine as pre-institutional while denying that there are any pre-institutional counterpart obligations or obligation holders; it must take a congruent view of the counterpart obligations. But this suggests that such rights must be special, institutional rights rather than universal human rights. There is, of course, nothing wrong or problematic about conventional or institutional rights, but if Declarations and Covenants create rights to goods and services, claims that they are universal or human rights lack justification. Declarations and Covenants cannot show that some particular configuration of institutional rights and obligations is universally optimal or desirable, or justifiable.

This dilemma might be fudged by allowing the idea of human rights to goods and services to drift between two interpretations. A view of rights to goods and services as independent of institutions and transactions could be cited as offering a basis for justifying some rather than other institutional arrangements. A view of rights to goods and services as the creatures of convention could fit with well-defined counterpart institutional obligations, but offer no claims about their justification other than the fact that (some) states have signed up to them. Equivocation is a desperate justificatory strategy. Yet this equivocation is disconcertingly common in discussions of human rights claims.

This dilemma within normative views of rights and obligations can be resolved in more than one way. We could conclude that liberty rights are fundamental and universal, and claim that they can be justified without reference to Covenants or institutions, but concede that rights to goods and services are special (institutional, positive) rights that can be justified only by appeal to specific transactions, such as signing and ratifying Covenants. We could try to justify a configuration of special rights and the institutional structures that secure them and their counterpart obligations. For example, we might argue that certain rights to goods and services and their counterpart obligations protect basic human needs or interests, or that they have utilitarian or economic justification. Or we could justify institutional structures that define and secure special rights and obligations more deeply by appealing to a theory of the good (moral realists) or a theory of duty (Kantians).

The option that is closed is to claim that human rights and obligations are corollaries of normative claims, but that there are some universal rights without counterpart obligations. So there are plenty of possibilities – although each may raise its own difficulties. If none of these possibilities can be made to work, the default position would be to reject normative views of human rights and to see human rights claims as aspirational (noting that aspirations need justification too) and to treat the task of establishing institutions that allow for justiciable claims as a task to be guided in part by appealing to those aspirations. And then, it may seem, we in effect endorse a cynical reading of the human rights Declarations and Covenants.

State obligations

These are awkward problems, but I think that others may lie deeper. The deepest problem may be that the obligations assigned to states by some of the most significant Declarations and Covenants are *not* the corollaries of the human rights that the documents proclaim. The Covenants assign to states not straightforward obligations to respect liberty rights (after all, liberty rights have to be respected by all, not only by states), but rather second-order obligations to *secure* respect for them. Equally, they assign to states not obligations to meet rights to goods and services, but rather second-order obligations to *ensure* that they are met. For example, Article 2 of the CESCR proclaims that

> Each State Party to the present Covenant undertakes to take steps, indi-
> vidually and through international assistance and co-operation, especially
> economic and technical, to the maximum of its available resources, with a
> view to achieving progressively the full realisation of the rights recognized in
> the present Covenant by all appropriate means, including particularly the
> adoption of legislative measures.[12]

'Achieving progressively the full realisation of . . . rights . . . by all appro-
priate means' is evidently not merely a matter of respecting the rights recognised in CESCR. It is a matter of ensuring that others – both individuals and institutions – carry out the obligations that correspond to those rights. Later comments by the Office of the High Commissioner for Human Rights spell out some of the obligations that states are taken to assume if they ratify the two Covenants.[13]

An immediate and encouraging thought might be that if the obligations assigned to states by the international Declarations and Covenants are *not*

---

[12] Art. 2 CESCR at www.unhchr.ch/html/menu3/b/a_cescr.htm.
[13] *The Nature of States Parties' Obligations*, Art. 2, para. 1 of the Covenant, Fifth session, 1990, Office of the High Commissioner for Human Rights, CESCR General comment 3, www.unhchr.ch/tbs/doc.nsf/(symbol)/CESCR+General+comment+3.En?OpenDocument.

the counterparts of the human rights proclaimed, but second-order obligations to ensure or secure respect for such rights, then this may resolve the allocation problem for rights to goods and services.

States party to a Covenant would be seen as acquiring special obligations by signing and ratifying the instrument. It would then be clear that those special, second-order obligations did not have counterpart rights, let alone counterpart universal human rights. They are second-order obligations to secure some configuration of first-order rights and obligations. This thought may be helpful: since obligations without counterpart rights are normatively coherent (unlike rights without counterpart obligations), we can take a normative view of the obligations assumed by states that sign and ratify the Covenants, and can see them as setting requirements. Human rights enter into the Covenants only indirectly as aspects of the content of second-order state obligations.

But a second thought is far less congenial to those who would like to see human rights as normative. If the obligations that the Declarations and Covenants assign to states are *not* the counterparts of the human rights these instruments declare or recognise, then they also do not define the first-order obligations that are the counterparts of human rights. Rather the problem of giving a coherent normative instantiation of Declarations and Covenants is devolved to the states party, which may (or may not) set out to secure positive rights for their citizens. If the claims of the human rights documents have normative force they must be matched by obligations; if they are not matched by obligations, they are *at best* aspirational.

As I suggested earlier, it may not be wholly a misfortune if the supposed rights declared in the Declarations and Covenants are seen as aspirations. Legal commentators might be willing to say that there is still substance in there, in that the States party take on real obligations to realise these aspirations. Non-lawyers may habitually make the mistake of thinking that Declarations and Covenants claim that there are pre-institutional universal human rights, but their mistake is not necessary – although politically convenient – for progress towards the realisation of the underlying aspirations, once states have signed up. This is a coherent position, but unlikely to be popular with those who seek to base ethical and political claims on appeals to human rights, which they see as normatively fundamental rather than as the creatures of the convention that are anchored in the Covenants that assign obligations to realise aspirations to states.

And there are further difficulties. If we read Declarations and Covenants as instruments by which states assume second-order obligations to define and allocate first-order obligations that correspond to certain human rights (now no longer seen as universal rights), why should all the obligations lie with states? A plausible answer would be that states, and only states, have the powers necessary to carry the relevant second-order obligations to define and allocate first-order obligations and rights to individuals and institutions. The story is told of the FBI agent who asked the bank robber Willie Sutton why he robbed banks and got the puzzled answer: 'That's where the money is.' Similarly we might reply to anyone who wonders why Declarations and Covenants assign obligations that are to secure human rights to states by pointing out that that's where the power is.

But the thought that it makes sense to assign all second-order obligations to define and allocate first-order obligations to states because they, and only they, have the power to discharge these obligations is often less than comforting. Many states violate rather than respect human rights. Assigning second-order obligations to define and allocate first-order obligations and rights to agents who do not even reliably respect the first-order obligations that correspond to those rights may be rather like putting foxes in charge of hen houses. It is true enough that those who are to achieve progressively the full realisation of human rights must have capacities to do so – but it does not follow that those with (a good range of) the necessary capacities can be trusted to do so. Some states – not only those we think of as rogue states – disregard or override many of the Covenant rights. Some sign and ratify the relevant international instruments, but make limited efforts to work towards their full realisation.

Other states lack the power to carry the obligations to 'achieve progressively the full realisation of the rights recognised' in Declarations and Covenants. Weak states – failed states, quasi states – cannot carry such demanding obligations. Although they may not always violate them, they cannot secure their inhabitants' liberty rights; still less can they ensure that their inhabitants have effective entitlements to goods and services. It is an empty gesture to assign the obligations needed for human rights to weak states, comparable to the empty gesture made by town councils in Britain in the 1980s that proclaimed their towns nuclear free zones. Indeed, even strong and willing states may find that they cannot 'achieve progressively the full realisation' of the rights recognised in Declarations and Covenants. Strong states may have a monopoly of the legitimate use of force within their territories; but they seldom have a monopoly of the effective use of other forms of power. There are plenty of reasons for thinking carefully about the specific character of state power, and for questioning the assumption that powerful – let alone weak – states can carry the range of second-order obligations that they ostensibly take on in signing and ratifying human rights instruments.

Given these realities, it may be worth reconsidering whether all second-order obligations to secure human rights should lie with states. Perhaps some of them should lie with powerful non-state actors, such as transnational corporations, powerful non-governmental organisations, or major religious, cultural, and professional and educational bodies. The assumption that states and states alone should hold all the relevant obligations may reflect the extraordinary dominance of state power in the late twentieth century, rather than a timeless solution to the problem of allocating obligations to provide goods and services effectively. For present purposes, I shall leave these unsettling possibilities unexplored, but say a little more about some of the cultural and political costs that are linked to persistent confusion between normative and aspirational views of human rights.

Control and blame

If human rights are not pre-conventional universal rights, but are grounded in the special obligations assumed by states, then there is – at the very least – an awkward gap between reality and rhetoric. The second-order obligations of states are discharged by imposing first-order obligations on others and enforcing them. The reality is that state agency and state power, and that of derivative institutions, is used to construct institutions that (partially) secure rights, and that to do this it is necessary to control the action of individuals and institutions systematically and in detail. If states party are to discharge the second-order obligations they assume in signing and ratifying human rights Covenants, they not only must ensure that liberty rights are respected by all, but must assign and enforce first-order obligations whose discharge will deliver rights to goods and services to all. Human beings, it is evident, will not merely be the intended *beneficiaries* of these obligations, but will carry the intended *burdens*.

The system of control that states must impose to ensure that these obligations are discharged is likely to be dauntingly complex. Yet, as Burke pointed out, what we really need if we are to have food and medicine is the active engagement of 'the farmer and the physician'. Can that active engagement be secured or improved by imposing detailed and complex obligations on those who are to carry the relevant first-order obligations? There is much to consider here, and I offer very brief comments under four headings: complexity, compliance, complaint and compensation.

Complexity

Detailed control is needed to 'achieve progressively the full realisation' of very complex sets of potentially conflicting rights, which must be mutually adjusted. It is no wonder that legislation in the age of human rights has become prolix and demanding. Those who frame it have to seek to ensure that individuals and institutions conform to a very large number of constraints in all activities, so have to set and enforce very detailed requirements.[14] It is now common in developed societies to find that legislation imposes highly complex procedures that bristle with duties to register, duties to obtain permission, duties to consult, rights to appeal, as well as proliferating requirements to record, to disclose and to report. Such legislation is typically supplemented by copious regulation, relentless 'guidance', prolix codes of good practice and highly intrusive forms of accountability. These highly detailed forms of social control may be unavoidable in a public culture that aims to 'achieve progressively the full realisation' of an extraordinarily complex set of rights, so has to impose complex demands and burdens on all activities and all areas of life.

The results are demanding for the state agencies that are supposed to set the requirements and police the system. They can be dementing for the institutions and individuals that are to carry the first-order obligations – not least for the farmer and the physician. Complex controls risk stifling active engagement. Those of whom too much that is extraneous to their basic tasks – growing food, caring for the sick – is required are likely to resent the proliferating and time-consuming requirements to obtain permissions, to consult third parties, to record, to disclose, to report and to comply with the demands of inspectors or regulators. These requirements for control and accountability impose heavy human and financial costs, and are often damaging to the performance of primary tasks. Those who face these burdens on their attempts to perform demanding substantive tasks – the farmer and the physician – may comply and resent (and sometimes engage in defensive practices); they may protest and complain; or they may withdraw from activities that have been made too burdensome. The costs of complex control systems are paid in increasing wariness and weariness, scepticism and resentment, and ultimately in less active engagement by 'the

---

[14] Michael Moran, *The British Regulatory State: High Modernism and Hyper-Innovation* (Oxford University Press, 2003). Moran argues that the new regulatory state is neither liberal nor decentralising, despite its commitment to human rights. Rather, it is both interventionist and centralising in ways that colonise hitherto relatively independent domains of civil society – including those of the farmer and the physician.

farmer and the physician', and by others who come to see themselves primarily as obligation-bearers rather than as right-holders.

Compliance

Individuals who are subject to hyper-complex legislation, regulation and control are offered two roles. As obligation-bearers their role is compliance; as right-holders they are permitted and encouraged to seek redress and to complain when others fail to comply. The individuals and institutions on whom first-order obligations are imposed in the name of securing human rights are offered limited options: they can soldier loyally on in compliance with the obligations states impose; they can voice their discontent; they can exit from the tasks that have been made too burdensome by the excess complexity of legislation and regulation.[15] Loyal compliance becomes harder and more burdensome when the sheer number and complexity of requirements imposed damages the quality with which substantive tasks can be achieved. Voicing concern and objecting to these controls provides some, but limited relief. Exit from the activities that have been made too burdensome may often be the most reasonable and the preferred option. For 'the farmer and the physician', exit means giving up growing food and caring for the sick.

There may be ways of extending human rights that do not carry these costs, that use a 'lighter touch', that achieve 'better regulation'.[16] But the jury is out on this matter. At present, and certainly in the UK, the juggernaut of human rights demands, at every stage of legislation and of the regulatory process, tends to increase complexity even when the costs for 'the farmer and the physician', and the damage to the services they provide, are high and well known.

Complaint

First-order obligation-bearers are also right-holders, and it may be that the burdens their obligations impose are recompensed by the rights they enjoy as a result of others discharging their obligations. However, the experience

---

[15] See Albert O. Hirschann, *Exit, Voice and Loyalty: Responses to Decline in Firms, Organizations and States* (Cambridge, MA: Harvard University Press, 1970), for a classic analysis of these options. See also O'Neill, 'Trust, trustworthiness and accountability'.

[16] The United Kingdom government established a Better Regulation Task Force in 1997, which has ramified into a range of Better Regulation units and activities. The aim has been to promote the 'five principles of better regulation' which are said to be Proportionality, Accountability, Consistency, Transparency and Targeting (consistency is a nice touch!).

of right-holders is not symmetric with that of obligation-bearers. Individuals act as right-holders when they claim or when matters go awry and they complain, seek redress and compensation. The legislation and regulation of states that take human rights seriously often provide a range of remedies – for those with the time, energy, courage (or foolhardiness) to pursue them. When complaints work, redress may be achieved and compensation may be secured. But often the experience of complainants is less than happy because the process of achieving redress is complex, exhausting and frustrating, and the remedies less than would satisfy and assuage a sense of injury. Since the role of complainant is too often one that exhausts, demoralises and undermines active engagement, many who are wronged do not choose this course of action. For 'the farmer and the physician' and for many others the choice is mainly between loyalty and exit: giving voice is not generally a positive experience, since it requires complainants to see themselves as victims rather than as actively engaged.

Compensation and blame

The best outcome of the voice option is that, with luck and persistence, those who take on the role of victim or complainant achieve redress and compensation, or some opportunity for the dubious pleasures of casting blame. Compensation clearly has its positive side – although it may be hard to achieve, and limited in amount, and is not always worth the struggle through the complexities of process. Blaming by contrast is a readily available and cheap pleasure – even for complainants whose case is not upheld. Those who cast blame can appropriate, enjoy and prolong their role and status as victims, can enjoy indignation and a feeling of superiority, even if they cannot quite identify or demonstrate the failings of others. If it proves impossible to identify a blameworthy culprit, they can at least blame 'the system', that is to say the institutional framework that is failing to achieve 'progressively the full realisation of the rights recognized . . . by all appropriate means, including particularly the adoption of legislative measures'.

There is a dark and tempting undercurrent of pleasure in blaming. Nobody has written about the psychology of blaming, or about its murky appeal and insidious psychological effects, more brilliantly and darkly than Nietzsche. Some of his comments are particularly apt to the realities of the farmer and the physician:

> Suffering people all have a horrible willingness and capacity for inventing pretexts for painful emotional feelings. They already enjoy their suspicions,

they're brooding over bad actions and apparent damage. They ransack the entrails of their past and present, looking for dark and dubious stories, in which they are free to feast on an agonizing suspicion and to get intoxicated on their own poisonous anger. They rip open the oldest wounds, they bleed themselves to death from long-healed scars. They turn friends, wives, children, and anyone else who is closest to them into criminals. 'I am suffering. Someone or other must be to blame for that.'[17]

I do not wish to suggest that the human rights culture inevitably promotes this rancorous approach to life. But I do not think we should accept at face value the view that it is all about respect for persons and treating others as agents. Much of it is indeed about protecting the weak and vulnerable. But it is also about extending the power of states over non-state actors and human individuals, about establishing systems of control and discipline that extend into the remotest corners of life, about running people's lives for them while leaving them with the consoling pleasures of blame. As Bernard Williams puts it, blame is 'the characteristic reaction of the morality system' in which obligations and rights have become the sole ethical currency.[18]

We find it unsurprising that the ruling ideas of past eras have been superseded and modified, and we can hardly doubt that human rights are a central ruling idea of our age. Yet we do not find much current discussion of the likelihood that the idea of human rights may suffer the same fate. Public discourse is for the most part admiring, and often represents human rights as unquestionable truth and progress: we may question anything – except human rights. Indeed, unlike some earlier dominant ideologies, the human rights movement has acquired the beguiling feature of being an ideology not only of and for the ruling classes, but an ideology for – and increasingly of – the oppressed. This seems to me a good reason for thinking particularly carefully and critically about the internal structure of human rights claims, for trying to be less gestural about their basis and their limits, and for being more explicit about their costs as well as their benefits. The farmer and the physician, and others whose work and commitment are indispensable, are the key to securing a decent standard of life for all: their active enthusiasm and efforts are more valuable than their dour compliance with prescribed procedures, their resentful protest, let alone their refusal to contribute.

---

[17] Friedrich Nietzsche, *The Genealogy of Morals*, Part III, section 15. This translation, which draws on earlier received versions, can be found at *The Nietzsche Channel*'s website at www.geocities.com/thenietzschechannel/onthe3.htm#3e15.

[18] Williams, *Ethics and the Limits of Philosophy* .

PART IV

Health across boundaries

CHAPTER 13

Public health or clinical ethics: thinking beyond borders[1]

Most work in medical ethics has centred on the ethics of clinical medicine. Even work on health and justice has, in the main, been concerned with the just distribution of (access to) clinical care for individual patients. By contrast, the ethics of public health has been widely neglected. This neglect is surprising, given that public health interventions are often the most effective (and most cost-effective) means of improving health in rich and poor societies alike.

In this chapter I explore two sources of contemporary neglect of public health ethics. One source of neglect is that contemporary medical ethics has been preoccupied – in my view damagingly preoccupied – with the autonomy of individual patients. Yet individual autonomy can hardly be a guiding ethical principle for public health measures, since many of them must be uniform and compulsory if they are to be effective. A second source of neglect is that contemporary political philosophy has been preoccupied – in my view damagingly preoccupied – with the requirements for justice *within* states or societies, and (until very recently) has hardly discussed justice across borders. Yet public health problems often cross borders, and public health interventions have to measure up to the problems they address.

An ethically adequate approach to health questions needs to look beyond the clinical context, and beyond the boundaries of states and health care systems. Health ethics must cover more than clinical ethics; accounts of health and justice must cover more than the just distribution of clinical care within health care systems.

Individual autonomy and public health

Contemporary medical ethics emerged in rich societies, in particular in the United States, during the 1970s. Unsurprisingly, it took for granted the

[1] 'Public health or clinical ethics, thinking beyond borders', *Ethics and International Affairs* 81 (2005), 427–39.

medical practices and institutions of such societies. The new medical ethics addressed ethical problems that were typical of professionalised, hospital-based clinical practice that could provide expensive, high-tech medical interventions. Traditional one-to-one, long-term physician–patient rela-tionships, based on patient trust and physician beneficence, did not fit well into the new clinical settings, which deployed large teams of professionals in the care of individual patients. The new medical ethics advocated an end to all forms of medical paternalism, in favour of what is now usually called patient autonomy.[2]

The various conceptions of individual autonomy deployed in medical ethics view it as a predicate of individual persons. Autonomous patients are independent agents who decide for themselves whether they will accept or refuse treatment; professionals are to respect patients' autonomy and undertake treatment only on the basis of informed consent. Compulsion and coercion are always unacceptable in clinical practice. The new medical ethics had relatively little to say about public health, where interventions are often (and sometimes necessarily) compulsory.[3]

Even in clinical practice, unqualified demands to respect individual autonomy proved problematic. As sociologists and anthropologists of medicine have long pointed out, the individualistic frameworks within which conceptions of individual autonomy can most easily be thought of as central to medical ethics correspond poorly with the realities of clinical practice. Professionals are linked in complex institutional networks; patients come encumbered with family and other responsibilities.

Nor was individualism the only problem. Since ill health so often limits individual independence in minor and major ways, it was harder to build respect for individual autonomy into medical practice than into most other areas of life. Children and the senile, the comatose and the confused, the cognitively impaired and the mentally disturbed, and all of us when we are feeling ill and frail, have reduced or no capacity for individual autonomy.

Showing what it takes to support patient autonomy and professional respect for that autonomy amid – almost despite – the realities of limited

---

[2] Tom L. Beauchamp and James F. Childress, *Principles of Biomedical Ethics* (Oxford University Press, 1979) became a standard text placing individual autonomy at the heart of medical ethics. Consistent opposition was voiced from an early date by Daniel Callahan, 'Autonomy: a moral good, not a moral obsession', *Hastings Center Report* 14 (1984), 40–2, and 'Can the moral commons survive autonomy?', *Hastings Center Report* 26 (1996), 41–2.

[3] Even discussions of health and justice have often been more concerned with the just distribution or allocation of clinical care to individuals, rather than with public health. See Norman Daniels, *Just Health Care* (Cambridge University Press, 1985).

capacities proved hard work. The social and medical realities were typically reconciled with individual independence by relying on minimal interpretations of individual or personal autonomy that reduced it to requirements to institute and respect informed consent procedures.[4] In cases where capacities to give and refuse consent were impaired, medical ethicists looked for more inclusive or accessible ways for patients with limited capacities for individual autonomy to give and refuse consent. Patients nevertheless seldom experience medical care as an arena for individual autonomy or independence. This is hardly surprising: if individual autonomy is reduced to respect for informed consent procedures, it amounts only to freedom to refuse what others offer. Patients who are offered only the standard treatment for their disease may (even if consent and refusal of consent are within their capacities) feel that their choices were pretty limited, that they had little scope for any robust expression of individual autonomy.

In consequence the forms of autonomy discussed in contemporary medical ethics had very little to do with the Kantian conception of autonomy, whose pedigree was nevertheless frequently but misleadingly invoked.[5] Unlike individual autonomy, Kantian autonomy is predicated of principles, rather than of persons. It demands that action be based on principles that can be adopted by all. It therefore demands that we reject principles such as those of injuring or coercing, of manipulating or deceiving, of extorting or false promising, of oppressing or victimising, and the like, whose universal adoption would *at least sometimes* be expressed in like action, so *at least sometimes* prevent others from adopting like principles. Such principles cannot be universalised.

Proponents of Kantian and individual autonomy converge in regarding compulsion, and the coercive sanctions by which it is achieved, as generally wrong. The advocates of individual autonomy generally take a Millian view of the limits of acceptable coercion, which argues that it is permissible to coerce individuals only to prevent them from harming others. Kant and proponents of Kantian autonomy argue more broadly that human societies need public authorities with power to compel individuals to act in order to

---

[4] Tom L. Beauchamp and Ruth R. Faden, in collaboration with Nancy M. P. King, *A History and Theory of Informed Consent* (Oxford University Press, 1986).

[5] For some of the differences see Thomas E. Hill, Jr., 'The Kantian conception of autonomy' in *Dignity and Practical Reason in Kant's Moral Theory* (Ithaca, NY: Cornell University Press, 1992), 76–96; and Onora O'Neill, *Autonomy and Trust in Bioethics* (Cambridge University Press, 2002), and *Constructing Authorities*, Part II.

support a larger scheme designed to limit restrictions on freedom. They advocate an approach that does not give automatic priority to individual autonomy, and a framework within which some public health measures may – and others may not – legitimately be compulsory, and backed by coercive sanctions if necessary.

Compulsion in clinical medicine and public health

If the ethically acceptable practice of medicine prohibits compulsion of individuals, except in narrowly drawn circumstances, it is clear enough why contemporary medical ethics has little to say about public health. Yet since public health measures are particularly effective ways of improving health, particularly (but not only) in poorer societies, this silence has striking results. Reading in many fields of medical ethics one could be forgiven for thinking that health interventions and improvements are the preserve of medical systems and the medically qualified, that they always require individual consent, and that the very health interventions most likely to be most effective in poorer and richer societies are not ethically acceptable. The fact that aspects of clinical practice rest on forms of compulsion, and so ultimately on the possible use of coercion, is simply overlooked.

I am personally sceptical of attempts to make individual autonomy the central value of medical ethics. However, here I do not want to say more about my underlying reasons for this scepticism, but rather want to look more closely at ways in which a focus on individual autonomy can marginalise and even undermine adequate consideration of public health ethics, and also distort discussions of justice and health care. The basic reason why contemporary medical ethics has so little to say about public health is, in my view, that its focus on individual autonomy suggests that *all* compulsion for the sake of health is wrong. Yet many public health measures have to be compulsory if they are to be effective, and all compulsion ultimately relies on sanctions, hence on the possible use of some sorts of coercion. If we start from the assumption that individual autonomy is the key to medical ethics, and that all compulsion and all coercion are wrong, public health measures are unavoidably suspect.

In fact, some sorts of compulsion are basic even to clinical medicine, as practised in all parts of the world. Most obviously, the costs of health care are usually funded in part, or even entirely, out of taxation, which is compulsory and whose collection ultimately rests on the use of coercive sanctions. However, this compulsion is perceived as 'external' to medical practice. Secondly, the practice of clinical medicine is heavily controlled by legislation and regulation, and these are ultimately enforced by coercive sanctions. The controls within health care systems bear in the first instance on professionals rather than on patients, and are generally seen as acceptable conditions of professional certification and employment rather than as threats to professional autonomy (nobody is forced to practise medicine). Equally, institutional certification, inspection and quality control also are compulsory, but again are generally viewed as acceptable conditions for being permitted – sometimes even funded – to practise medicine. By contrast, the health care systems and policies of rich societies limit compulsion of patients to emergency and exceptional measures, such as detention of those whose illness may endanger others, quarantine, vaccination (in some cases), or notification of certain diseases. (In the vaccination case some rich societies, including Germany and the United Kingdom, have allowed individual autonomy to trump public health concerns, and some communities in both societies have hovered on the edge of measles epidemics.)

The need for compulsion, however, and the possibility of coercion are evident in the area of public health. Some public health measures have to be compulsory because variation in provision to suit individual preferences is not technically feasible. For example, standards for public goods such as air and water quality, food safety and waste disposal, and road and building safety have to be imposed. Because they are organisationally external to the health care system, their imposition is not seen as violating demands for individual consent and autonomy that have been so prevalent within medical ethics.

By contrast, we can allow some variability in the standards to which consumer goods are produced. Yet here too we accept some compulsion in setting uniform safety standards, because we know that individuals cannot judge the safety of complex products themselves. Only in marginal cases where the effects of individual consumption are wholly on that individual, and where consumption is optional – cigarettes, safety helmets for cyclists – may we sometimes think it enough to warn and educate. Even in these cases there is constant debate as to whether health education and health promotion, which preserve individual autonomy and avoid compulsion (at least for adults), are enough.

Evidently, then, public health policies are often imposed, and imposed for good reasons. They are imposed on populations and groups at common risk – that is why they can be so effective. So it is not surprising that they have been so largely exempted from demands that individual autonomy be built into health provision. Yet this is often obscured because mainstream writing in medical ethics has ignored public health requirements. They are often seen as external to medicine, perhaps because they are the responsibility not of medical practitioners or ministries of health, but of other agencies and ministries. During recent decades a concentration on autonomy in medical ethics, combined with the assumption that public health can properly be separated from provision of clinical care, has distracted us from thinking as broadly or as well as we might about health ethics, and in particular about the ethics of public health.[6]

Health, justice and boundaries

A focus on clinical medicine has (rather surprisingly) been extended into many discussions of health and justice, which often focus mainly on the just distribution of individual (access to) clinical care.[7] If health provision consisted entirely of clinical provision, it could in principle be based on voluntary, consensual relationships between patients and physicians that respect individual patient autonomy (however conceived). The good to be distributed could not then be health care itself (let alone health!), but rather access to health care or opportunity for health care. This way of thinking preserves the view that health measures are the province of clinical medicine, and that compulsion is unacceptable outside narrowly defined areas.

Discussions of health and justice that focus on the distribution of (access to) clinical care marginalise public health in two ways. Like medical ethics that focuses on clinical medicine, they tend to leave public health measures out of the picture. They also usually marginalise public health by taking existing boundaries – whether the boundaries of states or the (often coinciding) boundaries of health care delivery systems – as fixing the *scope* of justice.

In taking this view of the scope of justice, discussions of health and justice follow the statist focus of most contemporary conceptions of justice. They view questions about just health care, medical rationing and medical resource allocation as internal to states and health care delivery systems. Health economists and health policy analysts typically focus on (just) health care provision within boundaries, and bracket ill health beyond

---

[6] I leave aside the question of whether processes of democratic legitimation could show that some compulsion is acceptable, though we would probably not judge health and safety standards and requirements acceptable if they inflicted or permitted serious harms, however strongly they were endorsed by a democratic process.

[7] Daniels, *Just Health Care*; Dan W. Brock, Allen Buchanan, Norman Daniels and Daniel Wikler, *From Chance to Choice: Genetics and Justice* (Cambridge University Press, 2000).

boundaries. The huge health problems of poorer parts of the world, for which public health interventions are often of decisive importance, are then seen as matters for development programmes and development studies, rather than as part and parcel either of mainstream theories of justice or of mainstream medical ethics.[8]

The frequent neglect of ill health beyond borders reflects well-entrenched features of contemporary political philosophy, which has typically confined questions of distributive justice within societies, and viewed trans-border justice (at best) as a secondary matter. The conceptions of justice most favoured in developed societies have often been statist – they have assumed that states are the primary agents of justice, and that justice is primarily 'domestic'. These claims may seem surprising in view of the fact that some prominent contemporary conceptions of justice have explicitly repudiated the view that justice is state-centred. For example, John Rawls, whose philosophical approach has been so widely followed in writing on justice in welfare and health care provision, insists that the locus of justice is not the state but the 'bounded society'. In my view, the supposed difference between states and bounded societies is less robust and less convincing than Rawls claims. For he thinks of a 'bounded society' as a society that is politically organised, that protects its territory and its boundaries, and that excludes outsiders.[9]

The costs of assuming that the context of justice, including that of justice that bears on health, must be either a 'bounded society' or a state are high. In failing to look beyond boundaries we fail to take into account the fact that boundaries are now multiply porous. Health problems travel across boundaries not only because diseases travel, but also because the mirror image of a global configuration of social and economic power is a global configuration of poverty and ill health. Work in political philosophy

---

[8] The scene has changed – up to a point. More recent literature on health inequalities is not confined to inequalities within states, and connections between normative reasoning and health inequalities are being drawn more frequently. See some of the papers in David A. Leon and Gill Walt (eds.), *Poverty, Inequality and Health: An International Perspective* (Oxford University Press, 2001); and in Sudhir Anand, Fabienne Peter and Amartya Sen (eds.), *Public Health, Ethics, Equity* (Oxford University Press, 2004).

[9] Rawls's reasons for thinking that such societies are not states is, I suspect, that he adopted a realist conception of the state, and consequently assumed that state action would be irredeemably self-interested, and thus that states provide an inadequate basis for thinking about justice beyond borders. But not all conceptions of the state are realist. See O'Neill, 'Political liberalism and public reason'; and Kuper, 'Rawlsian global justice'.

that assumes that boundaries can define and separate discrete domains of justice is increasingly unrealistic.

Yet looking beyond boundaries in building an account of justice, including health justice, is not simple. Adopting a wholly abstract or moral cosmopolitanism ostensibly takes the moral standing of all individuals in all societies equally seriously – but often at the expense of moving thinking about justice remarkably far from the realities of power and the capabilities for effective action. Such thinking is likely to identify at most certain targets or ideals: for example, an ideally just distribution of resources, or of health care. Further lines of argument to show *who* ought to do or provide *what* for *whom*, and specifically *who* ought to do *what* to protect or restore *whose* health, are then remarkably hard to identify. Knowing that some distribution (equal, maximin or whatever) of resources, or of health care, would be *ideally* just does not take us far towards knowing *who* should do *what* for *whom* in order to work towards that distribution.

Nor can approaches to justice that assign priority to 'bounded societies' or states get very far by pointing out that states construct international institutions, such as the United Nations and the WHO. If states are the primary global actors, they may be able to secure some forms of international justice, but 'domestic' justice will remain the primary focus and the primary locus of any legitimate use of force. Political philosophy that starts with states is therefore unlikely to offer a full account of global or cosmopolitan justice, in which any boundaries have to be justified rather than presupposed. Any political philosophy that assigns basic moral standing to societies (or to other bounded entities such as nations, peoples or states) will be hard pressed to justify a more cosmopolitan conception of justice, including health justice. As we know all too well (in this respect realists in international relations are not wrong), states and other bounded entities usually pursue self-interest in constructing and supporting international institutions.

In my view, we need to be both more practical and more philosophically rigorous if we are to identify norms for health policy that can guide action without marginalising public health, and without assuming arbitrarily that justice is to be pursued primarily within borders. To do so we need to engage as fully with political philosophy as we do with (medical) ethics, and to set aside – or rather relegate to their proper context – exaggerated views of the importance of individual autonomy. In starting with political philosophy, we must make it explicit that just health provision has to be based on a reasoned view of the limits of justified compulsion, and hence of the limits of permissible coercion, not only in transferring resources (whether within or across borders) but also in maintaining and enforcing public health policies.

Norms for health policies

Norms for health policies could be approached by a number of types of argument. To many writers it has seemed most plausible to derive them from an account – complete or partial, subjective or objective – of the good. Such accounts are hard to establish, but supposedly can provide a strong anchor for normative reasoning, and thereby for health ethics and health justice, including public health ethics. I am sceptical on various counts. Some brief reminders will have to stand in for long and complex arguments.

First, it is worth recalling the standard difficulties with subjective conceptions of the good, such as those preferred by utilitarians or more narrowly by those whose approach to health ethics is based on some measure of experienced health (for example, the Quality Adjusted Life Years measure). Subjective measures of the goodness of outcomes are problematic, in matters of health as elsewhere, because each person experiences benefit and harm, including good or ill health, in a certain light. The problems of adaptive preference (in health debates: the 'contented invalid') and of expensive tastes (in health debates: the 'worried well') are ubiquitous. Aggregating with elastic units of account cannot lead to reliable conclusions, even if the units are purportedly worth attending to.

If health norms are to be derived from a conception of the good, it had better be from an objective conception of the good, measurable in objective units and providing a basis for objective judgements of aggregate and comparative good. It is easier to wish for an objective account of the good than to find one. Broadly speaking, few philosophers now expect to find an objective account of the good, complete with a standard unit of account, for measuring and comparing differing goods. Most contemporary accounts of the good are pluralistic: they claim that a good life includes a plurality of goods, but that we lack any common metric for ranking their goodness. For example, in *Women and Human Development*, Martha Nussbaum proposes a rich, pluralistic conception of the good.[10]

Without a common metric for aggregating goods and comparing different bundles of goods, however, a conception of the good cannot shape

---

[10] Martha C. Nussbaum, *Women and Human Development: The Capabilities Approach* (Cambridge University Press, 2000).

public policy, including health policy. The reason is simple. Just as a
shopping list – a list of heterogeneous goods that cannot be measured,
ranked or compared in terms of any common unit – does not tell us which
purchases should have priority, so a pluralistic account of the objectively
good without a common metric does not tell us which policies or interventions should have priority. These problems are not overcome either by
confining discussion to 'basic' goods (which still need to be ranked or
compared if we are to draw normative implications), or by treating public
discussion and collective decision making as a source of normative justification. The philosophical demands of arguments that define basic goods or
demonstrate how and when political legitimation provides normative
justification are formidable.

Another way of reaching action-guiding health norms would be to
ask what ought to be done, rather than what results ought to be
achieved. A favoured way of doing this across the last fifty and especially
the last thirty years has been to look at action from the recipient's point
of view and to propose an account of rights.[11] A common problem with
rights-based approaches is that rights are usually identified using
highly ambiguous substantival phrases such as 'right to life' or 'right
to health', 'right to development' and 'right to work', 'right to equal
opportunity' and 'right to access', as well as latterly 'right to know' and
'right not to know'. Most of these phrases have multiple interpretations:
they cannot be disambiguated without sorting out *who* has to do *what*
for *whom* – in short by specifying which *obligations* correspond to
various more specific interpretations of each supposed right. Taking
rights as basic to ethics, including health ethics, does not get close
enough to the action.

Theories of rights generally assume that there is a single answer to the
question 'Who should ensure that rights are respected?', and that the
correct answer is that this is the task of states. Yet some states are either
unwilling or incompetent, or both. Rogue states are not going to secure
justice or just health care for their citizens, let alone for the citizens of other
states; weak and failing states cannot secure justice or health care for their
citizens, let alone for the citizens of other states. States of either sort

[11] Typically rights are justified by reference to well-known public documents such as the
UN *Universal Declaration of Human Rights* of 1948. As justifications, such arguments from
authority are pretty unconvincing. See Griffin, 'Discrepancies between the best philosophical
account'; and Chapter 7 'Pluralism, positivism and the justification of human rights', above
120–33.

sometimes make it hard for other agents or agencies to step into the breach, but weak states sometimes allow them to do so.[12]

My own view is that if we want to establish intellectually robust norms for health policies it would be preferable to start from a systematic account of obligations rather than of rights. One rather simple reason why this is preferable is that a focus on required action, rather than on entitlements to receive, makes it easier to spot incoherence. For example, it is easy and rather fetching (and regrettably common) to talk about a universal 'right to health', but plain enough when one considers *who* has to do *what* for *whom* that universal health cannot be provided, so that there can be no such right. Even the notion of a universal 'right to health care', while not glaringly incoherent, is multiply ambiguous and may or may not be compatible with other equally important – or more important – obligations in particular cases and circumstances. It is easier to judge the coherence of proposed sets of obligations than of proposed sets of rights, because requirements for action are more explicit when we start with obligations.

This is not the place to show how fundamental principles of obligation can be derived from underlying conceptions of action or of practical reason. I simply state that in my view a promising route for doing this goes by way of a minimalist Kantian conception of reason and action that can establish (for example) basic obligations to reject coercion and deception, victimisation and oppression, and to assist others in permissible forms of action – hence specifically to support others' health. These obligations are, of course, not fully specific: but it is clearer *who* holds the obligations than it is when obligations are derived from accounts of the good or of rights. Some obligations fall directly on *all* agents; others fall indirectly on *all* agents in the form of obligations to support the construction and maintenance of effective practices and institutions that allocate obligations to identifiable agents and agencies. The need for an internally coherent allocation of obligations, including trans-border obligations, is more explicit, hence more readily addressed, than it is in rights-based accounts of justice.

Just health policies and practices cannot be identified without relying on the core arguments of political philosophy. It would, for example, be quite arbitrary to assume that health policies can do entirely without compulsion, and the possibility of coercion. On the contrary, any society and any

---

[12] For a significant example see Abbas Bhuiya, R. Chowdhury and A. Mushtaque, 'Do poverty alleviation programmes reduce inequities in health? The Bangladesh experience' in Leon and Walt, *Poverty, Inequality, and Health*, 312–32.

world that seeks to limit coercion will have to permit some coercion – for example the forms of coercion needed to enforce just laws. Considered abstractly, coercion may be wrong, but it does not follow that actual health policies can all be optional. Considered abstractly, deception may be wrong, but it does not follow that actual health policies can require total transparency. Under real-world conditions of communication, elements of deception – for example, those that we think of as silence or tact – may be necessary components of any reliable culture that seeks to limit deception and to support agents who seek to judge where to place and where to refuse their trust. Where excessive demands for total disclosure are made, such as those to which we gesture in invoking supposed ideals of complete transparency or openness, we may end up with a public culture which makes it harder rather than easier to distinguish true from false, trust-worthy from untrustworthy, significant from trivial.[13]

This is particularly evident in providing health information, where excessive disclosure by health providers (often in the name of supporting some version of patient autonomy!) may overwhelm rather than support patients' abilities to judge for themselves. Still less can we assume that obligations to assist or support others can be owed to all others: nobody can help all others in all ways on all occasions. Each of these caveats also applies to policies that affect health: here too we are unlikely to be able to avoid all coercion and all deception, let alone to provide maximal health care for all.

Since total compliance and comprehensive provision are never feasible, we need to choose among less-than-ideal policies, including less-than-ideal health policies. Health policy choices can never be made in isolation from other practical and ethical goals and requirements. A demand that we be totally dedicated to others' health is not achievable; even a demand that we always give priority to health improvements over other action is unachievable. Health care needs time and resources, and giving unconditional priority to the demands of health and health care would be self-defeating since it would undercut capabilities to provide health care. But it is reasonable to make some judgements about the health interventions most needed in particular times and places, and about the ways in which these can be most effectively supported. In my view, these are always likely to include the construction and the maintenance of institutions and practices that support public health, simply because these interventions are known

[13] Onora O'Neill, *A Question of Trust: The BBC Reith Lectures 2002* (Cambridge University Press, 2002).

to produce effective health improvements for large numbers, often at low cost.

This does not mean that there will be general agreement about the range of medical policies that fall under public health provision. In the developed world, for example, views differ on whether prenatal provision and provision for substance abusers should be classified as public health provision or individual, refusable treatment. Both are often classified as medical treatment of individuals, even where individuals who refuse treatment inflict huge costs on others. Those who are less convinced of the primacy of individual autonomy may view prenatal and family planning care and vaccination programmes, whose full benefit to communities requires full compliance, as matters of public health rather than of individual choice.

Who should act?

Who should do or provide *what* for *whom* for the sake of better public health? Who are the agents of justice, and specifically the agents of public health provision? In my view, accounts of obligations offer a clear general answer to this question: basic obligations fall on *all* agents, and *all* institutions. These obligations are then made more specific and concrete by constructing institutions and cultures that embody coherent and effective allocations of obligations, and by developing the necessary capabilities. A realistic process for instituting health policies begins from the *actual* configuration of agents and institutions and their capabilities.

The most effective agents of justice may therefore be different bodies and different institutions in different situations. In some situations an international institution, or a certain sort of non-governmental organisation (NGO), or a religious group, a women's group, or even a transnational corporation (TNC), may be able to take an effective role in improving public health, and contribute thereby to just health policies. Given the dire level of public health provision in many parts of the world, I do not think we should to be too fastidious in insisting that specific types of institutions should take on specific obligations to support public health. In a politically and economically well-ordered society it might be quite wrong for a women's group to take control of a sewage scheme, or for a TNC to provide health education, or for a religious group to take control of food provision, or for an NGO to provide family planning programmes – and doubly wrong if there is any element of compulsion, backed by coercion, in the way in which they proceed. I believe that in many poor or politically disorganised societies it is too rigid to assume that all interventions can or will be initiated and directed in a well-ordered way by the central authorities.

These thoughts have implications for any account of the part that rich societies ought to play in supporting public health in poorer societies. Since obligations of justice fall on all, there is no reason to think that rich societies and institutions are systematically exempt from basic obligations to those who are far away, or beyond various sorts of borders. But since abilities to act effectively may have varied configurations, there is also no reason to assume that one type of intervention will generally be the most effective, or that states may work only with other states and their governments. Often richer states and institutions located in richer states will be able to act only in partnership with state and non-state institutions within a poorer society. Again, there is no reason to assume that the only partners with whom they may cooperate, or whom they may fund, must be of any one sort. Assistance and funds may reasonably be provided to any group or institution that can use them effectively and accountably to improve public health without doing injustice. In saying this I am not arguing for lack of accountability, or for across the board permission to coerce: evidently just health policies, like all other just policies, should not proceed by compulsion when it is avoidable. Equally, however, they have no reason to assign such priority to demands for individual independence and autonomy that they impede or fail to support action that is indispensable for even basic public health.

CHAPTER 14

Broadening bioethics: clinical ethics, public health and global health[1]

From narrower to broader

Since the 1970s bioethics has had an intense focus on medical ethics, and specifically on clinical ethics. One of its central aims has been to reconceive relationships between patients and medical professionals, in particular doctors. This preoccupation has, unsurprisingly, mainly focused on clinical practice in rich societies, and has paid less attention to the ethics of public health, to the health problems of poorer societies (which suffer a high share of the global disease burden), or to connections between health and environment.

This approach to medical ethics emerged in a period during which the delivery of health care in the rich world shifted from a one-to-one, direct and often long-term relationship between patient and doctor, where each party knew the other and could make reasonable judgements about the other, to one in which increasingly complex health care was provided in complex institutional settings. Patients often encountered a phalanx of professionals, each with a fleeting presence in their lives, which made it harder to judge their probity and competence, and therefore harder to place and refuse trust with discrimination. Medical research changed in parallel ways. It was undertaken less and less by individual doctors, and increasingly by research teams with many members, complex organisation and multiple sources of funding, and often enough multiple locations. These transformations were described over twenty-five years ago in David Rothman's aptly titled *Strangers at the Bedside*[2] and have been analysed in many works, including Renée Fox and Judith Swazey's perceptive *Observing Bioethics*.[3]

---

[1] Given to mark the twentieth anniversary of the Nuffield Council on Bioethics in May 2011. An earlier version was posted on their website; this is the first publication.

[2] David J. Rothman, *Strangers at the Bedside: A History of How Law and Bioethics Transformed Medical Decision Making* (New York: Basic Books, 1991).

[3] Renée C. Fox and Judith P. Swazey, *Observing Bioethics* (Oxford University Press, 2008).

In some respects Rothman's arresting title underplayed the magnitude of the transformation: those who appeared (briefly) at bedsides (and many others who never even appeared) were no mere strangers: they were strangers with highly specialised and valued knowledge and considerable power to provide or refuse specific interventions. A heightened imbalance in power and knowledge was seen as a source of risk to patients and research subjects, and one of the aims of modern bioethics was to contain this risk.

As is well known, a central claim of those who sought to refocus medical ethics was that traditional relations between doctors and patients were paternalistic, and those between researchers and research subjects potentially dangerously defective. In both contexts more formal relationships and procedures were needed to protect patients and research subjects. This was to be achieved in part by requiring the *informed consent* of patients or research subjects – now promoted to 'research participants'! – to any treatment or research, and in part by regulating and restructuring health care systems and research governance to meet more explicitly formulated ethical and other requirements. These transformations were often seen as a matter of replacing relations of trust with procedures that ensured respect for what is conventionally thought of as the autonomy of patients and research subjects. This transformation has taken place in various forms in most developed countries, and is now often seen as uncontroversial. Here I shall not discuss this preoccupation with individual autonomy and informed consent procedures in biomedicine,[4] but focus on ways in which this preoccupation has marginalised a range of other important matters.

This has happened in large part because modern medical ethics has been radically individualistic. It focuses on the individual patient or research participant and his or her consent to medical treatment or research interventions; it has a lot to say about the rights, or supposed rights, of individual patients and research subjects. When it addresses questions of justice, it often focuses on the just distribution of goods and services, such as specific forms of health care, to individuals. An enormous amount of work in medical ethics has addressed the use – and possible misuse – of technologically sophisticated interventions, such as those enabling

---

[4] See O'Neill, *Autonomy and Trust in Bioethics*, and *Constructing Authorities*, Part II; and Neil C. Manson and Onora O'Neill, *Rethinking Informed Consent in Bioethics* (Cambridge University Press, 2007).

assisted reproduction[5] or genetic investigation and enhancement,[6] and their availability or unavailability to individuals – sometimes ignoring the wider familial context of reproduction and of genetics.

Although more work in bioethics published after 2000 has considered the population and public health implications of new technologies, this shift of concern has not been as complete as one might hope or expect.[7] For example, Norman Daniels, who had focused largely on health care in his 1985 work *Just Health Care*, took a broader approach to health and justice in his 2008 book *Just Health*.[8] However, *Just Health* also focuses mainly on 'health care', which it takes more broadly as including 'both medical services and public health measures, since both are functionally aimed at individual and population health'.[9] I am unsure whether this formulation articulates a sufficient broadening of focus, but it takes us some way. It seems to me that a focus on clinical care, supplemented by a focus on those public health interventions that are 'functionally aimed' both at individuals and at populations, still looks at distributable goods and their just allocation to individuals. Only a broader form of bioethics could take on the full range of ethical questions about public health and global health. However, to do so it would be important not only to limit preoccupation with requirements for autonomy and informed consent, and the strong forms of individualism that they assume, but to articulate the aims of a broader bioethics.

Targeted and non-targeted public health interventions

More recently things have been changing beyond public health circles, and in this some of the Nuffield Council on Bioethics' reports have been

---

[5] The ethical issues of reproductive medicine have persistently been viewed as matters of individual reproductive choice. Much of the earliest publication on reproductive ethics was resolutely individualistic, and the perspective still dominates discussions. See Ronald Dworkin, *Life's Dominion* (London: HarperCollins, 1983); John Harris, 'Rights and reproductive choice' in John Harris and Søren Holm (eds.), *The Future of Human Reproduction: Ethics, Choice and Regulation* (Oxford: Clarendon Press, 1998), 5–37; and John A. Robertson, *Children of Choice: Freedom and the New Reproductive Technologies* (Princeton University Press, 1994).

[6] For individualistic work on genetic enhancement see Brock et al., *From Chance to Choice*.

[7] For a brief example of non-individualistic discussion of some implications of new reproductive technologies see Theresa M. Marteau and Lyn Chitty (eds.), 'Fetal sexing: global perspectives on practices, ethics and policy', special issue of *Prenatal Diagnosis* 27 (2006), 646–7.

[8] See Norman Daniels, *Just Health Care*, and *Just Health* (Cambridge University Press, 2008). I am unsure whether this is a sufficient broadening of focus.

[9] Daniels, *Just Health Care*, 12.

trendsetting. This reflects its remit, which requires it 'To identify and define ethical questions raised by recent advances in biological and medical research in order to respond to, and to anticipate, public concern.'[10] This focus not merely enables but requires the Council to investigate ethical questions that bear not only on the implications of scientific advances for patients, or more generally for individuals, or for the distribution of health care, but on their implications for public and population health. Although the aims of public health interventions are often geographically restricted, they are not intrinsically individualistic.

Some public health measures evidently do not target interventions on identifiable individuals, yet protect or improve the health of many. For example, measures to protect or improve air and water quality, food and product safety, or the design of housing, roads, transport and other products, aim to protect or improve population health. So do measures that set standards for medical training or drug safety. We cannot sensibly talk about the level of benefit that each individual receives from these measures, although we can make statistical generalisations about the average health of persons in populations with and without these measures, and note significant differences. This sort of public health measure is *not* targeted on particular individuals, and the benefit produced is dispersed among a population: neither the intervention nor the benefit is targeted. We cannot tell who is benefited to what degree, or who would have fared just as well without a specific public health measure, or indeed who may (in the event) have been harmed by an intervention that benefits a population.

This case differs from that of public health measures that use individually targeted interventions, such as immunisation, where individuals who are immunised obtain a clear benefit, but others may benefit indirectly from the resulting herd immunity. Here it makes sense to speak both of a level of benefit to an individual and of a level of benefit to the population. *The intervention is targeted, but benefit spreads beyond the target.*

Both non-targeted public health measures and targeted public health interventions often have to be paid for by public funds. Where a public health measure is not targeted on any individual, although its benefits are to reach some or many members of the population, individuals may have insufficient interest in funding or accepting its provision. Even where a public health measure is targeted on individuals, but benefits accrue more

---

[10] See http://nuffieldbioethics.org/about and links on that page to their publications on topics such as GM crops, emerging biotechnologies and biofuels.

widely, some individuals may be tempted to free-ride, for example by relying on the fact that *other* people have their children vaccinated to provide indirect protection for their own children. In either case, market failure would be likely if the intervention had to be paid for by individuals, and collective provision or legal enforcement, or both, are needed. This means that public health measures are often politically contentious: a further reason why excessively individualistic approaches to bioethics are unlikely to address them effectively.

Global public goods?

Some discussions of global public health have claimed that certain public health provisions are 'global public goods', and so in everybody's interest. If true, this would be politically important. Where everybody benefits, it should be easier to persuade everybody to contribute or participate (although free-rider problems would remain). However, this seems to me too fast: some public health measures provide public goods; others do not.

Public goods in the strict sense are *non-rivalrous* or *non-excludable*, and often both.[11] Goods are *non-rivalrous* if they are not depleted by use. For example, safe streets, a medical database, or knowledge of how to manage a safe maternity service are all non-rivalrous goods. Nobody will have less of them if others too enjoy them. By contrast, the safe delivery of a baby is rivalrous (as well as excludable: a midwife or obstetrician who is delivering one baby will not be available at that time to deliver another). Goods are *non-excludable* if it is impossible to exclude others from enjoying them if they are provided to some, or at least impossible to do so cheaply, and their enjoyment by additional people has no or little additional cost. Systems for ensuring food safety or a stable currency or a public broadcasting service are examples of *non-excludable* goods; by contrast a plateful of safe food is an excludable (as well as rivalrous) good.

Are there any *global public goods* of high relevance to health? If so, providing them for all would be important for public health policy, and in particular for public health programmes that aim at global impact. Providing them would be in the interest both of those able and willing to contribute and for those who cannot or are reluctant.

---

[11] I shall not comment on *common goods*, which are rivalrous but non-excludable; or on *club goods*, which are excludable but in context non-rivalrous, although they may sometimes be important for public health.

This line of thought became prominent in the work both of the United Nations Development Programme and of the World Health Organisation, and has been promoted as a basis for building coalitions and programmes to secure the provision of global public goods for all.[12] When he was Secretary General of the United Nation, Kofi Annan championed the approach, claiming that 'no country can achieve these global public goods on its own, and neither can the global marketplace. Efforts must now focus on the missing term of the equation: global public goods.'[13]

In some cases this was a plausible view of public health measures. For example, the eradication of smallpox is a benefit to everyone, wherever they live. The disease is highly transmissible and serious: even when controlled in some countries and regions, it remained prevalent elsewhere and created risks beyond the areas of prevalence that could be managed only by immunisation and travel restrictions.[14] Another example of a global public good might be a programme of effective action to prevent and to treat a rapidly spreading and highly transmissible disease, which will almost inevitably cross boundaries. For example, had SARS proved as transmissible as was initially feared, then, given its death rate and seriousness, there might have been a case for international action, ranging from mandatory monitoring of those exposed to infection, to mandatory immunisation (if a vaccine had been developed), to restrictions on travel or quarantine.[15] Should SARS or another serious infection mutate and become more rapidly transmissible between humans, this situation might arise. And it could also arise if an infection such as Ebola, that was previously geographically confined, spread more widely. However, it is much less plausible to regard the eradication of the diseases of poverty as a global public good. Reducing the incidence of these diseases requires a reduction of poverty, which is a great good, but in large measure a distributable rather than a public good.

It is true that high-level characterisations of projects that aim to eradicate or contain serious transmissible diseases *look* like cases of global (or regional)

---

[12] See R. Smith, R. Beaglehole, D. Woodward and N. Drager (eds.), *Global Public Goods for Health: Health Economics and Public Health Perspectives* (Oxford University Press, 2003).

[13] Kofi Annan, Executive Summary in Inge Kaul, Isabelle Grunberg and Marc A. Stern (eds.), *Global Public Goods: International Cooperation in the 21st Century* (Oxford University Press, 1999).

[14] Similar things might be said about diseases that create risk for anyone entering certain regions without the necessary precautions, although here the claim is less strong because those who live far away need not take such precautions. The eradication of malaria, yellow fever or Ebola would benefit everyone, but the benefit is far greater for those living where these diseases are most prevalent.

[15] Angela McLean, Robert May, John Pattison and Robin Weiss (eds.), *SARS: A Case Study in Emerging Infections* (Oxford University Press, 2005).

public goods with high relevance to public health. However, many specific components of programmes to eradicate or contain these diseases are not public goods, let alone global public goods. Programmes that target HIV/AIDS are a good example. Although a programme for containing HIV/AIDS, *considered in the abstract*, may count as a global public good, many of its components cannot. For example, providing subsidised antiretroviral therapy (ART) to AIDS sufferers in low-income countries is not a case of providing a public good.

As Richard D. Smith and Landis MacKellar point out:

> ART is rivalrous (therapy made available to one person or nation cannot be made available to another) and excludable (persons can be barred from receiving it).

However, they contrast providing ART with other interventions which they see as providing global public goods:

> by contrast, AIDS prevention, in the form of media campaigns, condom distribution, voluntary counselling and testing, reduction of sexually transmitted infections, and encouragement of male circumcision, is non-rivalrous (if A remains HIV-negative as a result of a prevention program, his sex partners B and C are protected equally) and non-excludable (no one can prevent C from enjoying the same protection as B).[16]

But, while they offer a sober correction of some of the more enthusiastic claims about the possibility of basing public health policies on arguments for the importance of global public goods, there are grounds for being yet more sober. Some of the elements of HIV/AIDS prevention programmes may be cheap, *but they are not public goods*. When clean needles are distributed to drug users, or condoms to sex workers, what is distributed is rivalrous and excludable, although the benefits of providing them may be widely shared.[17] Indeed, public education about HIV/AIDS and safe sex, health promotion leaflets or education, advertisements or nudges, are also provided to individuals, although their benefit may spread to others. These interventions may be cheap, but they are rivalrous and excludable, and are not strictly speaking public goods. Health promotion is a *targeted* intervention, aimed at some recipients and not at others.

---

[16] Richard D. Smith and Landis MacKellar, 'Global public goods and the global health agenda: problems, priorities and potential', *Globalization and Health* 3 (2007).

[17] For a comparative account of the *effectiveness and ineffectiveness* of the HIV/AIDS policies adopted in many jurisdictions see Norman Fowler, *AIDS: Don't Die of Prejudice* (London: Biteback, 2014). The evidence is that punitive and moralistic HIV/AIDS policies are dramatically less effective than policies that do not rely on criminal sanctions.

Probably the *best* examples of genuine public goods are *systems* that have to be universally provided (a stable currency, clear rules of the road) and *abstract entities* that in the nature of the case are non-depletable, non-rivalrous and non-excludable. Ideas, knowledge, standards and laws are genuine public goods, and some of them genuine global public goods (laws are non-global, since limited by jurisdiction). It needs a lot of effort to treat abstract entities as private goods. As we all know, intellectual property law successfully construes abstract entities such as texts, musical works or inventions as ownable, tradable items that are rivalrous and excludable. But this has required the definition of points of control for excluding non-owners and non-payers from obtaining free access to abstract entities, typically by regulating free access to *material copies* or *performances*, or to *activities* and *transactions* by which ideas are shared, knowledge is transferred or standards are promulgated.

Although abstract entities are not rivalrous or excludable, copyright law treats *uses* of copyrighted works as rivalrous and excludable. We live in an era of persistent attempts to *extend* intellectual property regimes by ensuring that *uses* and *copies* of abstract entities are treated *not* as public goods, but as proprietary assets that may be controlled by their owners. This is a shifting and contested frontier. On the one hand, some proponents of extensive intellectual property regimes have become more militant. Patents are filed on smaller inventive steps; steps are taken to control manufacturing and marketing of generic drugs. Holders of copyright seek to exert stricter control of secondary rights, putting pressure on some of the traditional 'fair use' exemptions that allow(ed) individuals to copy limited amounts of material for private study, review, criticism and research. However, this more aggressive approach probably reflects the reality that major holders of intellectual property – among them pharmaceutical companies and publishers – are under great pressure. They are often fighting a rearguard commercial battle in a world of increasing open access publishing, open data, violations of patents, plentiful piracy and rampant plagiarism, all of which weaken intellectual property rights and erode both their traditional role as the reward for originality and their current role as tradable assets.

So it is not surprising that various public health initiatives challenge current intellectual property regimes and seek to change them. Some of these initiatives are highly relevant to public and global health, including the Health Impact Fund,[18] which seeks an alternative to the current patent

---

[18] See http://healthimpactfund.org.

regime for rewarding innovation in pharmaceutical research,[19] and the Drugs for Neglected Diseases Initiative.[20]

However, such initiatives, interesting as they are, do not provide a general basis for thinking that *uses* of ideas, as opposed to the ideas themselves, can be genuine global public goods. *Uses* of ideas are not abstract entities, and they may be organised to make them targeted, rivalrous and excludable. Perhaps unsurprisingly, the definition of public goods used in the UNDP sponsored work *Global Public Goods: International Cooperation in the 21st Century*[21] is much weaker than the economists' definition. The report characterises public goods as 'having benefits that cannot easily be confined to a single "buyer" (or set of "buyers")'. This is not a standard view of public goods, and is met by many goods, including not only non-targeted public health measures but public health interventions that target individuals where the benefits spread to others. An intervention may be rivalrous and excludable, but its *benefits* may nevertheless be (in part) non-rivalrous and non-excludable. Many public health measures are targeted interventions with beneficial externalities, rather than genuine global public goods.

The political point of claiming that certain policies promote global public goods is clear enough: it is meant to suggest that everyone has an interest in ensuring that these goods are provided. However, a focus on targeted goods with dispersed benefits is, I think, likely to be more fruitful for a broader bioethics than any search for global public goods, in the strict sense of that term.

Targeted interventions with dispersed benefits

So, while it is tempting to think that the problem of securing coordinated international action that addresses global health problems would be helped by identifying genuine global public goods, this is not likely to be enough. Much that is needed for public health improvements – locally and globally – consists of non-targeted health measures or of targeted health interventions

[19] See Thomas Pogge, 'Human rights and global health: a research program', special issue of *Metaphilosophy* 36 (2005), 182–209; and Aidan Hollis and Thomas Pogge, *The Health Impact Fund: Making New Medicines Accessible for All*, downloadable from http://healthimpactfund.org/wp-content/uploads/2012/11/hif_book.pdf.

[20] See www.dndi.org.

[21] Inge Kaul, Isabelle Grunberg and Marc Stern, *Global Public Goods: International Cooperation in the 21st Century* (Oxford Scholarship Online, 2003).

that spread benefits beyond their targets. Both are unlike clinical treatment, which is targeted on individuals whom it is intended to benefit. Non-targeted interventions often benefit others who were not targeted. (They sometimes do not wholly fail if they provide *no* benefit to the targeted individuals. Anti-smoking advice might be targeted on A, who remains regrettably indifferent, but the message might reach B and C who stop smoking; HIV containment policies might be directed to a population who ignore it, but have good effects if others who were not targeted grasp the message and benefits are dispersed.)

The importance of structuring targeted public health interventions with an eye to the distribution of their benefits beyond targeted individuals can be illustrated by contrasting the differential effects of a pragmatic HIV/AIDS prevention campaign, emphasising safe sex and clean needles, such as that used in Australia, particularly in New South Wales, with the more moralistic approach such as that used by some US HIV/AIDS prevention policies, that in some cases promoted individualistic interventions aimed at lower-risk individuals (for example: encouraging teenage sexual abstinence; discouraging multiple-partner sex).[22] Pragmatic responses that target those *most* at risk and *spread* benefits have proved more effective than policies that target those less at risk. Some of the restrictions on programmes under the US PEPFAR programme in the President's Emergency Plan for AIDS Relief placed constraints on interventions targeting high-risk groups (e.g. commercial sex workers; injecting drug users), but proved relatively ineffective.[23]

Targeting and benefits

A focus on public health interventions that appeals to global public goods is *at best* moderately helpful. The most relevant goods are often not public goods, a fortiori not global public goods, in the strict sense of the term. They are a mixture of non-targeted policies that benefit many, and

---

[22] The contrasts have been discussed in the many publications and reports of the HIV/AIDS project of the Lowy Institute in Sydney. They conclude that countries that used pragmatic HIV containment policies (e.g. clean needles for substance abusers, working with sex workers, making condoms available) secured substantially better HIV outcomes than programmes based on promoting sexual abstinence, criminalising prostitution or zero tolerance for injecting drug use: www.lowyinstitute.org/HIVAIDSProject.asp. See also Fowler, *AIDS*.

[23] See Smith and MacKellar 'Global public goods and the global health agenda'. They conclude: 'It is hard to consider PEPFAR as collective provision of a GPG when ... Its prevention programs are designed to cater to a domestic political constituency.' Online only at www.globalizationandhealth.com/content/3/1/9.

targeted policies with benefits that spread wider than their targets (just as the harms of some targeted malign activities, such as violent crime, spread harm beyond their targets).

Both non-targeted and targeted public health activity raise distinctive ethical questions for a broader bioethics. *Non-targeted public health measures* are not a minor aspect of public health ethics. They are present in the infrastructure of all but the most rudimentary clinical interventions. Modern clinical medicine needs many structures, facilities, technologies and standards, which have to be provided at agreed levels. These provisions cannot be matters for choice, nor therefore for informed choice, by individual patients. Individual patients may give or refuse consent to treatments, but cannot (for example) choose the level of training of their doctors, the safety standards for licensing drugs, or the safety culture of hospitals. All of these systems and structures are debatable matters in other contexts, but for individual patients at the point of deciding whether to accept an intervention, they are simply given. Medical practice is not just a set of transactions between free-standing agents: it is framed by public health and other provisions that are not and cannot be matters for consent or choice by individual patients, or indeed by individual practitioners. This, it seems to me, gives us reason to think of public health ethics as more fundamental than clinical ethics.

Targeted public health interventions too must be judged not only by the extent to which they benefit their immediate or intended targets, but also by the extent to which they benefit (or harm) a population more widely. For the individualistic bioethics that has been dominant for the last thirty years, this looks problematic. Is not using an individual in ways intended to benefit others exactly what we have long been telling one another is ethically unacceptable?

Yet clinical ethics too constantly faces situations in which interventions that are intended to benefit an individual on whom they are targeted also affect others. In treating an individual patient, benefit is intended primarily for that patient, but everyone knows that others too will benefit. The patient's family, friends and carers will benefit if health improves. If the condition is transmissible, effective treatment may benefit others who might have been infected. If it is a rare condition, successful treatment may benefit future patients by improving the knowledge base for treating them. In other cases, treatment for the benefit of a particular patient may harm others. Medically futile treatment will use up resources that might have saved other patients. Poor decisions about the treatment of transmissible diseases or psychiatric conditions may lead to third party injury. And in medical research the dispersal of benefit is even more fundamental: the central aim of clinical research is to acquire knowledge to be used for better treatment of subsequent cases.

Both non-targeted public health measures and targeted public health interventions may benefit many. Although the incidence of wider benefit cannot be foreseen, its amount can often be estimated prospectively and measured retrospectively by comparing population health before and after measures are introduced or interventions undertaken. These facts suggest to me that an excessive focus on individual choice and informed consent by patients or research subjects will not only marginalise public health and the ethical questions it raises, but hide much that is ethically fundamental to clinical practice and biomedical research.

Some ethical conclusions

If bioethics is to address the broad range of ethical issues raised by public health policy effectively, it must locate discussions of individual choice, consent and autonomy in the context of a wider range of ethical issues. Consent procedures are a useful way, but not the only way, of assuring ourselves that an intervention is not (for example) forced, coercive, deceptive or manipulative, and not likely to injure.[24] Needless to say, consent does not provide total assurance that an intervention will not injure individuals who consent. Assurance is limited because there may be inadequate information about the effects of an intervention; because individuals do not grasp the relevant information when consenting; because they choose against their own interests; because risks are hard to foresee; because consent cannot be sought from all who may be affected – or just because something goes awry. None of these cases is unusual.

Fortunately, consent procedures are not the only way of assuring ourselves that basic ethical norms are not breached – as we know from the many cases in which persons without competence to consent are treated on the basis of considering their best interests. What matters in many cases is not the formality of obtaining consent, but the reality that fundamental obligations not to force, coerce, deceive, defraud, manipulate or injure, which consent *generally* protects, are met in medical and research practice.

---

[24] The Nuremberg Code that forms the backdrop to countless demands for informed consent in bioethics treats consent not as ethically fundamental, but as a means of preventing more fundamental ethical failings such as 'force, fraud, deceit, duress, over-reaching, or other ulterior form of constraint or coercion'. See Manson and O'Neill, *Rethinking Informed Consent in Bioethics*.

Both non-targeted public health measures and targeted public health interventions can meet these underlying standards. Non-targeted measures have to meet them without using consent procedures, because it is impossible to pick out individuals whose consent would be relevant. For example, safety standards for medicines and medical devices, training standards for surgeons and measures for infection control are non-targeted measures, which cannot require consent from each individual whom they may affect. Adding fluoride to water that lacks it, or folic acid or iodine to staple foods, can disperse benefit without injury to individuals, but cannot be based on consent from each affected individual. Such policies can only be justified by good evidence of their effects, and clarity that adopting them so would not breach fundamental obligations. Similarly for targeted interventions. Measures that make it harder for individuals with contagious conditions to transmit them (quarantine or condoms, as the case may be) can be justified *provided* that they do not rely on force, coercion, fraud or deception, or injure without proportionate reason.

It might be said that this is impossible because any legal or regulatory measure will be backed by coercive powers, so coerces. This seems to me a mistake, though a common one; such a view unless qualified would make the rule of law itself an unacceptable form of coercion, on a footing with criminal activity. If both non-targeted measures and targeted interventions that individuals do not choose are to count as coercive, then almost any action that impinges on others would require consent if it is not to count as coercive! However, by and large legal and regulatory requirements do not work by coercion: often they work by formative, coordinating, persuasive and exemplary methods, and even when there are legal sanctions – coercive backing – coercion is rarely used. Coercive backing is not the same as coercion. Public health measures and the ethical arguments that support them operate in this domain, and do not assume that everything that does not or cannot receive consent requires actual coercion, although it may need coercive backing.

Health promotion measures and other targeted public health interventions that are likely to benefit many do not require consent from all affected parties. There will of course be empirical questions to be settled, and questions about the limits of harm that non-targeted measures or targeted interventions where effects spread more widely may risk. But there is no reason to think either that the only tolerable level of harm is zero, or that any activity that risks harm will be permissible only if all affected consent to it. The world we live in transmits and disperses benefits and harms among agents in ways that are neither wholly foreseeable nor wholly assignable to individuals. It is an illusion to imagine that we need to obtain consent from each individual for everything that might happen to them. The most we can do is to try to ensure that what is done to protect or promote public health neither risks disproportionately serious injury nor breaches other fundamental obligations.

Index

239

states and, 146. *See* states
to a nationality, 152, 181
to asylum, 152, 182
to compensation, 43–57
  for ancient and distant wrongs, 51–3
to fair trials, 129
to food, 34–5, 129–30, 195
to goods and services, 155, 181, 194, 196, 199, 203
to health, 34, 195, 221
to life, 26, 127, 129
to marry, 127
to not be enslaved, 128
to not be killed, 13–28
to not be tortured, 128
to privacy, 127, 129–30
to secession, 61
to security, 127, 129
to self-determination, 76
to subsistence, 36
to work, 127
universal, 126, 162–3, 183
Rousseau, Jean-Jacques, 67, 69, 83
Ruggie, John
  Protect, Respect and Remedy Framework, 147

safety standards, 237
Sandel, Michael, 80–1
SARS, 230
scarcity, 13–28
scope of ethical principles, 61
self-defence, 13–16, 20–1
self-determination, 61
self-interest, 185
self-legislation, 112
Sen, Amartya, 6, 123, 187
Singer, Peter, 4, 17, 31, 84, 162
  Famine, Affluence, and Morality, 17
Sittlichkeit, 80–98
slavery, 51, 53
social contract, 113
socialism, 79
society, 121
  bounded, 99, 104, 184, 217–18
  civil, 106
sovereignty, 77, 107, 158–9, 170, 185–6
starvation, 17, 29. *See* hunger
state of nature, 115
states, 63–7, 79, 99–119, 137–50, 156, 160–1, 165, 177–92, 218. *See also* agents
  agents, 158
  bounded, 64, 70, 152, 160, 182
  dependent, 179
  failing, 165. *See* states, weak

imperial, 160
league of, 116
minimal, 50
plurality of, 66
power of, 207
quasi- 179. *See* states, weak
republican, 101, 116–17
rogue, 165, 179
sovereign, 64
sovereignty of, 64
state boundaries, 61–78
system of, 177, 186
unjust, 164
weak, 147, 165, 169, 174, 179, 187, 189, 202, 220
world state, 63, 76, 101, 155, 177
statism, 151–3, 157, 161–2, 164, 175, 183.
  See also justice
sufficiency situations, 18–23
supererogation, 37, 54

tasks, 176. *See* obligations
territories, 63–70, 105–7, 155–8, 184–5, 217.
  See also states
  bounded, 162
tradition, 103, 142. *See* constitution
  shared political, 141
transnational corporations (TNCs) 165. *See*
  institutions, non-state

underdevelopment, 20. *See* development
United Nations (UN), 101, 105, 123, 147, 153, 164, 169–70, 172, 183, 218, 230
Universal Declaration of Human Rights, 34, 99, 122–8, 137, 139, 152–3, 155, 161, 177, 180–3, 195, 198, 220. *See also* international covenants
Universal Principle of Justice, 113–16
universal principles, 100
universal rights, 61, 161. *See* rights
universal scope, 71, 79, 83, 114, 126, 148, 162
universalisability, 213
utilitarianism, 30–4, 37, 41, 50, 55, 84, 162–3

value monism, 121–2, 125–6, 132–3
value pluralism, 121. *See* pluralism
victims, 43–57, 206

Walzer, Michael, 62, 80, 152
Weil, Simone, 37, 42
Westphalian, 146–7
Williams, Bernard, 80, 166–7, 207
World Health Organization (WHO), 195, 218, 230. *See also* United Nations
world state, 155. *See* states